Plotting Women

PLOTTING WOMEN

Gender and Narration in the Eighteenth- and Nineteenth-Century British Novel

ALISON A. CASE

UNIVERSITY PRESS OF VIRGINIA
Charlottesville and London

BRESCIA COLLEGE
LIBRARY
68785

The University Press of Virginia
© 1999 by the Rector and Visitors of the University of Virginia
All rights reserved
Printed in the United States of America

First published 1999

∞ The paper used in this publication meets the minimum requirements of the American National Standard for Information Sciences—Permanence of Paper for Printed Library Materials, ANSI Z39.48-1984.

Library of Congress Cataloging-in-Publication Data

Case, Alison A., 1961–
    Plotting women : gender and narration in the eighteenth- and nineteenth-century British novel / Alison A. Case.
        p.   cm.
    Includes bibliographical references (p.   ) and index.
    ISBN 0-8139-1895-2 (cloth : alk. paper)
    1. English fiction—18th century—History and criticism. 2. Women in literature. 3. English fiction—19th century—History and criticism. 4. English fiction—Stories, plots, etc. 5. Sex role in literature. 6. First person narrative. 7. Narration (Rhetoric) I. Title.
PR858.W6C37 1999
823.009'352042—dc21   99-28818
                                                             CIP

For Elinor, who tells wonderful stories

CONTENTS

ACKNOWLEDGMENTS

$\mathscr{I}$ would like, firstly, to thank the early teachers who helped me to reach the point where I could write this book: especially Katherine Beckwith, Rick Yeiser, Pat Murphy, Laurence Buell, and Sandra Zagarell.

Harry Shaw read, critiqued, debated, and encouraged this project throughout. I owe a huge debt to his generosity and critical intelligence. Laura Brown, Dorothy Mermin, and Paul Sawyer taught the courses that inspired its central argument, and they helped to shape its development from the early stages onward. Wendy Jones also gave me warm support and intelligent help throughout.

I am grateful to my current and former colleagues at Williams College for their welcome support and encouragement: I would like to thank Bob and Ilona Bell, Carol Benedict, Deb Brothers, Steve Fix, Larry Graver, Kiaran Honderich, Scarlett Jang, Cathy Johnson, Sherron Knopp, Andy and Beth Koch, Chris Pye, Jana Sawicki, Thandeka, and Steve Tifft. Suzanne Graver, Karen Swann, and Anita Sokolsky, in particular, lent their intelligence and expertise by commenting upon numerous drafts and versions of part or all of this book. My students at Williams College have helped in innumerable ways to complicate my thinking about the books I teach. In particular, the wonderful participants in my two seminars on "Writing the Female 'I,'" most especially Ticien Carlson, Thomas Wong, Maria Agosto, Meredith Johnson, and Stephanie Bird, contributed materially to the argument of this book.

James Phelan contributed his valuable advice to the introduction. To Herbert Tucker's generosity I owe thanks for favors too numerous to list. Many other people helped, directly and indirectly, to make this book possible. In particular, I am grateful to Julie Corwin, Libby Gruner, Kabi Hartman, Geraldine Heng, Tamar Katz, Elsie Mitchie, Louis Schwartz, and Lauren Wenzel. Many thanks also to Clara Park and her family for permission to reproduce the portrait of her great-grandmother Justine Lockett, alleged Confederate spy and ancestress of many fine writers.

I thank my family, especially my father, my brothers, and Ilon Specht, for the support they have always given me. Their persistent desire to understand what I was doing and why I was doing it has helped to keep my own thinking clear. To James Pethica, I owe an even greater debt, since he has combined the roles of supportive spouse and scholarly adviser. He has been my most persistent and helpful reader, and without his love, patience, and encouragement, this book could not have been completed.

An earlier version of chapter 4 appeared in "Gender and Narration in *Aurora Leigh*" in *Victorian Poetry* 29 (1991), and an earlier version of chapter 6 appeared in "Tasting the Original Apple: Gender and the Struggle for Narrative Authority in *Dracula*," in *Narrative* 1, no. 3 (1993), © 1993, Ohio State University Press; permission to reprint this material is gratefully acknowledged.

Plotting Women

INTRODUCTION

*W*hat does it mean for a woman to tell a story? to tell her own story? As asked of the novelist, the question directs us toward the links between authorial gender and the real or imagined gendering of narrative theme, form, or style. The question of what constitutes, characterizes, enables, or circumscribes the female novelist within any given literary tradition has been central to a wide range of feminist critical projects. But if "being a woman" has come to be seen as a more problematical and contradictory state than we once believed—a matter of staging an obligatory "performance" of womanhood as one's culture defines it—producing "a woman's voice" in fiction is even more so, shaped by the codes and expectations of a literary as well as a social milieu. Hence, we can also take "What does it mean for a woman to tell her story?" as a question about the literary conventions that govern the representation and interpretation of female storytellers in fiction within a particular tradition.

As a way of approaching this question, I want to begin by discussing the openings of two first-person narratives—one male, one female—that appear in a popular, mid-nineteenth-century British novel, R. D. Blackmore's *Lorna Doone*. The first is the opening of the novel itself, which introduces its first-person narrator John Ridd:

> If anybody cares to read a simple tale told simply, I, John Ridd, of the parish of Oare, in the county of Somerset, yeoman and churchwarden, have seen and had a share in some doings of this neighborhood, which I will try to set down in order, God sparing my life and memory. And they who light upon this book should bear in mind, not only that I write for the clearing of our parish from ill-fame and calumny, but also a thing which will, I trow, appear too often in it, to wit—that I am nothing more than a plain unlettered man, not read in foreign languages, as a gentleman might be, nor gifted with long words (even in mine own tongue), save what I may have won from the Bible, or

> Master William Shakespeare, whom, in the face of common opinion,
> I do value highly. In short, I am an ignoramus, but pretty well for a
> yeoman.[1]

Ridd's opening is apologetic and self-deprecating, but in ways that indirectly authorize him to tell this story. He is disclaiming a certain kind of narrative authority and competence, a kind he associates with "gentlemen," learned in "foreign languages" and well-versed in the Latinate neologisms of the day (the novel is set in the seventeenth century). By disclaiming this high literary authority, though, Ridd is also claiming the authority of the "simple tale told simply." Nor is it entirely clear that Ridd is apologizing for what distinguishes him from the literary authorities of his day, as he unhesitantly proclaims his literary allegiance to William Shakespeare "in the face of common opinion"—an allegiance, of course, that marks him for the Victorian reader as possessed of better literary taste than those authorities. Thus, if what Ridd offers is ostensibly only "a simple tale told simply," the implication is that such a tale may offer as much pleasure and profit as the most learnedly elaborated literary productions of the day.

Several chapters into the novel, Ridd includes a narrative in Lorna Doone's own voice of her life before meeting him. Whereas Ridd's narrative is presented as a written document—one identical with the text of *Lorna Doone* the novel—Lorna's is a much briefer, oral narrative composed of two consecutive chapters titled "Lorna Begins Her Story" and "Lorna Ends Her Story." In introducing the narrative, Ridd tells us that he initially intended to tell Lorna's story in his own words, but found himself "beset . . . with heavy obstacles," the two greatest being "the one that I must coldly speak, without the force of pity, the other that I, off and on, confused myself with Lorna, as might well be expected" (150). He thus decides to have Lorna "tell the story, with her own sweet voice and manner," as she originally told it to him at one of their early meetings. Lorna's story begins, "I cannot go through all my thoughts, so as to make them clear to you, nor have I ever dwelt on things, to shape a story of them. I know not where the beginning was, nor where the middle ought to be, nor even how at the present time I feel, or think, or ought to think. If I look for help to those around me who should tell me right and wrong (being older, and much wiser), I meet sometimes with laughter, and at other times with anger" (151).[2]

Like Ridd's, Lorna's opening is apologetic and self-deprecating. But unlike Ridd, she seems to be disclaiming the very qualities that would make it possible to "shape a story" at all. Her opening denies both the ability to order temporal events into a proper beginning, middle, and end and any grasp of their larger psychological or moral significance. And whereas Ridd proclaims his independence from prevailing authorities, Lorna explicitly ascribes her narrative shortcomings to an unfortunate lack of suitable authorities willing to tell her how she "ought to think." What she claims to offer, then, is not so much a coherent narrative as the raw material of narrative, which requires an external authority to give it shape and significance.

There are a number of questions we could ask about these two openings: Why are these narrators self-deprecating? Is their self-deprecation sincere? Is it accurate? And if not, how should their initial misrepresentation of their abilities affect our understanding of their narratives? More to the point, why is Lorna's opening so much *more* self-deprecating than Ridd's? Finally, are these really Lorna's own words? How can Ridd possibly remember them verbatim after all these years? If they are not, how might Ridd be distorting Lorna's story?

I address most of these questions below, but for now I would like to point out that reading *Lorna Doone* competently—in the way that Blackmore's intended audience would have read it[3]—does not in fact require us to ask any of these questions, in the way that it does require us to ask questions like, Who is Lorna really? and, Will (or how will) Ridd and Lorna surmount the numerous social and practical obstacles to their union? We do not need to ask them because, for the most part, the answers are provided by the conventions associated with the novel as a genre at the time Blackmore is writing. Take the question about the reliability of Ridd's retelling of Lorna's story. Realistically, it is unlikely that Ridd could reproduce Lorna's language exactly, or that his approximation thereof would not be shaped in some ways by his own (possibly distorting) understanding of Lorna and her story. But the assumption that first-person retrospective narrators are able to recount verbatim lengthy narratives told to them years earlier was a familiar one by the Victorian period, and *Lorna Doone* offers nothing to suggest that it is not in operation here. Most readers would (quite rightly, I think) take for granted that we should accept these two chapters as a mimesis of Lorna's own language as she originally told her story to Ridd.

Readers familiar with a given genre will tend to take the operative conventions for granted—they may not even be aware that they are operating: hence, Peter Rabinowitz titles his study of some of the broadest conventions governing the reading of fiction *Before Reading.* A large part of the task of teaching literature, particularly at the introductory levels, is familiarizing students with the conventions at work in the texts we ask them to read. Outside of that pedagogical task, literary conventions tend to come to critical attention either because, 1. there seems something worth pointing out about the convention as a whole, such as the way the convention of perfect recall operates in general as a tool in the production of certain effects of realism that we might find either laudable or suspect; or, 2. there is something anomalous or otherwise intriguing about the deployment of the convention in a particular text—hence, we might conclude (though in this case I would not do so) that Blackmore is *playing* with or mobilizing the convention of perfect retrospective recall in ways that could give us an interesting purchase on the novel. In my discussion of a gendered convention of first-person narration, both approaches will be apparent: on the one hand, the convention itself has an ideological force that is worth calling attention to; on the other hand, awareness of its general outlines highlights interesting features of its anomalous deployment in particular texts.

In the *Lorna Doone* passages, it is fairly easy to see that the self-deprecation these openings share is also conventional—though in this case the convention is as much cultural as literary. In both fiction and life, it is commonplace (if not invariable) for people who are about to claim the prolonged attention of an audience to begin with apologies about the inevitable inadequacies of their presentation. In this case, the narrators' apologetic characterizations of their stories exist primarily to assure us that these are decent people aware of the presumptuousness of assuming narrative authority in the first place—a presumptuousness heightened by Ridd's class and by Lorna's gender.

But I want to argue that the differences between these two openings are also conventional, in detailed and important ways. In particular, the qualities of narrative confidence, competence, and control implicitly claimed in Ridd's narrative and explicitly disclaimed in Lorna's are the markers of a gendered convention of first-person narration in the British novel of the eighteenth and nineteenth centuries. Feminine narration, I will argue, is characterized by the restriction of the female narrator to the role of narrative *witness;* that is, by her exclusion from the active shaping of narrative form and meaning—from what Lorna calls "shap[ing] a story" and telling "right" from "wrong" within it, or from what I shall term *plotting* and *preaching.*

In these terms, the femininity of Lorna's narrative is signaled not only by her opening but by the way her narrative is framed. Ridd's introduction of it calls attention to the rhetorical considerations involved in offering the story in this form: frustrated by the emotional and grammatical distancing involved in telling the story himself, he turns to Lorna's "own sweet voice and manner" to produce an effect of both temporal and personal immediacy. But the impact of that immediacy—its status as a conscious rhetorical choice within the larger narrative of *Lorna Doone*—is attributed to Ridd, not Lorna. Her contribution is, again, only the raw material of narrative artistry.

The features of feminine narration clearly derive from and exemplify broader cultural strains of gender ideology in the eighteenth and nineteenth centuries, which associate femininity with passivity and lack of discursive authority. Why, then, identify these features as part of a distinct literary convention at all? Would it not make equal sense just to say that Lorna is (unsurprisingly) exhibiting various features of conventional Victorian femininity in her behavior as both a character and a narrator?

In giving feminine narration the status of a convention, I am suggesting that it takes on a degree of autonomy in the subsequent development of the British novel, relative to the continuing shifts and contestations of gender ideology in the culture at large. It becomes a distinct term in the set of literary and cultural negotiations any text necessarily carries out. In the case of *Lorna Doone,* positing a convention of feminine narration helps to explain why Lorna's opening, rather than expressing the vague diffidence, shyness, fear of boring her audience, and so forth that we would associate with a generalized Victorian femininity, instead so explicitly and thoroughly disclaims the power to shape narrative and give it moral significance—despite the fact that Lorna does go on to tell a reasonably coherent story, and that her ability to hold onto clear-cut moral standards, despite her total isolation from anyone who affirms them, is central to both her character and the plot of the novel.

In *Lorna Doone,* Blackmore's deployment of the convention of feminine narration is . . . well, conventional, and even perfunctory. It is artistically useful, for a variety of reasons (some of which Ridd points out), to shift to Lorna's voice at this point. Since the author wants us to approve of Lorna, he takes pains, in introducing her story, to ensure that she will not be seen as violating norms of proper femininity, including the literary conventions of narrative femininity. That done, he can get on with the story. In *Lorna Doone,* then, the convention of feminine narration can be read both as a resource and as a restriction. On the one hand, feminine narration offers Blackmore a way to create certain useful artistic effects—such as a break from Ridd's voice and a sense of immediacy difficult to achieve with his more self-conscious retrospective narration—while emphasizing Lorna's positive qualities as a heroine. On the other hand, given the desire to have Lorna narrate, the author is obliged, if he does not want to call Lorna's virtuous femininity into question, to provide at least superficial conformity to the norms of feminine narration.

Conventions generally *are* both resources and restrictions. They are not hard and fast rules—in fact, it can sometimes seem that they are made to be broken. But neither are they simply neutral, take-it-or-leave-it resources: they help to shape the very terms on which a literary text is made meaningful to its expected audience.[4] Certainly, not all female narrators in this period are consistently feminine, nor are all feminine narrators female.[5] But as I hope to show, feminine narration represents the "unmarked" case for a female narrator, just as narrative confidence, competence, and control do for the male narrator. Deviations from the model are marked by virtue of their deviation: they draw attention to themselves, requiring some form of more or less explicit explanation or compensation.

Much of this book is concerned with the forms these deviations take. When Walter Scott, for instance, gives the male protagonist of *Redgauntlet* a femininized narrative voice, he also has him compelled to dress up as a woman, and Wilkie Collins's granting of a more masculine authority over plotting and narrative to the villainess/narrator Lydia Gwilt in *Armadale* poses a problem the remainder of the novel must resolve. And when Charlotte Brontë and Elizabeth Barrett Browning create first-person narrators who challenge women's conventional exclusion from narrative authority, they also create pairs of alter egos for them who represent the narrative roles they have rejected.

Later in this introduction, I discuss the particular sources and features of feminine narration in more detail, but I turn first to the way my formulation of the convention relates to more general questions about gender and narration.

Feminist Narratology

My primary focus on narration, on the *how* rather than the *what* of narrative presentation, aligns my work with the emerging field of "feminist narratology," which Robyn Warhol defines as "the study of narrative structures and strategies in the context of cultural constructions of gender."[6] One of the greatest strengths of narratology has been its development of a precise vocabulary—or, more accurately, a range of often competing vocabularies—for talking about exactly how stories are told, or understood. These range from broad binary distinctions like Seymour Chatman's between *story* (the events of a narrative) and *discourse* (the way those events are told) to Gerard Genette's dazzlingly fine-tuned array of neologisms for identifying shifts in the temporal movement of a story or variations in the narrator's relationship to it. Genette, for example, distinguishes usefully between first-person narrators in general, which he terms *homodiegetic,* and those who are protagonists of their own tales, or *autodiegetic.* In offering clear, distinct terms for such textual features as the different narrative functions characters serve,[7] or the "rules" readers need to grasp intuitively to make sense of any novel,[8] narratologists have demonstrated that a well-developed set of terms has the merit not just of making it easier to *talk about* particular features of texts, it makes it easier to *see* them. As feminist critics become more interested in analyzing the textual construction of gender, narratology offers valuable tools.

At the same time, feminist critics have themselves posed a valuable challenge to traditional narratology's tendency to abstract texts from their social setting, and to make global claims about the features of narrative in general based on a predominantly—and often exclusively—male pool of texts. In this, feminist narratologists have been aligned with what is often termed the *rhetorical* strain of narratology, associated with theorists like Wayne Booth, James Phelan, Peter Rabinowitz, and David Richter, who focus on narrative primarily as "an act of communication between author and reader," rather than as a set of abstract "codes,"[9] and who are consequently more likely to recognize the ways that the *how* of narration—or of reading—can be inflected by categories like ideology or ethics.

Nowhere is the relationship of rhetorical narratology to the emergence of a feminist narratology clearer than in Susan Lanser's work. Her first book, *The Narrative Act,* proposes a "speech-act" model of narration, the purpose of which is "to broaden the discussion of narration beyond the consideration of its vantage-point for perceiving events or the degree of omniscience it permits," to take into account the "psychological and ideological relationships the text creates between narrators, characters, textual events, author, and audience." Though not itself explicitly a work of feminist criticism or theory, Lanser's book laid the groundwork for reading gender as a significant factor in narration, since, as she observed, gender is "one of the strongest determinants of social, linguistic, and literary behavior in patriarchal societies."[10] In particular, a narrator's "status"—that is, "the authority, competence, and credibility which the communicator is conventionally and personally allowed"—is dependent to a large extent on the conventions of *social* authority, competence, and credibility that operate at the time, rather than being determined solely by the relationships between elements in a story.[11] In her later work, Lanser builds on these insights to begin to develop a "feminist poetics of narrative voice,"[12] illuminating some of the patterns that emerge in women writers' efforts to produce "fictions of authority"—that is, both authoritative fictions and fictional constructions of authority.

Warhol has joined in Lanser's appeal to feminist critics to turn from the analysis of *story* (plots, characters, etc.) to that of *discourse,*[13] but her project takes a different tack. Whereas Lanser begins from the presumption that women in modern Western culture occupy a radically different discursive position from men, and from that premise seeks corresponding differences in female-authored texts, Warhol begins with a textual phenomenon already loosely associated with female authors in the nineteenth century: the use of direct address to the reader by an omniscient narrator to promote greater emotional engagement with the story. This phenomenon, Warhol argues, is unaccounted for (and thus rendered invisible) by the theory and terminology of narratology, which had classed direct address to the reader as a distancing device. By distinguishing and defining a little-noticed narrative device, *engaging direct address,* she provides an opening for a broader analysis of the gender politics of both novelistic narration and the critical and theoretical responses to it.

Both Warhol and Lanser present themselves—quite rightly—as pioneers of a new field they term *feminist narratology.* Lanser's work takes her "toward a feminist narratology"—words she used as the title of a 1986 article; and Warhol, in the title of her opening chapter, asks, "Why Don't Feminists 'Do' Narratology?"[14] In the few years since that question was posed, the answer has been that clearly they now do: Kathy Mezei's *Ambiguous Discourse: Feminist Narratology and British Women Writers* contains thirteen essays identified as works of "feminist narratology," and her bibliography lists dozens more, most published since 1989.

Because it arose partly in response to the tendency of traditional narratology to address texts by men, feminist narratology has tended to focus primarily on female-authored texts. Mezei's introductory overview of "the rise of a feminist narratology" uses the term interchangeably with the narratological study of women's texts.[15] Most feminist narratologists are clearly resistant, at least theoretically, to any essentializing notion of "female narrative." Lanser, for example, reminds us that "both narrative structures and women's writing are determined not by essential properties or isolated aesthetic imperatives but by complex and changing conventions that are themselves produced in and by the relations of power that implicate writer, reader, and text";[16] Warhol, for her part, sees her project as contributing to an understanding of gender as a social construct.[17] Nonetheless, feminist narratology has tended to aim at formulations meant to illuminate the distinctive strategies of women writers. Even Warhol's study, while it treats both male and female novelists, is directed primarily toward identifying and reevaluating a narrative strategy seen as distinctive of (if not exclusive to) women writers. In other words, the "gender" with which feminist narratologists have concerned themselves in their analyses of narrative has been, first and foremost, the gender of authors.[18]

This study, by contrast, will take as its starting point a notion of gender that is already textually constructed: the gender of narrators. Because the use of female narrators in the English novel has by no means been limited to female authors—indeed, Defoe and Richardson, and to some degree even Fielding, put female narrators at the center of what have long been considered the foundational texts of the English novel—I have chosen to treat the literary construction of female narrators by both male and female authors as part of a single (albeit internally contested and evolving) tradition. However great the tendency of writers to define themselves in a gendered tradition—for male authors to construct a literary history that renders women largely invisible, or for female authors to motivate and assess themselves largely in relation to female peers and predecessors—male and female British novelists throughout this period wrote for a shared audience and were influenced by a shared tradition.

This is not to say that I consider authorial gender irrelevant. A literary convention governing the propriety, and even the possibility, of textual women making narrative sense and meaning is bound to carry a different kind of weight for women writers seeking to do just that than for men. In general (although not exclusively), male writers have tended to reinforce conventional restrictions on what a female autodiegetic narrator can say or do, whereas women writers—particularly those I discuss here—have been more likely to subvert or expand them. But such generalizations are not the primary method or aim of my analysis.

Although this project thus diverges to some degree from the current feminist narratological practice of working primarily toward generalizations about the narrative strategies of female authors, it is consonant with its larger aims.[19] In the broadest terms, feminist narratology has emerged as a practice that, by merging feminist criticism's attention to the politics of representation with the formalist analytic tools and terminological precision of narratology, seeks to reveal the ways gender is woven into the dynamic of novelistic narrative itself, and into our responses to it as narrative. That is a goal this project fully shares.

In part, this study seeks to add a new concept—*feminine narration*—to the toolbox of narratologists, feminist or otherwise. But *feminine narration* as a term is at least as important for what it draws together as for what it distinguishes. It is defined by the narrator's conceptual relationship to the shape and meaning of the narrative as a whole, not by a particular narrative technique. Hence it appears in epistolary and diary narration as well as in retrospective narration, in narrators who are *intradiegetic* (addressing an audience *within* the story) or *extradiegetic* (addressing the audience *of* the story), and in narrators who are either reliable or unreliable, in a variety of ways. Furthermore, the convention is notable in part for the cluster of issues that tend to accompany it, issues whose implications regularly cross the boundaries between story and discourse. In mapping these issues, I have drawn more on the terminology of the novels themselves than on the specialized vocabulary of narratology: *plotting* and *preaching, artful* and *artless,* and later, *resolution*—all these are words that recur in similar contexts from novel to novel, and emerge as loaded terms in their application both to the actions of characters and to the activity of narration.

By taking the gendering of narrators rather than authors as my starting point and focusing on a shared tradition, I believe I can offer a richer and more nuanced sense of the terms and stakes of the contestation over women's narrative authority in this period. This contestation occurs not just between men's and women's texts but within and between texts by men, and also within and between texts by women. It is frequently staged, and thematized, in works with feminine (or female) first-person narrators. *Lorna Doone* aside, nearly all of the novels I have chosen to discuss, by men or women, are ones in which the convention of feminine narration is mobilized in dynamic ways, being challenged, reasserted, and sometimes reshaped, in the course of the narrative. My readings of individual novels will focus on their distinctive negotiations with literary and social conventions, and the unique and complex gender dynamics of narration that result. Part of that negotiation, too, is their engagement with each other: *Jane Eyre* rewrites *Pamela; Bleak House* and *Aurora Leigh* rework both novels; *Armadale* evokes (and inverts) *Clarissa,* and *Dracula* closely parallels, but also complicates, *The Woman in White.* Most broadly, understanding how feminine narration works in these novels gives us a different kind of purchase on the gender dynamics of reading—again, not the way women read differently from men, but the way readers of novels from this period are conditioned by the texts to respond to women who tell stories about themselves.

Plotting and Preaching

The autodiegetic narrator—a narrator who is him- or herself a central character in the story he or she tells—is a particularly rich locus for narratological analysis in that he or she partakes of the roles of both created and creator, being both a literary construct of the author's and the (fictional) constructor of the narrative we experience as reader. Autodiegetic narrators often trouble the line between discourse and story. Although it may be analytically useful to make a distinction between the narrating self and the narrated self (particularly when there is a substantial temporal gap between them), the fact that they share the same *I* keeps them closely intertwined for the reader: as Lanser observes, readers' responses to the narrator's acts are inflected by their response to the character's actions, and vice versa.[20] A reader responds to such a narrator both as character and as pseudo-author, sometimes becoming conscious of the gap between implied author and narrator, as in moments of "unreliability," and sometimes merging the two.

In particular, in creating a dramatized autodiegetic narrator—that is, someone we are made conscious of as actually writing or speaking the story we read[21]—a writer typically must provide not only a plausible (i.e., conventionally acceptable) character, but also a plausible narrative authority for that character: a reason and a right to write (or speak) within the fictional world that character inhabits. In the case of those accorded greatest social authority and credibility—primarily, in the period I am concerned with, educated gentlemen—the authority may be largely implicit, but the further one moves from that position (a "plain, unlettered man" like John Ridd; women; servants; etc.) the more overt the construction of narrative authority—to whatever degree it is granted at all—is likely to be.[22]

As Genette observes, *plausibility* is itself a literary convention, a matter of what readers expect from stories (or from a particular kind of story). Nancy Miller has shown how the demand for plausibility in the novel has policed the representation of women in particular, referring less to any form of real-life likelihood than to cultural notions of what women ought to be.[23] The female first-person narrator, as one who is both the object of the story and the speaker of narrative discourse, is thus the locus for a rich interpenetration of literary and social conventions. Gender cannot help but inflect the use of first-person narrators in a culture in which men's and women's voices are accorded very different kinds and degrees of authority, and in which men and women's actions are judged by very different standards.

The potential for gender to "make a difference" also comes into view when we consider what Peter Brooks calls "the dynamic aspect of narrative—that which makes a plot 'move forward,' and makes us read forward, seeking in the unfolding of the narrative a line of intention and a portent of design that hold the promise of progress toward meaning."[24] Brooks's model in *Reading for the Plot* has been roundly critiqued by Susan Winnett for its elevation of a male model of sexual experience to a universal norm of narrative shape.[25] Phelan has also compellingly argued that Brooks's strongly teleological model somewhat overstates the controlling force of the endings of novels, while his psychosexual focus inappropriately narrows the intellectual and emotional range of the reading experience.[26] Nonetheless, like Phelan, I find useful Brooks's attention to the power of plotting, the "activity of shaping" event into meaning, in the reader's experience of a novel. Winnett suggests that taking alternative (female) trajectories of sexual experience as a model might more adequately account for the narrative forms produced by women authors. But even if we accept that sexual experience provides the primary model for narrative, the model Winnett identifies as male—the gradual buildup of tension leading directly to climax and release—is also one (if not the only one) of the forms women's sexual pleasure can take. Furthermore, since I suspect that writers are influenced at least as much by the nature of the pleasures they have had from reading as by their sexual pleasures, it seems likely that the prominence of a teleological model for narrative shape in the nineteenth-century novel gave it considerable conventional pull for women novelists of the period. Again, my interest is less in identifying how women authors do things differently than in illuminating the gender dynamics of narration, in texts by either men or women. Hence, I argue later that Brooks's inattention to gender and its impact on narration imposes limitations even on his readings of texts by men.

In conventional novelistic narrative—the kind of narrative that predominates in the eighteenth- and nineteenth-century British novel— "plotting," that "activity of shaping," is performed first and foremost by the narrator, and by the reader only in tandem with, or in opposition to, that initial shaping. Plotting as carried out by a narrator is, in relation to the story, a purposive activity, because plots themselves are, as Brooks says, "intentional structures, goal-oriented and forward-moving."[27] In relation to the reader, plotting is an act of authority: the narrator poses as the one to assign the shape, and hence the meaning, we are to derive from the story. The granting of this (provisional) authority is part of the implicit contract between a narrator and a reader. In a certain sense, we become disciples, relying on the narrator to give us the information we need, in the order and with the emphasis and analysis needed to make the story comprehensible, engaging, and meaningful. We may, of course, given sufficient evidence of narrative "unreliability," become rebellious disciples, constructing an alternative meaning in opposition to the narrator's, but we still recognize the authority even if we partially or wholly decline to submit to it.

Since some of the most consistent threads in Western gender ideology concern women's purported inability to take purposive action—to be goal oriented—and the inappropriateness of their assuming certain kinds of authority over others, it should come as no surprise that women's relationships to narration are often problematical.

In the tradition I am considering, this is reflected in the development of a literary convention that excludes female narrators from the process of shaping the experiences they narrate into a coherent and meaningful story. As we saw in *Lorna Doone,* a feminine narrator typically provides only the raw material of narrative, which is usually shaped and given meaning by a male "master-narrator" within the text, or by an authorial or editorial frame that serves the same function. To borrow Roland Barthes's terms, the feminine narrator is closed out of the proairetic and hermeneutic codes that structure linear narrative, while remaining (unconsciously) subject to them. She may, in effect, tell her own story, but in doing so she must be seen neither to *plot* nor to *preach.*[28]

Narrative authority necessarily retains an intimate link with social authority. Particularly as the British novel begins to define itself as a privileged source of social and moral wisdom—most obviously with novels like *Pamela* and *Clarissa* in the eighteenth century—the reader potentially becomes the disciple of an authoritative narrator in more than his or her subjection to the unfolding of this particular narrative. Such authority—particularly that of a master over disciples—has never been gender-neutral. Saint Paul forbade women to teach in the church on the grounds that there was something inherently offensive and unnatural about women holding such authority over men, a pronouncement that became the scriptural basis for official church bans on women preaching.

Indeed, the analogy between female preachers and female narrators is a useful one in several respects. The question of women's qualifications, or their right, to preach the gospel was publicly reopened with the rise of the Protestant sects in the mid-seventeenth century, the same period in which the English novel had its early roots, and the rise of Methodism in the late eighteenth century again brought women preachers into public debate—a debate that eventually resulted in a renewed ban on such activity. Christine Krueger, in *The Reader's Repentance,* argues that the experience of Methodist women preachers became the foundation for the social and moral authority claimed by such authors as Hannah More, Elizabeth Gaskell, and George Eliot, and Warhol suggests that the practice of "engaging direct address" to the reader developed by Gaskell, Stowe, and others arose as an alternative to the public exhortation, via preaching or public speaking, denied to women in the period.[29] But this transference of preacherly authority to women's novels is dependent on the abstraction and at least partial degendering of an omniscient narrator. The woman preacher who appears as a character in Eliot's *Adam Bede,* for example, is silenced at the novel's close, whereas the novel's omniscient narrator adopts an explicitly male voice. This potentially preacherly authority is also partially obviated by the critical denigration of direct address as a sleazy feminine trick, as Warhol points out. In reading work of the eighteenth and nineteenth centuries, when the novel increasingly took upon itself the task of defining the social order and giving it moral coherence, and even addressing specific social evils with the aim of reform, the analogy between preaching and narration becomes increasingly useful.

Even where authors or contemporary readers do not explicitly associate authoritative narration with preaching, the conditions under which women of the time could make themselves heard on religious subjects without being seen to usurp the authority of preachers often parallel those under which they appear as first-person narrators. Those conditions can be best understood on the basis of a distinction between *witnessing* and *preaching;* in other words, between the recounting of significant personal experience and the interpretation of that experience (or anything else) explicitly for the benefit of the congregation. John Wesley, who was generally supportive of Methodist women preachers, offered the following distinction to authorize their speech without violating Paul's injunction: "Say, 'you lay me under a great difficulty; the Methodists do not allow women preachers; neither do

I take upon me any such character. But I will just nakedly tell you what is in my heart.'"[30]

The same distinction between witnessing and authoritative exposition, I would argue, determines the implicit etiquette of female first-person narration in the early English novel. That is, feminine narrators ideally do not so much claim possession of moral truth—in fact, like Lorna, they are likely to disclaim it explicitly—as embody it. Of course, as Methodist women and their audiences perceived, it is difficult to maintain an absolute distinction between witnessing and preaching—one can hardly put one's experience into words without giving it some shape or significance, and that significance can easily be structured in such a way that it is instructive without being explicitly didactic. Pamela's monologue to Mrs. Jewkes before the second attempted rape is a perfect example of a sermon couched in the form of witnessing.[31] Nonetheless, the fact that the line cannot be very clearly drawn seems less significant than the need, in theory, to maintain and enforce its existence. Richardson and his descendants devote a good deal of literary energy to policing this boundary.

The potential impropriety of assuming a preacherly authority in relation to a reader is equalled by that of assuming the control over events necessary to shape them into a "story." Women's virtue in the period was more concerned with *being* than *doing*. Margaret Doody cites Richard Allestree's *The Ladies Calling* (1673) for an early, socially commonplace view of female virtue as "consist[ing] more largely in an attitude of soul than in action," and Victorian social tracts would continue to stress women's role as influence and inspiration rather than as an active force in their own right.[32] Under such a view, women who act according to a plan to achieve particular results become morally suspect simply by doing so.

This view comes to infect the retroactive shaping of events in narrative as well. As Brooks points out, *plot* refers both to the structure or outline of a story and to a plan to carry out some illicit purpose. The association is a fertile one, referring, again, to the status of plots as "intentional structures."[33] Female narrators always run the risk of being associated with female plotters of another and more unsavory sort. As we will see, Richardson's epistolary narration operates in part to insulate his virtuous female narrators from such moral infection; but even here, the narrator's troubled relationship to plotting, in both senses of the term, becomes central to the novel.

In fact, this double valence of *plotting* is one of the most striking ways that story and discourse interact in novels with female narrators. In general, such novels exhibit a clear parallel between the heroine's power to plot actual events at the level of story—to manipulate patterns of cause and effect in action—and her power to shape her narrative at the level of discourse. What Lanser terms "the plot of narration" thus often parallels, prefigures, or even catalyzes changes in the "story plot"—and does so precisely via the implicit analogy between, and moral anxiety about, narrative and material plotting.[34]

To the extent that female narrators are excluded from plotting, their role again becomes, in a different sense, that of a witness. While a preacher or a plotter assumes authority over his listener, a witness does the opposite, submitting her testimony to the readings of others, who may understand it in ways that she cannot. In the novels I discuss in this book, female narrative witnesses, whether reliable or unreliable, virtuous or otherwise, are likely to be more interesting for what they do not know—about the people and events around them, or about themselves—than for what they know. Indeed, a great part of the pleasure feminine narration provides is that it thus appears to reverse the power relations of narrator and reader. This is not to say, though, that it reverses those of *novelist* and reader—even in novels like *Pamela* that are told almost entirely by means of a feminine narrator. If witnessing seems in theory to open a space for what Barthes would call a "writerly" relation to a text, in practice that space is quickly filled by the male master-narrator, who provides either a model for the reader's relationship to the witness's "testimony," like Mr. B. in *Pamela,* or an authoritative perspective within which to understand it, like Matthew Bramble and Jery in *Humphrey Clinker.*

I have emphasized the terms *witness* and *testimony* because they seem linguistically loaded in fruitful ways. Because they are terms that refer to religious speech, they focus the issues of moral authority that are so important in the eighteenth- and nineteenth-century novel. They evoke as well, especially for modern readers, the world of the courtroom, where testimony provides data that lawyers, and ultimately a jury, can shape into a coherent narrative that legally counts as truth. The testimony of a courtroom witness is always to be understood within the framework of meaning (usually a narrative) provided by a lawyer. Indeed, the less stake in, or understanding of, the lawyer's master-narrative a witness has, the more reliable he or she is likely to be viewed as a witness. My description of feminine narrators as witnesses, then, suggests their relationship to the twin novelistic concerns of *virtue* and *truth.*[35]

Given the continual back-and-forth slippage throughout this period between accounts of what women are and accounts of what they ought to be, questions of feminine propriety in narration intertwine themselves with questions of female capacity. As we shall see, particularly as regards sexuality, feminine virtue becomes linked not just to the refusal to tell a story, but to the inability to do so.

Virtue vs. Narration: Peter Brooks and Fleur-de-Marie

Brooks's discussion of Eugene Sue's *Les Mystères de Paris* in *Reading for the Plot* is particularly illuminating about the implications of being able or unable to tell a story about one's own life. What Brooks fails to recognize, I argue, is the role gender plays in that ability. My rereading of his reading of *Les Mystères de Paris* is intended to make visible the gender issues in narration that his approach obscures, and to reveal how far the categories of the narratable and the unnarratable can be seen as a function of who narrates —and specifically of an opposition between authoritative narration and feminine virtue.

According to Brooks, Fleur-de-Marie, the innocent child-prostitute of Sue's novel, never fully understands how "soiled" she is by her sordid past until she finds herself unable to exchange life-histories with an innocent and sheltered girlfriend, Clara Dubreuil: "Fleur-de-Marie has discovered[,] in juxtaposition and contrast to the normal existence of the unsullied girl of her age[,] that her own life, her own past, is not narratable. The story of the mark she bears cannot be told, the past cannot be recovered in a full, candid narrative of her life. Hence the mark is ineffaceable, the past irremediable."[36] But as Brooks continues, it becomes clear that this "ostensibly unnarratable life" is far from unnarratable. In fact, it "comprises the very definition of the 'narratable'"—that is, "the deviant, the shameful, the criminal"—at least in the nineteenth-century novel, "and perhaps in some degree [in] all narrative, which in general has precious little use for the simple, calm, and happy [i.e., Clara Dubreuil's life story], since whatever moral obeisance one makes to these, they lack narrative interest."[37]

Brooks himself never seeks to resolve the "apparent paradox" whereby Fleur-de-Marie's "unnarratable" story becomes, in Sue's hands, the most "narratable" story of the nineteenth century. Its existence should suggest, though, that the subject-position from which narration is undertaken can affect more than the perspective on a story: it can determine its very narratability. Fleur-de-Marie cannot narrate her story; Eugene Sue cannot stop doing so. What accounts for the difference?

To answer this, we must consider what it would mean for Fleur-de-Marie to be able to narrate her story to Clara Dubreuil. It would mean more, in Brooks's own terms, than being able to tell "what happened." Fleur-de-Marie does in fact do this early in the novel, recounting all the elements of her past to Rudolph in response to his questions and promptings, but far from being able to shape them into a coherent narrative, she confesses that "since my birth, this is the first time that I have recalled all these things at once to my memory."[38] To make a narrative of "all these things" would mean that she was able to structure the events of her life teleologically, to "bestow meaning on the [sordid] beginning and . . . middle"[39] of her life by showing their essential relationship to a redeeming "end" in the present—an end in which she can be judged an appropriate companion for the likes of Clara Dubreuil. This is essentially the story Sue narrates—one in which Fleur-de-Marie's fundamental moral purity is established all the more emphatically by the fact that it has survived through scenes that ought to have destroyed it. But for her to construct this narrative for herself would mean that she had sufficiently internalized and accepted her sexual past to be able to incorporate it into a narrative of her life—and this in turn would make her "impure" after all. The real paradox here lies in the fact that the soiled innocent can be judged as "pure" only to the extent that she is unable to see herself as other than soiled.

This is because the narrative of the innocent debauchee—and this is as true of Richardson's *Clarissa* as of *Les Mystères de Paris*—inevitably comes to rely on a divided and seemingly contradictory notion of feminine virtue: the one a rather crude notion of innocence and virtue as ignorance coupled with virginity, a matter of what has never been "known" either physically or mentally, and the other as an inherent quality that keeps the moral purity of the victim "intact" despite exposure to the very dregs of sexual knowledge. For either definition to take over entirely would collapse the story. In the former, the debauched woman, now morally "fallen," would inspire pity, but little interest or admiration; in the latter, the debauchment would not be a sufficiently important event, since its *moral* effect would be so minor.

It is tempting to see the internalized notion of virtue as more profound and more humane than the crudely literal equation of virtue and virginity. In fact, though, the positions are not so different. Both are equally far from the conception of masculine virtue that prevails in these same novels—one that sees sexuality, among other temptations, as a force to be recognized and resisted or controlled. If in the crude version of feminine virtue innocence can be maintained only by insulating a girl against exposure to sexual knowledge, in the latter it consists of an incapacity to internalize sexual knowledge when exposed to it. If in the former a girl's mind is a blank slate, in the latter it is a shattered one, whose owner cannot make the pieces cohere into a meaning, a narrative, a plot.[40] In a certain sense, then, feminine virtue comes to be marked by the inability to construct a proper narrative, either because, as for Fleur-de-Marie, the "deviance" necessary to generate plot cannot be accepted, made part of a broader, redemptive meaning, or because, as for Clara Dubreuil, there is no deviance, and hence there is really nothing worth narrating.

Narrating Deviance: *Moll Flanders* and the Lust for Plotting

If Fleur-de-Marie cannot narrate "the deviant, the shameful, the criminal," Moll Flanders, it seems, can do little else. As the first retrospective female narrator—the first female storyteller—in the canon of English novels, Moll is obviously no model of feminine virtue, or she would not have so much to tell—nor such relish for telling it. I would argue, though, that she is also no model of narrative authority. Though she seems to fall on the wrong side of the opposition between virtue and narration, she is, in her own way, a feminine narrator.

The narrative proper is framed by an editorial "Preface" that calls into question Moll's relationship to what is supposedly "her" story. Though we are told that "the Author is here supposed to be writing her own History," the editor hastens to add that "the original of this Story is put into new Words, and the stile of the famous Lady we here speak of, is a little alter'd, particularly she is made to tell her own tale in modester Words than she told it at first; the Copy which came first to Hand, having been written in Language more like one still in Newgate, than one grown Penitent and Humble, as she afterwards pretends to be."[41] Nor is the editor's task limited to adjusting Moll's diction, for as he says, that style itself casts into question the ending of her story—her "pretended" penitence—and hence the shape and significance of the story as a whole. Moll's story as told in her own words might well lead a reader to different conclusions than the moral ones the editor says he intends. Thus he also claims to have omitted altogether several episodes that would not tend toward his instructive purposes (viii), and to have ensured throughout that the story recommends "how to make the good Uses of it" (viii): "In a Word, as the whole Relation is carefully garbled of all the Levity and Looseness that was in it: So it is applied, and with the utmost care to vertuous and religious Uses" (ix). Finally, the editor goes on to enumerate specifically some of the "serious Inferences which we are led by the Hand to in this Book": accounts of Moll's successful crimes "intimat[e] to [honest people] by what Methods innocent People are drawn in, plundered, and rob'd, and by Consequence how to avoid them," while her penitence assures other "unfortunate Creatures. . . . that no Case can be so low, so despicable, or so empty of Prospect, but that an unwearied Industry will go a great way to deliver us from it" (x).

The status of Moll's narration after such a preface is ambiguous in important ways. While the reader is assured that the actual experiences on which the narrative is based are Moll's own, the mass of silent emendations to which the preface confesses leaves open the question of how much hand Moll has had in the shaping of that experience into a meaningful narrative —or at least, into the particular meaningful narrative that is here presented in her name. Specifically, whatever moral force the narrative has, it is suggested, is to be attributed largely to the editor's careful recasting of Moll's dubious "original" narrative. In other words, while Moll is undoubtedly witnessing—recounting experiences—on her own behalf, the transformation of that witness into preaching is implicitly attributed elsewhere. In case any suspicion remains, Moll also frequently disclaims her ability to offer moral instruction to her readers in the midst of her attempts to do so. "But it is none of my Talent to preach" (1.64) she apologizes at one point; and at another: "but I leave the Readers of these things to their own just Reflections, which they will be more able to make effectual than I, who so soon forgot my self, and am therefore but a very indifferent Monitor" (1.135).

The insertion of this ambiguity in the preface is extremely useful for Defoe. It allows him to construct a narrator with access to all the tantalizing experience of female deviance without overstepping the bounds of decorum, either by taking her sexual and acquisitive delights on their own terms, or by investing a wiser, penitent Moll with undue moral authority. And of course, it means that the reader can enjoy that deviance on the same terms.

Moll is hence a doubly fictionalized narrator, one whose (fictionally) "true" narrative has been in turn *re*fictionalized by the editor, who reshapes and rewords her tale while retaining the "fiction" of Moll as autonomous narrator. But the fiction *is* maintained: the reader is to perceive Moll as a reasonably coherent personality narrating her own story, and this in itself is also important to the novel's effect.

Even without the preface, Moll's narrative would generate doubts about her own sense of the meaning of her story. While she maintains, on a broad scale, the confessional mode of a story of error or deviance told from the perspective of later repentance, on a more local, episodic level Moll frequently seems more proud of her successes than contrite for her sins. It is as if these small local plots have a teleology of their own, one that temporarily overcomes the wider providential teleology of the novel as a whole. In fact, it is not only within her narrative, but in the life she narrates, that Moll is led astray by such plots. Just as, in the narration of certain episodes, the sincerity of Moll's repentance is undercut by her delight in narrating her own successes, so, in the course of her life, Moll is continually seduced by the success of her own schemes and contrivances, which become a pleasure in themselves: the most notable example is her inability to give up stealing even after accumulating a fortune sufficient to retire comfortably. Moll has been overcome by her own lust for plotting—or rather, for generating subplots, for the problem with these is precisely that they distract Moll from broader aims or structures. Moll in her life is unable to subordinate stealing to the aim of material security, just as in her narrative she often fails to subordinate local triumphs to her eventual debasement and then salvation. Indeed, her conversion itself comes to seem like little more than a particularly clever way out of a particularly difficult situation, and even a Moll who is now converted and contrite is not cured of the need to "plot" her way out of her difficulties.

In other words, if Moll has early parted company with the virtuous of her sex by entering into the joys of plotting, she reassures us of her more fundamental femininity by her inability to construct more broad-ranging "intentional structures." The charm of *Moll Flanders* for a reader lies precisely in its moral incoherence: it is the sign of Moll's "earthiness," her believability as a "real" woman of a certain kind.

My point here is not that Moll's perspective as a narrator is necessarily readily distinguishable from that of the fictional Editor, or, for that matter, from an extrapolated authorial voice of Defoe himself. Indeed, some of the most eminent critics of the English novel have concluded that it is not. Ian Watt, for example, argues that Defoe identifies too closely with Moll—that she is merely an extension of himself, and hence not really "feminine."[42] Dorothy Van Ghent also notes a similarity between Moll's moral crassness and the viewpoint of the "Preface," though she resists extending this to Defoe himself.[43] But whether or not one can actually measure the ideological gap between Moll as feminine narrator and the authoritative voice that presents her, the presumption of that gap has a particular value for Defoe and his readers. Having a woman—particularly a sexually deviant woman —as narrator enables him to explore the potential overlap between criminal desire and capitalist fervor to the limit, without needing to resolve the contradictions such an overlap reveals. In other words, Moll's deviant femininity serves the same function as the shipwreck and desert island do in *Robinson Crusoe:* both allow us to participate imaginatively in the excess of material acquisitiveness that their central characters display, while distancing ourselves from the antisocial implications of that acquisitiveness. But the distancing in *Crusoe* does not require the limitation of the narrator's authority: Defoe's "editorial" preface to that novel explicitly endorses Crusoe's narrative and moral authority.[44]

Writing Female Virtue: Pamela as Narrator

Though *Moll Flanders* demonstrates some of the special uses a feminine narrator can be put to, it is not as central to the development of a convention of gendered narration as Richardson's first novel.[45] In its exploration of the relationship between exemplary female virtue, plotting, and preaching, *Pamela* provides one of the most influential "feminine" voices in English fiction, and indeed becomes a foundational text for the literary conventions of feminine narration.

In writing *Pamela,* Richardson had two distinct but related didactic purposes. First, the novel grew out of Richardson's project of writing model letters to be emulated by the newly literate servant and petit-bourgeois classes: they would establish conventions of literary decorum for written self-representation. But beyond that, Pamela herself was to be a *moral* model for her behavior in a trying situation. Within this framework, Richardson created a work with a psychological intensity and unity of plot that entitled it, by some standards, to be called the first "true" novel in English. Certainly the phenomenal popularity of *Pamela,* and later *Clarissa,* profoundly influenced the characterization and presentation of literary heroines by male and female authors long after their publication. From the very roots of the English novel, then, the question of female virtue was closely allied to that of female self-representation in prose.

The epistolary form of Richardson's heroine-novels is significant in itself. Pamela—or any epistolary heroine—makes a good example of the first-person female narrator as witness of, rather than master of, her story. There is no formal reason why this feature of epistolary narration should be limited to women, but in fact epistolary heroes in the eighteenth-century English novel are hard to find. Most of the letters that make up *Sir Charles Grandison*, for example, are written by the female characters, and Richardson goes to sometimes absurd lengths—such as secreting an admiring scribe in a closet for one encounter—to save Grandison from having to narrate his own manly exploits. (Lovelace is a somewhat different case, and will be discussed at length in the next chapter.) The conventional association of epistolary narration with women is one feature of the gendering of narrative voice during this period.

The epistolary novel in general, even when consisting of only one correspondent, is, like the diary novel, something of a special case in narrative, in that it offers a story without a storyteller who knows himself or herself to be one. This means that the ordering principle of the story as narrative must be presumed to lie elsewhere than with the consciousness through whom we perceive the story. The question the reader is faced with is not just "what is the *telos* of this plot," but "whose plot is this?"[46]

When we ask this question of *Pamela*, the immediate answer is, "Certainly not Pamela's!" Indeed, as has been repeatedly noted in criticism of the novel, it is crucial to Richardson's presentation of Pamela as moral exemplar that the novel's ending—or even its progression from one stage to another—at no point be seen as active contrivance on her part. As Fielding amply demonstrated in *Shamela*, all that is required to collapse Pamela's "virtue" into its opposite is to represent whatever happens to Pamela as the result of her own plotting.

The problem is by no means limited to the peculiarities of Pamela's situation, as Richardson's 1751 *Rambler* essay "Advice to Unmarried Ladies" demonstrates. The writer nostalgically recalls a time when church was the primary place for single men to look for prospective wives. At the same time that he recommends this system specifically to today's "Unmarried Ladies," however, he condemns those women who had gone to church with an eye to their effect on men as "Seekers," arguing that the attractiveness of a woman in church stems precisely from the male observer's belief that she is "earnest in her first duties" and unconscious of her effects on others: "Her eyes were her own, her ears the preacher's." Male "seekers," by contrast, pose no particular moral problems. For the men, a proper action performed for the wrong reason (i.e., going to church to look at the girls) reads not as hypocrisy but as a step in the right direction: "some good often resulted, however improper might be their motives. . . . The men were often the better for what they heard. Even a Saul was once found prophesying among the prophets whom he had set out to destroy." Even what seems real hypocrisy, such as making an artificial "show of good principles" to a prospective bride's family, is only a sign of incipient reformation: if the heart is not "yet quite right," the author implies, it soon will be. With a male ethic based on action rather than a state of being, a virtuous consciousness is seen to follow from the habit of virtuous actions, however the habit may be acquired. (Hence, men are particularly suited to advice that demonstrates the unity of virtue and self-interest—Richardson's "policy"—a tactic Richardson used frequently in his treatments of male virtue, particularly in *Sir Charles Grandison*.) For women, though, it is the state of mind that must validate the action. This makes it difficult to imagine how an "unmarried lady" could be expected to take Richardson's "advice" without being open to the "mark of infamy" as a "Seeker" herself. Ultimately, such advice seems to demand a mind that, while able to accept in a general sense arguments about the good effects of certain kinds of behavior, is constitutionally unable to calculate effects from causes in a particular case, or at least to base actions on such calculations.

Unsurprisingly, given such a model of feminine virtue, Pamela's own "Plots" to escape from her predicament—her correspondence with Parson Williams, and then her attempt to run away—are a conspicuous failure. She herself attributes this to the disabilities of her sex: "Oh why are poor foolish Maidens try'd with such Dangers, when they have such weak Minds to grapple with them!" (137). There is one point in the novel where Pamela is faced with a genuine strategic choice—that is, where clear-cut notions of virtue and duty to superiors can no longer safely determine her actions without need of any reference to results—when she is asked by B. to return to him of her own free will. At this point, Pamela does make an effort to weigh the probable consequences of her act, only to find that in this instance they can provide no reliable guide to her conduct: "if he should use me ill, then I shall be blamed for trusting him. If well, O then I did right, to be sure!—But how would my Censurers act in my Case, before the Event justifies or condemns the Action, is the Question?" (218). With the possibility of effective calculation eliminated, Pamela is forced to act on her feelings—and this, of course, is the very thing that validates her decision, guaranteeing that it is based on no motive of mere "policy."

If Pamela's virtue is ensured in part by her inability to plot her actions to achieve particular results, it is equally so by her exclusion from the narrative plotting of her story as it unfolds. As Cynthia Baughman has argued, part of the function of the whole machinery of intercepted and appropriated letters in *Pamela* is to give Mr. B. a form of access to Pamela's experience unshaped by any consciousness of him as audience—and, more particularly, by any suspect "design and intention" of narrative. If Mr. B. is to provide a satisfactory denouement to the "pretty Novel" (201) shaping up in Pamela's letters, it is only on the condition that their writer has no such teleological aim. (Pamela herself, on her way home after her expulsion by B., recognizes the potential of her experience as a narrative only with an implicit disclaimer of her own ability to "tell" it as such: "Well, my Story surely would furnish out a surprizing kind of Novel, if it was to be well told" [213]).

Pamela is more subtly distanced from the suspect activity of narrative shaping by her periodic inventories of portions of her journal that have passed out of her hands. These consist simply of long lists of the episodes covered: the second portion of her journal to be handed over to B., for example, is described in part as

> A Confession of mine, that notwithstanding his bad Usage, I could not hate him. My Concern for Mr. Williams. A horrid Contrivance of my Master's to ruin me; being in my Room, disguised in Cloaths of the Maid's, who lay with me and Mrs. Jewkes. How narrowly I escaped, (it makes my Heart ake to think of it still!) by falling into Fits. Mrs. Jewkes's detestable Part in this Sad affair. How he seem'd mov'd at my Danger, and forbore his abominable Designs; and assur'd me he had offer'd no Indecency. How ill I was for a Day or two after; and how kind he seemed. How he made me forgive Mrs. Jewkes. How, after this, and great Kindness pretended, he made rude Offers to me in the Garden, which I escaped. How I resented them. (205-6)

Aside from their obvious value in keeping the reader up to date on the ever-shifting subject of who has read what, I would suggest that part of the function of these lists lies in the refusal of narrative they represent. Faced with the opportunity—even the need—for some kind of retrospective summary, Pamela provides only lists of isolated events conspicuous for their lack of narrative linkage. The lists serve to emphasize the status of Pamela's writings as merely the raw material of narrative. Indeed, as raw material, the lists might equally be termed, at least in their effect on a reader, invitations to narrative. This is a function they have in common with the summaries at the opening of chapters used in many novels, which they most closely resemble in style. The latter are intended, by their fragmentary and often

incongruous listing of episodes to come, precisely to excite readerly specu-
lation about how such disparate elements are to be united in a coherent
narrative.

Pamela is hence discounted as a "plotter" of her own story. Her story
emerges rather as a dialectic between two plots: Mr. B.'s plot to "have"
Pamela, and the providential plot, whose telos, of course, is "Virtue Rewarded." Pamela herself suspects the intrusion of the providential plot at the
point where her own contrivances fail: "And how do I know, but that God,
who sees all the lurking Vileness of my Heart, may not have permitted
these Sufferings . . . to make me rely solely on his Grace and Assistance,
who perhaps have too much prided myself in a vain Dependence on my
own foolish Contrivances?" (153).

Mr. B. sees himself as the plotter of her story (it is, after all, his "plot" in
which she is so charmingly entangled)—a position that gives him, in his
eyes, a certain right to the writings in which the working out of that plot is
recorded: "as I have furnished you with the Subject, I have a Title to see the
Fruits of your Pen.—Besides, . . . there is such a pretty Air of Romance, as
you relate them, in your Plots, and my Plots, that I shall be better directed
in what manner to wind up the Catastrophe of the pretty Novel" (201).

B. provides a model for the reader of the novel, who, reading with an eye
to teleology, imposes an order on Pamela's experiences as an act of authority
over her. What B. recognizes in the course of reading Pamela's unfinished
story is that the position of the Providential Plotter is by far the most
authoritative one for him to occupy, in that it places him in the position of
God, and enables him to reclaim the whole story as both spiritual autobiography (his own change of heart) and a Griselda-like "trial" of Pamela.
(The switch is rendered easier by the fact that B. has no great stake in his
own plots. Lovelace's far greater investment in his plots as an ordering force
will mean that the conflict can result only in Clarissa's death.)

B.'s narrative authority comes into its own after the marriage, in which
he emerges both as the retailer of Pamela's story to the neighborhood
(Pamela never actually "tells" her story to anyone—B. tells its outline and
result and then provides Pamela's papers as a kind of witness), and as con-
troller of Pamela's virtue. With the conflict between providence and B.
essentially eliminated, Pamela is to slip back into the feminine mode of
acquiescent and uncalculating virtue that was apparently hers before the
story began. Many of the scenes and "Injunctions" of the postmarriage section of Pamela have to do with reasserting this "natural" order, which has
been upset by the conflict. Pamela's most heinous sin in this section is her

attempt to act on assumptions about the effect she has on B., in begging for forgiveness for Lady Davers (360). Her chief anxiety in her conversations with B. is that she will overstep the boundaries he has prescribed, in his injunctions and elsewhere, for her moral discourse—boundaries that could be most accurately defined by reinvoking the distinction between preaching and witnessing. In Richardson's later continuation of the novel (sometimes known as *Pamela in Her Exalted Condition*), Pamela quickly learns to interpret the comment "pretty preacher" as a hint that she has overstepped this limit: "I never dare to urge matters farther, when he calls me by that name."[47] Richardson must continually stage occasions, in the latter half of *Pamela* and more notably throughout the continuation, that will compel Pamela to reflect out loud or on paper on the moral grounds for her actions in various dilemmas, because to have her simply expound her views independently of experiential response would elevate her to the authoritative role of a preacher.

Pamela's epistolary form emerges as a necessary consequence of the ideology of feminine virtue that Richardson promotes. For Pamela's virtue to be believable, it must remain uncontaminated by its effects—by what it has achieved, materially and socially, for her. This is difficult or impossible to achieve with a retrospective narrator, who by the very nature of narrative must make clear the connections between actions and their results.[48] For B., by contrast, it is a case of "all's well that ends well": as with the young men in church, a virtuous ending confers a kind of retrospective sanction on the dubious actions that have directly led to it. B. makes this process explicit in his own retrospective account of the Pamela story in *Pamela in Her Exalted Condition*.

But even the epistolary form can provide no guarantee of privileged access to pure internal consciousness or raw experience, no sure inoculation against infection by results. A letter writer always has an audience, and hence potentially a consciousness thereof that shapes the writing of the letter. And even an intercepted letter gives us inside knowledge only if we can be sure that the writer had no knowledge of a possible interception. As Fielding showed, we can always imagine a Pamela who is one up on all of Mr. B.'s efforts to get access to what she "really" thinks, and such imaginings gain a certain plausibility by the fact that, after all, whatever she did worked: she got B.

Furthermore, as Ralph Rader explains, the need to signal, between the lines of Pamela's ostensibly innocent narration, the shape and direction of *Pamela*—to make readers recognize that it is a novel—inevitably casts doubt on her innocence as well. Pamela's letters must indicate to us, the readers, circumstances such as B.'s growing sympathy for Pamela, or her potential love for him, of which Pamela herself is supposed to be ignorant. But we may interpret these signals as signs of Pamela's own consciousness, not of the author's plotting. The tragic plot of *Clarissa* can be seen as in some sense a response to this problem: because Clarissa's principled choices always backfire for her in worldly terms, she, unlike Pamela, can scarcely be accused of having an eye to the main chance.[49]

Artfulness and Artlessness

But with a feminine narrator, even this strategy does not necessarily work. If Clarissa can hardly be accused of looking out for number one in material terms, she can be (and often is) accused of pandering to her own masochistic desires, or of maneuvering an elevation to sainthood as undeserved as Pamela's elevation to bourgeois opulence. This highlights an important point about "virtuous" feminine narrators. If there is one thing the textual and critical history of both *Pamela* and *Clarissa* makes clear, it is that no amount of narrative framing, rewriting, didactic footnotes, and critical insistence can secure an "artless" feminine narrator from accusations of artful narrative manipulation. The problem is simply implicit in the artistic (hence rhetorically self-conscious) construction of an "artless" first-person narrative. When we become conscious that we have been acted on rhetorically by a narrative—that is, when we become conscious of its designs on us —we have a choice between attributing the "design" to the author only, thereby rescuing the feminine narrator's reputation of artlessness, and attributing it to the narrator herself, thereby converting her into a manipulative, possibly negative, figure. The crux is that such a choice is radically undecidable based on evidence from within the narrative. Though it is customary for critics to argue for the artfulness of seemingly artless narrators by pointing to the rhetorical artistry of their narratives, such a strategy gets us nowhere, since it begs the question of whether the artistry is fictionally meant to reside in the character.[50] To convince us of something by means of a "genuinely" artless narrator, an author needs to employ rhetorically effective, "artful" means, and the artfulness of those means will then always be detectable by an astute reader, and attributable to the now-artful narrator instead.

Phelan suggests that, conventionally, lack of rhetorical self-consciousness is the "unmarked case" for homodiegetic narration in the novel. In the absence of overt signals—like Humbert Humbert's constant references to his own artistry in *Lolita*—he suggests, homodiegetic narrators should probably always be understood to be unconscious of the rhetorical aspects of their roles as narrators.[51] But I am not convinced that such a convention operates with any consistency in the eighteenth- and nineteenth-century novel (Phelan's most telling examples are from modern fiction). Certainly the issue seems a peculiarly vexed one in relation to female narrators, because the issue of narrative authority itself is more loaded. Female narrators have a way of winding up on this artful/artless seesaw, both within the novels in which they appear and in critical responses to them—a kind of narratological equivalent of the well-known angel/whore dichotomy. I am less interested in defending their virtue and artlessness than in elucidating the logic that links the two. Because conventionally no innate authority is granted to the female narrator, any perceived attempt to exert power over a reader is implicitly underhanded or suspicious. In the artful/artless dichotomy, there is no space for legitimate rhetorical artistry.

Feminine narration, as I use the term, then, can describe a narrative voice that falls on either side of the artful/artless divide: it can take the form of either Moll Flanders's deviant lust for plotting or Pamela's virtuous resistance to it. In fact, as the famous *Pamela/Shamela* pairing suggests, writers and readers of the period seem particularly drawn to the opposition—or oscillation—between the two.

Such a context sheds a different light on a text like "Female Ingenuity," the 1833 coded bride's letter from *Atkinson's Casket* that Lanser reprints and analyzes in detail in both "Towards a Feminist Narratology" and *Fictions of Authority.* The letter was printed with a simple "key" (that one read only every other line) that enables the reader to unveil a subtext of marital resentment beneath a seemingly innocent text of newlywed joy. Lanser notes that the two texts are able to coexist because of their shared reliance on a series of negative generalizations about what marriage means to women —generalizations whose personal application is denied in the top text and affirmed in the coded one. She concludes that the text as a whole is "politically motivated" and has as its primary intended audience someone who can "understand 'female ingenuity' as cultural critique."[52] But the relationship of the artful, coded text to the apparently artless surface text strikes me as too similar to the relationship of *Shamela* to *Pamela* to be obviously feminist in its aims or effects. Does the pleasure of reading this text come from identifying with "female ingenuity" as politicized resistance or from the triumph of unveiling the artful woman at work behind the mask of innocent artlessness?

Certain narrative forms—specifically, the epistolary and diary style—are more closely associated with feminine narration than others, in that they typically preclude the degree of retrospectivity needed for authoritative narrative shaping, and at least imply the presence of an intervening editor-figure who makes these private documents public. For this reason, the convention can also be linked to Lanser's useful gendered distinction between "public" and "private" forms of narration: "What came by the 1750s to stand for female voice—to be, indeed, among the novel's most marketable commodities—was a voice that modeled not public proclamation but private confidence," and one that constituted the textual woman "as a secret to penetrate."[53] But neither association is definitive: Lovelace's narrative position is technically as private and temporally immanent as Clarissa's, while Esther Summerson's narration in *Bleak House* is both "public" and retrospective, yet I will argue that both remain largely within gendered conventions of narration. "Femininity" in narrative is a function of the narrator's relation to the perceived structure and meaning of the narrative as a whole. Feminine narrators, whether they demonstrate their virtuous femininity by proving themselves unable or unwilling to generate coherent plots, or "artfully" construct them in ways we are invited to "see through," share in common the fact that we are expected to take our narrative pleasure at their expense. Rather than being subjected to their narrative authority, we are invited to assume authority over them—to construct a plot and a meaning out of their words that they themselves cannot understand, or do not wish us to know. This authority may be benevolent and paternalistic or triumphant and punitive, but characteristically it makes the feminine narrator the object, rather than the subject, of narrative manipulations.

The Functions of Feminine Narration

In a recent article, Booth has persuasively argued against assigning an a priori moral or ideological value to any particular narrative technique.[54] This observation is complicated in the case of feminine narration by the fact that the convention itself carries considerable—and from a feminist perspective, unsavory—ideological baggage. Novelists of this period, I would argue, did not have the option of ignoring that baggage, but they could, and did, unpack it and deploy it differently in different contexts. Darsie Latimer's function as a feminized male captive-diarist in *Redgauntlet,* for example, is radically different in its ideological implications from Jonathan Harker's, in a similar role, in *Dracula.*

Furthermore, in the context of some of the twentieth century's more thoroughgoing rejections of masterly narratives, the ideological significance of techniques that look like feminine narration might read very differently. At what point does a debilitating incapacity to "master" narrative, with its codes of clearly defined causality and moral and intellectual coherence, become a potentially revolutionary refusal of those codes and all they imply, making it not "feminine narration" but *écriture feminine*? This seems to me, as I am sure it would to Booth, to be a question that cannot be settled entirely in abstract, general terms. It would have to come out of a close reading of how the narration operates, particularly in relation to the narrative structure of the novel as a whole, in the texts in question.

Linda Kauffman provides a good example of how textual features I identify with feminine narration might be read instead as forms of resistance to masterly and coherent narrative. She links both *Clarissa* and *Jane Eyre* to the genre of the "amorous epistle," composed of fictional or actual letters from an abandoned woman to her lover, a genre she argues is characterized in part by its refusal of distance and its resistance to conventional narrative shape and closure. Kauffman's application of her model is at its most tenuous, though, with these two novels—the only British novels from this period she considers. *Clarissa* and *Jane Eyre* are the only texts she discusses that do not in fact conform to her definition of the genre (neither is presented as the letters of an abandoned woman to her lover), nor do they conform well to her summary of the genre's other major features. Finally, both are largely absent from the clear and convincing chain of influence and intertextual reference she traces among the other works she discusses, from Ovid's *Heroides* through Heloise and the Portuegese Nun to the twentieth-century reworking of that text. If the "amorous epistle" is an influence at all, I would argue, it is at best a buried subtext in these novels, in which the female narrative voices are demonstrably deeply involved—or entangled—in the drive for narrative shape and meaning, and consequently bound up in the dynamics of plotting and preaching.

Both Kaufman's argument and my disagreement with it underscore Booth's point about the final moral or ideological valence of any given narrative technique. Whether the narrator of *Jane Eyre* is refusing narrative coherence and closure through her evocation of the genre of the "amorous epistle," as Kaufman argues, or claiming them in a subtly crafted subversion of the convention of feminine narration—as I argue below—or in fact doing neither of these things, can be decided finally only by reading *Jane Eyre* itself, closely and carefully, with reference to its larger literary and cultural contexts. One of those contexts, I am arguing, is the convention of feminine narration, a convention that may be resisted, redirected, or transmuted, but not simply disregarded.

Like any other literary technique, feminine narration is likely to be overdetermined in its use, serving multiple, even conflicting purposes. But there are significant consistent features of its use. One of the pleasures feminine narration offers, and hence one of its functions, is its apparent empowerment of the reader. By appearing to offer only the raw material of narrative, feminine narration at its most pure provides the reader with a kind of do-it-yourself kit for narrative, in contrast to the ready-made article offered by a more conventionally authoritative narrator.[55] As one Victorian reviewer wrote in praise of Dickens's portrayal of Esther Summerson in *Bleak House:* "He does not draw his heroine's picture: he does not even make *her* do it: he leaves the reader to do it himself, and yet the latter (be he ever so dull-witted) can draw it only one way, under his unseen guidance."[56] Used exclusively, as in *Pamela,* feminine narration makes the novelist's own "designs" less obtrusive: the readers' relatively authoritative relationship to a female narrative witness may offset or obscure their subjection to the more "preacherly" ideological work of the novel as a whole. Used in conjunction with, or subordination to, an authoritative narrator, as in *Bleak House, Armadale,* and to a lesser degree *Humphrey Clinker,* it can provide crucial relief from the overt didacticism or narrative manipulations of such narrators.

Many deployments of female narrators can also be read as part of a buried debate about the place and authority of the female *writer.* That women novelists' constructions of female narrators should be inflected by their own relationships to and attitudes toward authorial "authority" comes as no surprise: if anything, the point is likely to be overemphasized, in the tendency to read the heroine of a female author as an authorial "self" rather than as a self-conscious narrative construct. My discussions of the female narrators produced by Brontë and Barrett Browning examine the negotiations these authors carry out between the conventions of literary femininity in narration and the desire to produce female voices who can serve as their own master-narrators.

But male writers' constructions of female narrative voices can also be read as a response to their female fellow authors: Richardson's interest in the limiting proprieties of female written self-representation coincides with the process of constituting himself as one of the male "founders" of a new genre hitherto well established among women writers.[57] Dickens responds to the phenomenal power and popularity of *Jane Eyre* initially with the male first-person narrator of *David Copperfield*—his first use of the form, and one that, particularly in the childhood sections, draws heavily on the plot and emotional effects of *Jane Eyre*—and then with *Bleak House*, which offers us a new female version of the abused but loving orphan, but one largely stripped of the conflicted self-assertion that made both Jane and David compelling as well as sympathetic children. Collins repeatedly stages the triumph of self-authorized male artist-figures over powerful and resourceful women who threaten their narrative preeminence. For these authors, in other words, the use of feminine narrators can be read as a corrective or compensatory response to the growing access to narrative authority (and all it implied) by the women writers who were in fact their direct competitors.

The use of feminine narrators, particularly in mixed narratives, sometimes has less to do with real women than with the process whereby troubling tensions or oppositions are mapped onto gender binaries as a way of stabilizing them. Novels like Collins's, which move toward an opposition between a subordinated feminine narrator and a hypermasculine master-narrator who gains a full command of narrative authority and agency, may be driven less by the fear that "mastery" could be made available to women than by the fear that it is not available at all. Early in *Armadale*, a character asks if we are "the masters of our own destinies"; can "mortal freewill . . . conquer mortal fate"?[58] The hard-won "yes" that the male protagonist in this novel eventually achieves is enabled in part by projecting the possibility of failure onto a competing female figure.

As the above should make clear, the literary history of feminine narration is by no means static over this period. While *Pamela* and *Clarissa* continued to exert considerable pull as foundational texts, later reworkings of their concerns—particularly such a radical and successful one as *Jane Eyre*—also necessarily become part of the field of influences on subsequent writers. In the latter part of the nineteenth century, the convention seems to come under increasing strain—as does the corresponding model of masculine narrative authority—making its most significant appearances in the sensation and Gothic novels of Wilkie Collins and Bram Stoker, which both challenge the convention more profoundly and reassert it more anxiously than most of their predecessors.

I present the following chapters largely in chronological order to emphasize the ongoing process of enforcing, challenging, reasserting, and reshaping the convention of feminine narration that goes on between as well as within these novels. But I am not primarily interested in presenting the kind of monolithic critical narrative that would subordinate these literary texts to a master-narrative of literary or cultural history, making them witnesses to broader cultural processes. Rather, I want to use the features of feminine narration as a critical tool to help reveal the gender dynamics operating on the level of form in these novels, both individually and in their dialogues with each other. Such dynamics, I suggest, are more hidden and often more recalcitrant than the overt thematics of gender.

One

THE TRIUMPH OF THE ANTIPLOTTER
Narration in *Clarissa*

*B*ecause of her intensive psychological self-scrutiny and her pervading awareness of her role as "exemplar" to her sex—both of which are provoked and encouraged by her correspondence with Anna Howe—Clarissa is a far more explicitly self-conscious narrator than Pamela, as well as more attuned to her impact on a broader social audience. She is also granted an unprecedented degree of moral authority. She frequently includes in her letters short essays on moral subjects that are only tangentially relevant to her own situation, and does not hesitate to lecture other characters on their "duty." Called "saint" and "angel" by those characters who have the benefit of her conversation, she has her moral reflections and injunctions copied and disseminated both within the novel and after its publication. This is the mark of Clarissa's moral supererogation of her own (and her author's) society: unlike Pamela, who has been only temporarily isolated from supportive authority figures, and who is pursued by a man of (we are told) ultimately sound principles, Clarissa is the only center of moral authority available for most of the novel. In all these respects, then, she seems at least potentially more authoritative, more "in control" as a narrator than I have suggested was appropriate for a feminine first-person narrator.

At the same time, though, as Castle and others have observed, much of what Clarissa's letters convey is a narrative of specifically linguistic disempowerment—what Terry Castle calls "hermeneutic violence":[1] Clarissa's speech and letters are continually interrupted, forbidden, misinterpreted and turned against her, or left unheard or unread. The "hermeneutic violence" Clarissa suffers is both the representation and the tool of the more material oppression of her, but it is in itself, for a character who ultimately cares more deeply about meaning than about her body, the unkindest cut of all.

Given this odd combination of power and victimhood, it is not surprising that critics, even those who share many of the same theoretical assumptions about language, should present such radically divergent versions of

35

Clarissa's narrative position. In William Warner's *Reading Clarissa,* Clarissa emerges as a kind of pious megalomaniac in her exercise of narrative authority, manipulating her own and others' representations to present a hegemonic narrative of her own spiritual triumph.[2] For Castle, by contrast, she is the novel's "exemplary victim of hermeneutic violence. Across the text, hers is that voice which repeatedly fails to make itself heard."[3] Terry Eagleton occupies both positions, though without attempting a reconciliation. Initially he suggests that Clarissa is a "masculine" figure who exerts "the fullest possible control over her meanings," and emerges as a "transcendental subject . . . whose relationship to writing is dominative and instrumental."[4] But in his efforts to read the novel as covert social critique, Eagleton, like Castle, winds up reading Clarissa as a victim of forces, including linguistic ones, over which she has no control.

If there is one point on which all three critics agree, it is that Clarissa does operate on the assumption that language is "representational"; that is, that "telling the truth" is an unproblematic intention and an absolute virtue—whether they see this as a canny form of self-empowerment or as evidence of fatal naïveté. In a certain sense, it is both: on the one hand, Clarissa's ideal of integrity, her refusal to stoop to the ungrounded permutations of language-as-strategy, or to assume that others are doing so, is what makes her so fatally vulnerable to the misconstructions of others. On the other hand, as Clarissa is well aware, her "integrity" is the foundation for whatever moral grandeur she will acquire, and also what will underwrite her power as an "exemplar" to an eighteenth-century audience. In this sense, Clarissa is neither (wholly) Castle's naive and pitiful victim nor Warner's prudish authoritarian. She is, above all, a powerful *figure.* That is to say, her representation as character and as epistolary narrator is the locus for the exercise of considerable narrative and ideological authority: narrative authority as a privileged source of "truth" and sincerity in a jumble of competing viewpoints, and ideological authority in her intra- and extratextual status as "exemplar" to her sex.

But the power of her representation cannot be equated with her own power as narrator or character. Indeed, I will argue that within the terms of Richardson's text the two are mutually exclusive. Despite Clarissa's narrative centrality and moral exemplarity—or rather, by means of them— the novel acts as a limit-case for what I have termed *feminine* narration. In *Clarissa,* Richardson is raising the processes and categories involved in *Pamela* to a different level of consciousness, just as the field of action in which the story can be conceived as one of "Virtue Rewarded" has been raised to include an afterlife. Clarissa is not freed from the limitations that made Pamela the object, not the subject, of the novel's competing "plots." A favorable reading of Clarissa as exemplary character is dependent upon perceiving her as closed out of "plotting" in all senses of the term, as *not* being the constructor of her own story. But rather than being, as Pamela is, closed out of it either by incapacity or by the imposition of an authority she recognizes as superior, Clarissa must continually choose to close *herself* out, in deference to a moral code whose ultimate logic demands of her the role of the ineffectually protesting victim. Her power as a representation, as an "exemplar," is founded upon her self-conscious self-exclusion from more wieldable forms of power, both linguistic and material— her self-exclusion, that is, from narrative and material authority.[5] Clarissa's reasoned, willed acceptance of the position of the feminine narrator, and the novel's linking of that acceptance with her moral exemplarity for women, makes *Clarissa* a powerful foundational text for the conventions of feminine narration.

Clarissa also complicates the narrative issues raised in *Pamela* through its multiplication of narrators: the novel is composed principally of two two-way correspondences between same-sex pairs of close friends—Clarissa and Anna Howe, and Lovelace and Belford. These dual correspondences offer not only contrasting perspectives on the same events, but also the correspondents' contrasting reflections on the nature of their own and each others' friendships and on the style and meaning of their correspondences. They consequently invite (and themselves often make) gender-based comparisons of characters' relationships to plotting and narrative. At the same time, differences within the pairs illuminate the parameters of the gendered divisions between them. Clarissa and Lovelace represent extremes of a kind: while Clarissa embodies the "feminine" virtue of submission to social/patriarchal and divine authority almost to the limit of human believability (and, some would argue, beyond), Lovelace exhibits a "masculine" ambition for mastery that overreaches human limitations in the other direction, through its defiance of social and divine laws. Their confidants, however, explore a more ambiguous middle region: Anna Howe questions and tests the boundaries of feminine propriety and capacity that cut her off from a male world of purpose and power; and Belford, in dialogue with both Lovelace and Clarissa, anticipates Grandison in seeking an active and manly moral stance that can yet do justice to the virtue of a Clarissa.

As we shall see, their status and activities as narrators parallel and reflect these positions.

The Plotting Correspondent 1: Lovelace

At first glance, *Clarissa* hardly looks like the place for locating stable gender roles, particularly in relation to Lovelace, who is often viewed as an androgynous or even a feminized figure. Eagleton, for example, having defined Clarissa's relation to language as "masculine," sees Lovelace as representing the "feminine," with his "more inward, bodily relationship to script."[6] Eagleton may owe this gender reversal partly to Warner, whose reading of Lovelace as playful deconstructor of Clarissa's logocentric false-consciousness would implicitly associate him with *écriture feminine* and her with patriarchal language:[7] Eagleton's later telling attack on Warner's reading challenges the values attached to these positions rather than the alignment itself. But Lovelace, too, occasionally identifies himself with women, most notably in his oft-quoted claim to have "a good deal of the soul of a woman,"[8] and also in his related habit of attributing to "the sex" (i.e., women) qualities, such as a love of plotting or of sexual adventure, that he must eventually concede that Clarissa does *not* have, and that he in fact exhibits par excellence himself. I would like to argue, though, that all of these forms of seeming feminization are in fact subordinated to—and sometimes directly in furtherance of—a broader aim of material and narrative mastery: an aim that the novel, and particularly Lovelace, constructs as a peculiarly masculine prerogative.

Eagleton later retreats from the clear gender reversal he articulates, concluding that Richardson's characters are more messily androgynous than it suggests ("the letter in *Clarissa* is masculine and feminine together").[9] But the difficulty lies elsewhere. By placing Lovelace simply on the "other" (and hence feminine) side of transcendence, order, control, or "truth, coherence and causality,"[10] and by making Clarissa unambiguously their self-conscious representative and promoter, his formulation obscures the more complex relations each character has to these concepts, and the very different kinds of power these relationships give them.

What Eagleton calls Clarissa's "dominative" control of meaning—the singlemindedness that makes her letters "orderly regimes of sense that brook no contradiction"—is in fact closely linked to what he elsewhere terms her "representational" model of language. Her conscientious adherence to the idea that language can be and should be a medium for telling the truth is precisely a *rejection* of the model of language as strategically powerful, as "dominative and instrumental." It is important not to confuse a commitment to *telling* the truth as one understands it with an authoritative claim to *possess* the truth, as I think Eagleton does here. It is those, like Lovelace, who feel no such commitment who are best able to manipulate claims to "truth, coherence and causality" for strategic ends. Nor should one attribute a more naively representational model of language to Clarissa than she in fact possesses. As her willingness to subject herself to Anna's critical readings suggests, Clarissa at least accepts the possibility of a disjunction between conscious intention and meaning.

This is what makes Clarissa's language so vulnerable to being used by others for ends beyond her control. As we shall see, this abdication of linguistic power is closely linked to her "feminine" conception of virtue. By the same token, if Lovelace feels free to violate notions of "truth, coherence and causality," it is not because he has no desire for the authority associated with them. Just as, for the con man, the ideal world is one in which everyone else is honest, so Lovelace envisages a world in which all others (and particularly women) are obliged to keep their promises, to say what they believe, and to believe what *he* says. In language as in action, Lovelace is less a revolutionary than an opportunist.

In fact, the conclusion Eagleton tentatively advances here on the novel's behalf—that "one falsehood [can] be countered only by another more fruitful falsehood, which in shifting the balance of power in one's favour may bring a deeper demystification to birth"[11]—is itself an excellent description of *Lovelace's* strategy, given that he sees his own elaborate and eminently fruitful falsehoods as a way of unmasking Clarissa's "mystified" notion of her own Virtue and of taking revenge on her sex and family, and hence as an advance for his version of "truth and justice." It is wrong, then, to suggest that Lovelace's relishing of the playfulness of his own writing and plotting stands in contrast to its calculated effectiveness: it is precisely Lovelace's more flexible approach to representation that enables his letters to be so "cruelly instrumental" in their very playful inventiveness.[12] Lovelace's "mercurial, diffuse, exuberant" prose has much in common with his equally mercurial social style, which his opponents come to suspect is more calculated and controlled than he wishes it to seem. "A sort of *manageable* anger, let loose to intimidate me" (392) Clarissa calls one of his outbursts, and Lovelace's own account of the same scene confirms the suspicion: "when humility would not do, I raised my voice and suffered my eye to sparkle with anger; hoping to take advantage of that sweet cowardice which is so amiable in the sex, . . . and to which my victory over this proud beauty is principally owing" (412). When Lovelace writes to Clarissa that, if she stops writing to him, "he will not presume to threaten either his own life, or that of any other man, [but] must take his resolutions as such a dreaded event shall impel him at the time" (100), he is obviously not really resigning himself to the momentary gusts of his passions as they "impel him at the time," but delivering a hint to Clarissa the effect of which has been careful-ly—and accurately—planned. Belford, too, describes him, in contrast to his public image, as "a man . . . not hurried, as most men, by gusts of violent passion," and notes the tremendous advantage this gives him as a plotter and seducer (501).

Part of the contradiction Eagleton puzzles at between the effectiveness of Lovelace's prose in the "end game of rape" and his seemingly playful rejection of "any vulgar *end* of writing" derives from his lumping together of Lovelace's letters to Belford with all his other correspondence as repre-sentative of his relationship to "writing" in general. In fact, though, the two fall on different sides of Lovelace's twin passions for "perform[ing] great actions by day, and [writing] them down at night" (74). While Lovelace's letters to other characters—Clarissa, Joseph Leman, Lord M., and so forth—are part and parcel of his material "plotting," on the same plane as his staged conversations with coached imposters or his faked rages, his let-ters to Belford are part of the process of reflecting on and savoring the progress of those plots—hence, the absence of any obvious *material* instru-mentality in their composition. This does not mean, however, that they constitute writing for its own sake, or indicate an "inward, bodily relation to script." *Their* instrumentality is rather that of narrative: they seek to engross their reader (i.e., Belford), to exert a power over his consciousness. And Lovelace relishes this kind of power at least as much as he does his power over Clarissa and the others he draws into his "plots." He glories in his narrative control—in the special effects created by withholding crucial information or adopting a particular style, in the power to manipulate a reader's impressions: "Now, Belford, for the narrative of narratives. I will continue it as I have opportunity; and that so dexterously, that if I break off twenty times, thou shalt not discern where I piece my thread" (767), he writes at one point; and elsewhere, as in his early accounts of meeting "Tomlinson," he describes scenes in such a way that Belford (and the reader) cannot be sure whether they are genuine or simply the product of more Lovelacean staging. Even his oft-quoted comment on his "lively *present-tense* manner" is a confession of the care and intent with which that "manner" is constructed: "Thoul't observe, Belford, that though this was written afterwards, yet (as in other places) I write it as it was spoken, and happened; *as if* I had retired to put down every sentence as spoken" (emphasis added)—and this is done specifically with an eye to its effect on Belford: "I know thou likest this . . . , as it is one of my peculiars" (882).[13] And Lovelace asserts his narrative authority over Belford even more insistently than he does his right as "general" to direct his actions, chiding him for daring to use his own words against him—for challenging the structure of significance he provides for his own information—and at one point even threatening to "punish" him by ceasing the narrative altogether (610). (This last hint is quickly abandoned, however, because it would mean losing himself the "pleasure in writing on this charming subject"; it seems that Lovelace cannot take pleasure in his writing without the consciousness of an appreciative audience.) As Janet Todd notes, Lovelace's letters to Belford "reiterate his domination over him . . . he largely ignores Belford's actual letters, instead dictating words and coercing his friend into attitudes of his own choosing."[14]

In other words, while Lovelace seeks to construct Clarissa as a character in his fictions—one who is (he hopes) largely unconscious of the complex structuring forces at work, and whose fate, and even identity, are ultimately to be determined by the plots he sets in motion around her—he constructs Belford as a model reader, who can on the writer's whim sometimes be made to share in a character's ignorance and at other times be given the inside knowledge that will enable him to appreciate the artist-narrator's careful teleological structuring: "I enclose the letter from Joseph Leman which I mentioned to thee in mine of Monday last, with my answer to it. I cannot resist the vanity that urges me to the communication. Otherwise it were better, perhaps, that I suffer thee to imagine that this lady's stars fight against her, and dispense the opportunities in my favour which are only the consequences of my own superlative invention" (493–94).

If Lovelace's "exuberant" and wide-ranging prose does not always give an impression of such an obsessive concern with mastery, it is partly because of the sheer reach of his ambition: he longs to absorb absolutely everything into his sphere of control. In spinning endless peripheral plots, whether carried into action or not, to take advantage of every chance occurrence and draw upon the analyzed weaknesses of every casually encountered character, Lovelace seeks to demonstrate at least his potential for absolute control of his environment. Hence his frequent association of his own plans with fate itself: "Why will this charming creature make such contrivances necessary as will increase my trouble, and my guilt too, as some would account it? But why, rather I would ask, will she fight against her stars?" (554). The same principle applies to Lovelace's elaborate justifications for his actions and explanations of his principles. These are applied in such a seemingly inconsistent and ad hoc fashion that it is tempting to see them as simply literary playfulness—Lovelace's way of proving again and again the plasticity of the language of justification: he can talk his way out of anything. But Lovelacean casuistry loses a great deal of its inconsistency and illogic when we consider that he continually casts himself as the ultimate dispenser of temptations and trials, rewards and punishments: his arguments have all the logic of a complex theodicy centered on himself. It is difficult, then, to see in what useful sense this striving for mastery over narrative, event, and meaning could be construed as "feminine."

Indeed, one problem with identifying Lovelace's prose with *écriture feminine,* or deconstructive playfulness, is precisely that it leads the critic to take his protean shifts at face value, obscuring the further-reaching, other-directed calculation—both literary and material—that underlies them. The most striking example of this is Eagleton's attempt to explore the psychoanalytic depths of the "baffling, bottomlessly interpretable dream-text" Lovelace recounts to Belford shortly after the rape, during the period of Clarissa's first attempts at escape.[15] Calling the dream "worthy of a whole study in itself,"[16] Eagleton goes on briefly to psychoanalyze the dream's multiple transformations—good-hearted "matronly dowager" into evil "Mother H.," and then into Lovelace himself; Clarissa into happy matron, and so on—as evidence of Lovelace's "polymorphous perversity" and consequent inability to enter the symbolic order, with its "stable system of gender roles."[17]

But a closer look at the letter's style and context raises questions about whether the text can be considered a true dream at all, or, at least, whether as such it can be said to offer any kind of raw material from the narrator-as-patient's unconscious for the critic-as-analyst to work on. The previous letter to Belford has closed with Lovelace considering how he might turn Clarissa's desire for escape to his own advantage: "Is there no way to oblige her, and yet to make the very act subservient to my own views?" (920). Introducing the dream text in his next letter, he notes that it is a product of his contemplation of the "precarious situation I stand in with my beloved"—that is, her desperate desire to escape from him—and calls it "a fortunate dream; which, as I imagine, will afford my working mind the means to effect the obliging double purpose my heart is now once more

set upon." Finally, before turning to the dream itself, he embarks on a
seemingly digressive paean to the joys of plotting: "What, as I have often
contemplated, is the enjoyment of the finest woman in the world, to the
contrivance, the bustle, the surprises, and at last the happy conclusion of a
well-laid plot?—The charming *roundabouts,* to come the *nearest way
home*—the doubts; the apprehensions; the heartachings, the meditated
triumphs—These are the joys that make the blessing dear" (920). (It is no
coincidence that this passage also describes perfectly the pleasures of reading traditional novels.)

The dream, then, is clearly to be read in the context of Lovelace's efforts
to plot his way out of his latest difficulties with Clarissa. And the dream
itself takes the form of an elaborately worked out plot: Mother H.,
disguised as a matronly dowager, will appear in the street; Dorcas, on
instructions from Lovelace, will pretend to appeal to her for help and then
convince Clarissa to escape with her. Back at Mother H.'s house, the setting
and staffing of which are calculated to inspire Clarissa's confidence, inci-
dents will be arranged to induce Clarissa to share her hostess's bed, where-
upon Mother H. can stage an excuse to get out of bed and go to her closet,
enabling her to switch places with Lovelace, who has been secreted there by
prior arrangement. Finally, Lovelace concludes his account of the dream
with the claim that, as he is a "strange dreamer . . . it is not altogether
improbable that something like it may happen; as the pretty simpleton has
had the weakness to confide in Dorcas" (922). The additions he makes to
the dream after this point are closer to conscious finishing touches on the
plot than to a dream-text, full of practical details like the date of her uncle's
birthday, or the advantages of Mother H.'s more plausibly virtuous appearance. By the end of the letter, Lovelace is already referring to the whole
thing as a "scheme" or a "happy invention," his "present contrivance" (923).

To psychoanalyze such an account as the pure product of Lovelace's
unconscious, then, seems to miss the point. The substitutions the "dream"
makes—Mother H. for the dowager; Lovelace for Mother H.—need not
hold any particular psychic depths: not only are such impersonations and
bedroom substitutions habitual in Lovelace's own plots (he had planned
something very similar in the earlier Miss Partington plot), they are utterly
conventional in seduction tales of the period, the frequency with which
women at that time slept together making female disguise an inviting strategy for gaining access to a woman in bed. And if the rest of the "dream"
proper slips into something closer to fantasy than strategy—Clarissa's preg-
nancy, the parallel seduction of Anna Howe, and so on—it still remains

broadly consistent with Lovelace's previous (and subsequent) statements of his less virtuous long-term hopes and intentions toward Clarissa and her friend. If it is appropriate to consider this text as a real dream at all, its effortless translation into an eminently practical plot (which Lovelace indeed later attempts to put into execution) reveals little more than the extent to which even Lovelace's unconscious is in the service of his conscious desire for mastery.

But as I have suggested, there is reason to doubt that this is even meant to represent a real dream.[18] The other element of the text effaced by treating it as a kind of written free-association is the significance of its literary style and presentation. Lovelace frequently adopts literary genres that will obscure the background and mechanics of his plotting to present only its puzzling surface to a reader, as a way of revealing his devices to Belford with maximum artistic effect—as when he presents his first meeting with Tomlinson in the form of a dramatic scene, of which he only later reveals himself as the author and director. The dream-form he uses here has a similar effect, but with added implications from its distinctive style: for the main text of the dream, Lovelace quite self-consciously adopts the diction and syntax of biblical prophesy, using expressions like "Hasten, oh damsel," and "I lifted up mine eyes, and behold the lady issued out of the house"—and at times rising almost to the poetry of the psalms: "'my chariot shall be her asylum . . . my house shall be her sanctuary, and I will protect her from all her oppressors'" (921). By presenting his plot as a prophetic dream, Lovelace can implicitly cast himself as both prophet and God—a "strange dreamer" indeed, with the power to convert his own dreams to reality. Far from associating Lovelace with a "hermaphroditic" Satan who resides "outside" the symbolic order,[19] then, this "dream," like the self-centered logic of his casuistry, reveals him as the all-too-male oedipal Satan who seeks to usurp its central position.

An interesting contrast is provided by the dream of tumbling into a pit that Lovelace has after Clarissa's escape, at a point where his sense of control over the situation with Clarissa—and over his narrative to Belford— has eroded seriously. He tells Belford about the dream only because it has given him a "cursed fright," and he can find no significance in it other than "that, sleeping or waking, my Clarissa is always present with me" (1218)— though he later makes a conspicuously weak attempt to interpret it favorably. In contrast to the Mother H. dream, which was an extension of Lovelace's own plotting consciousness, this dream offers a glimpse of Divine plotting through the medium of Lovelace's unconscious guilt, and is hence an intrusion of genuine prophecy. Lovelace is consequently the only person in the novel or out of it who could fail to understand its obvious foreshadowing of Clarissa's salvation and his damnation, for he resists above all the acknowledgment of a plotter whose powers supersede his own.

What, then, are we to make of Lovelace's own claims to femininity? Tassie Gwilliam has provided a detailed account of Lovelace's "contradictory desires . . . both to identify with and possess women."[20] What I would like to stress in her account is the degree to which Lovelace sees identification with women as a source of power over them. Like many other self-proclaimed "hermaphrodites," Lovelace believes "that femininity is constituted by a secrecy that, once exploded, destroys the power of women."[21] Lovelace's claims to femininity, then, are not abdications of, but powerful supplements to, his manhood. Indeed, in the letter in which he compares himself to Tiresias, the one characteristic of "modest women" with which Lovelace does *not* claim to identify is their passivity: "The difference between us is only, what they *think*, I *act*" (441). And this, of course, makes *all* the difference. For Lovelace, as for Tiresias, the experience of womanhood is a detour on the road to a privileged position vis-à-vis women, a position that relies on his superior power and authority as a man: as Gwilliam notes, "Tiresias, as ex-woman, has usurped [Juno's] position [as an authority on women's sexual experience] by his ability to speak for women without the disability of speaking (only) as a woman."[22] Lovelace, like Tiresias, begins and ends as a man, and that is what constitutes his power as a (supposed) part-woman.

Lovelace's more stereotypically misogynist claims about women's evil propensities serve a different but related function in propping up masculine power. Taking such statements straight as indicative of Richardson's gender ideology leads to a reading like Judith Wilt's, in which both a virtuously asexed Clarissa and the well-intentioned masculine side of Lovelace are victimized by the evil plot-spinning womanhood within him and around them both—that is, Sinclair and company.[23] But it would surely be at least equally reasonable to accept, as the basis for a distribution of gender characteristics, Clarissa's and Anna's comments that Lovelace's proclivities are, if exaggerated in degree, still typically and predictably "male."[24] Anna frequently draws on Clarissa's experiences with Lovelace to draw conclusions about what women can expect from men in general (e.g., at 1015), while Clarissa casts herself as victimized by the "masculine passions" (992) of Lovelace and her male relatives. Even Bella's "hard-heartedness" is accounted for by the reflection that "she has been thought to be masculine in her air, and in her spirit" (309).

It is more helpful to see Lovelace's comments as part of a familiar process whereby a patriarchal ideology attributes to women an inordinate and dangerous proclivity for activities that are intended to be a solely a male prerogative.[25] Such desires may be represented as faults to which women are particularly prone, but only because in men they register not as faults but as normality. For this reason, the achievement of their desires tends to make such faulty women perversely "masculine"—or, at best, unwomanly. Thus, even Lovelace attributes Mrs. Sinclair's power to frighten Clarissa to her "masculine air" (882).[26]

Indeed, linked with Lovelace's comments on women's propensity for plotting is a kind of proprietorial outrage when he catches them trying to outplot *him,* together with an unbounded confidence that, as women, they lack the capacity to succeed. When he first gets access to extracts from Anna Howe's letters, for instance, Lovelace takes umbrage at a mysterious reference to "Norris," which he suspects is part of some plot. He interprets such an unnatural intrusion on his territory as justifying further efforts on his part: "If such innocents can allow themselves to plot, to *Norris,* well may I" (634). On the one hand, Lovelace suggests that there is something masculine about Anna's supposed efforts to outplot him—"This girl's a devilish rake in her heart"—but he also indicates that only as a real man would she pose any serious threat: "Had she been a man, and one of us, she'd have outdone us all in enterprise and spirit" (634). Similarly, while taking offense at her efforts to make sense of his behavior, Lovelace also pokes fun at her feminine inability to arrive at a consistent interpretation of it, and at the day-to-day variations in her advice to her friend that result: "How I do love to puzzle these *long-*sighted girls!" (636). A key distinction emerges in his exclamation that "Women can't swear . . . they can only curse" (636). While an oath calls on God to witness the swearer's intention to carry out an act himself—and therefore implies the power to do so regardless of opposition—a curse merely asks God to carry out some form of vengeance on the curser's behalf. That is, while an oath establishes a claim on the future: "I *will* do *X*," a curse is a tacit admission of powerlessness over it.

When further extracts from Anna's letter reveal the outlines of a genuine scheme for Clarissa's escape, Lovelace is outraged, but more confident than ever: "Now the contention becomes arduous. Now wilt thou not wonder, if I let loose my plotting genius upon them both. I will not be *out-Norrised,*

Belford" (639). He casts his project implicitly as one of punishing "girls" who overstep the bounds of their sex: "'Tis my pride to subdue girls who know *too much* to *doubt* their knowledge; and to convince them that they know *too little* to defend themselves from the inconveniencies of knowing *too much*" (639). In other words, women who plot represent to master-plotter Lovelace a challenge, an opportunity, and a kind of perverse responsibility. He is simultaneously annoyed that they have encroached upon his territory and pleased that they have taken him on in an area where he is confident of his superiority, while the very fact that they have stooped to plotting justifies the punishment of being outplotted.

"Clarissa" and Clarissa

Clarissa is, from the start, the force that undermines and eventually dissolves Lovelace's mastery. This occurs by, as it were, three different routes: by means of the impression she makes on Lovelace; by means of the impression she makes on Belford via Lovelace; and finally, and perhaps least important, by means of her own (usually ineffectual) material opposition to Lovelace's plotting. The first two of these routes represent aspects of her "power" of which she is often unaware at the time, and that she thus cannot self-consciously manipulate, or "plot," to produce desired effects. I will use quotation marks to distinguish between the idea or image of "Clarissa" that produces these effects, and Clarissa as an acting, thinking, writing character. It is precisely the gap in agency between "Clarissa" and Clarissa, I would argue, that renders "Clarissa" so effective.

"Clarissa" produces an internal division in Lovelace's consciousness almost from the start of his dealings with her: a part of him really does want to "reform" and settle down with her in virtuous wedded bliss, largely because she represents so effectively the values of that state. This is figured in the narrative, in female form, as Lovelace's "conscience." He consistently associates conscience with Clarissa herself, as when he identifies the unnerving "eye-beams" Captain Tomlinson feels emanating from Clarissa as "the dog's conscience," adding "I have felt half a dozen such flashes, such eye-beams, in as many different conversations with this soul-piercing beauty" (824). The most dramatic such identification occurs when Lovelace recounts his attempt to destroy his conscience, which has "stolen [his] pen" to plead for Clarissa, in terms that prefigure the rape itself: "Puling and *in-voiced*, . . . in vain implorest thou *my* mercy, who, in *thy* day, hast showed me so little! . . . And now will *thy* pain, and *my* pain from *thee*, soon be over! . . .

Had I not given thee thy death's wound, thou wouldst have robbed me of all my joys. Thou couldst not have mended me, 'tis plain. Thou couldst only have thrown me into despair. Didst thou not see that I had gone too far to recede? . . . Adieu, to thee, Oh thou inflexible and, till now, unconquerable bosom-intruder" (848).

The association here is so close that Eagleton identifies the "intruder" directly with Clarissa, who "is imitating [Lovelace's] handwriting as a kind of superior *Doppelganger* to himself."[27] Thus, in an ironic reversal of what Warner describes as Lovelace's salutary effort to decenter Clarissa "by introducing a small part of himself *into*" her,[28] "Clarissa" has already decentered Lovelace by introducing a part of herself into him—and as the above passage shows, he resists the process as violently as Clarissa ever could.

"Clarissa" also undermines Lovelace's narrative control through her indirect effect upon his correspondent, Belford. Lovelace initially professes to be pleased at Belford's pleading for Clarissa, since it gives him a chance to "exalt myself by proving thee a man of straw" (519), but as Belford persists despite his friend's reiterated counterarguments, Lovelace becomes decidedly less amused. Belford's claim to detect a counternarrative between the lines of Lovelace's own narrative implicitly challenges the latter's power over both his material and his literary "plots." Belford argues, first, that Lovelace is no more than the "tool" or "machine" of the Harlowes—that his own elaborate and inventive plots are really subordinate to the masterplot of Clarissa's siblings, or in service of the telos provided by her father's curse (604). Lovelace explodes in response: "*An instrument of the vile James Harlowe,* dost thou call me?—Oh Jack! how I could curse thee!" (609). This kind of enraged outburst against Belford is rare at this stage of the story, as Lovelace generally prefers to convey the impression that he is immune to any opposition Belford can offer. It is an indication, then, of just how much such a possibility disturbs him. Indeed, in the light of his own gendered distinction between cursing and swearing, made only a few letters later, Lovelace's impulse to "curse" on this occasion would seem to indicate that he perceives this suggestion as a profound threat to his sense of mastery.

More significantly, though, Belford throughout his correspondence disrupts Lovelace's elaborate casuistry, for if the former argument questions Lovelace's material power to control the destiny of himself and others, the latter questions his right to assign to them his own significance. As Belford's arguments begin to tell—that is, begin to correspond with the promptings of Lovelace's own "Clarissa"/conscience—Lovelace becomes increasingly insistent about the narrative authority he exerts, arguing that his status as Belford's only conduit for information about Clarissa gives him, in addition, sole authority over the meaning Belford assigns to it. Indeed, it might be argued that Belford's pleadings hasten Clarissa's "ruin," for the fact that Belford's moral challenges to Lovelace do correspond to those of his conscience only underlines for Lovelace the fact that his conscience itself poses a threat to his desired mastery.

These are, as we have said, aspects of Clarissa's "power" over which she has no direct agency. As she is not fully conscious at first of Lovelace's immoral designs on her, she cannot be aware either of the fight his "conscience" puts up on her behalf: the inconsistencies in his behavior that result register with her as merely puzzling, or as markers of his volatility, and she never tries to turn them to her advantage. And she is of course completely unaware of Belford's efforts on her behalf until long after the rape. These are, again, the effects of "Clarissa"—that is, of the image of herself produced by Clarissa's uncalculated *witnessing* to her own convictions. But "Clarissa" is really another name for Clarissa's exemplarity, so that although the power she exerts by means of her exemplary virtue is in one sense out of her knowledge or control, in another sense it is very much a part of her consciousness, in that she is continually concerned with her own exemplarity—that is, with maintaining, as far as possible, an absolute purity of motive and action.

Emphasis on the indirect power of Clarissa's exemplarity provides a necessary context for considering her refusal or incapacity to think and act strategically in her dealings with Lovelace. Critics (including both Lovelace and Anna Howe) have frequently expressed frustration at—and in some cases suspicion of—Clarissa's recurrent failure to "strike while the iron is hot" with Lovelace, which can at times seem almost deliberately self-destructive. But Clarissa's refusals of strategy are always in service of an ideal of virtue, which, in promoting her exemplary status, is ultimately more efficacious in defeating Lovelace's libertinism—albeit to her cost—than any plans she could have made or carried out to that purpose. To the extent that Clarissa triumphs over Lovelace, she does so by refusing to play his game—the game of "plotting"—at all.

Clarissa's position as a narrator exhibits a similar split between narrative authority and actual efforts to manipulate or control story and audience. For Lovelace, letter writing serves to show off his strategic and literary skills to best advantage. The epistolary mode, rather than limiting his stature as narrator by denying him the opportunity to shape his experience retroactively toward a known end, increases it by allowing him to demonstrate that events are shaped by his imagination before they even take place. His narration has a teleological power despite his immersion in events, because of his supreme confidence in a seamless continuum between the plot he has for the future and the plot of his unfolding narrative.

For Clarissa, by contrast (as for Pamela), the epistolary form becomes a way for Richardson to insure the heroine-narrator against the possible imputation of having shaped a plot in her own interests—though in this case the potential "plotting" has more to do with the narrating itself than with the events narrated. Anna Howe requests in her first letter that Clarissa "write in so full a manner as may gratify those who know not so much of your affairs as I do," reasoning that "[i]f anything unhappy should fall out from the violence of such spirits as you have to deal with, your account of all things previous to it will be your justification" (40). As Anna's reasoning implicitly suggests, "justification" cannot be retroactive, because it is then likely to seem motivated, its narrative shaped and selected, by the results that need "justifying." For Clarissa, justifying herself would be inherently suspect anyway, involving the assumption of a moral authority to which she is not entitled—though because it is important to her to be *justifiable* in all she does, it presents a continual temptation: "How dare a perverse girl take these liberties with relations so very respectable and whom she highly respects?" she asks, castigating herself, and then laments, "What an unhappy situation is that which obliges her, in her *own defence* as it were, to expose *their* failings?" (82).

This conflict between the desire to be justifiable and the impropriety of undertaking retroactive self-justification resurfaces later in Clarissa's rather puzzling behavior at Mrs. Moore's. On the one hand, she declines to tell her own story to the landlady, even though she knows that Lovelace is constructing behind her back an explanatory narrative that will put her at a disadvantage with her hostess. On the other hand, though, she expresses to Captain Tomlinson a great longing to have everything about herself known and judged: "Mr. Lovelace may have secrets. I have none. You seem to think me faulty: I should be glad that all the world knew my heart. Let my enemies sit in judgement upon my actions: fairly scanned, I fear not the result. Let them even ask me my most secret thoughts, and, whether they make for me or against me, I will reveal them" (822).

Clarissa's own explanation for her refusal to tell her story—that it "is too long, and too melancholy . . . and my time here is too short, for me to enter upon it" (791)—is conspicuously weak: she does, after all, have plenty of time to write long letters to Anna Howe, and it is surely important by any standard for her to gain the support of the only people who now stand between her and Lovelace. The point is rather that it is impossible for her to produce a narrative of explanation that will not seem—and indeed *be*—motivated by the need to justify herself. This is what generates the fantasy of being in a courtroom, where her enemies can "sit in judgement upon [her] actions." If she were merely a witness providing data at someone else's request, rather than, as it were, the defense attorney shaping a clearly "interested" narrative—if, best of all, she could somehow promise genuine access to her "most secret thoughts"—she could circumvent the logic whereby a narrative claiming to prove her innocence really proves only her skill at constructing such a narrative. In one sense, Clarissa is right that her time is too short. To establish her innocence decisively, nothing less than everything would do. Under the circumstances, all she could possibly provide to Mrs. Moore in her own defense would be a selected and "constructed" narrative. Instead, more self-consciously than Pamela with her lists, Clarissa demonstrates her feminine virtue through a refusal of narration. Clarissa has here internalized—and been silenced by—the same bind that motivated the use of the epistolary form in *Pamela*.

The Plotting Correspondent 2: Anna Howe

The special qualities of her correspondence with Anna provide a way for Richardson to get Clarissa out of this bind. Anna's professed interest in everything Clarissa has to say motivates *externally* her exhaustive inclusiveness of both the events in which she is involved and her reflections upon them: "It is not for a child to seek to clear her own character, or to justify her actions, at the expense of the most revered ones," she comments in a letter in which she has detailed her family's mistreatment of her, "yet, as I know that the account of all those further proceedings by which I may be affected will be interesting to so dear a friend. . . . I will continue to write as I have opportunity" (52–53). This inclusiveness in turn exonerates Clarissa by establishing that at no point has she intended or planned the effects that ensue from what she is and does. In other words, for Clarissa the epistolary form produces an unplotted narrative (that is, unplotted by her) that can verify the absence of plotting in her behavior.

The correspondence is further motivated by the opportunity it provides for self-exposure to a loving but critical friend, who can then (in theory) provide insight, guidance, chastisement to aid Clarissa's own self-guidance.

Rather than being shaped by any internally conceived "point" Clarissa wants to make, then, Clarissa's correspondence with Anna is avowedly instituted as a process loosely akin to the "free-association" demanded of a patient in psychoanalysis—particularly to the extent it is intended to give its audience access to her "most secret thoughts," including the ones she does not know she has.[29] Anna constitutes herself as an analytic reader of Clarissa's texts, taking them to reveal more than their writer consciously intends—the moral character of her family, for example, or Clarissa's emerging feelings for Lovelace. Clarissa does not, in principle, resent such suspicious reading (though she disputes particular readings), but rather sees it as a personal favor: her avowed purpose in writing to her friend is not to convince Anna of anything with regard to herself, but to reveal her mind fully, confident that such revelation will show her essential innocence, and eager that any dangerous or faulty thoughts or feelings of which she may be unaware be pointed out to her. Indeed, as Clarissa implicitly recognizes in her wish for full self-exposure at Mrs. Moore's, the fact that some of the "secret thoughts" Anna claims to detect in her letters do seem to "make against" her is itself a kind of guarantee of the genuineness of the whole—this is presumably why Clarissa tolerates, and even invites, the kind of hermeneutic "aggression" Castle detects in Anna's readings of Clarissa.[30] Clarissa is, of course, in another sense surrounded by readers of her speech and writing who systematically interpret her words against the grain of her conscious intention, her brother and sister being the most glaring examples. Anna is unique in being both "symptomatic" *and* sympathetic in her approach; that is, she gives Clarissa credit for ultimately wanting the truth about herself known, without necessarily accepting that this truth always resides in her self-conscious assertions. Clarissa's gratitude to her for this invites readers of the letters written for Anna's eyes to view the texts in the same way she does; in other words, to see the letters as witnessing to more than they consciously plan to convey.

Anna's suspicious reading of Clarissa's letters is of course part of a mutual pact of critical reading between the two friends: Clarissa returns the favor in her own reflections on Anna's letters. This in itself stands in sharp contrast to Lovelace's intolerance of criticism and jealousy of his own narrative authority over Belford.[31] There is, however, also an important difference between the two female correspondents: while Clarissa "properly" reflects on Anna's letters with reference to abstract proprieties, which sometimes (as in her own case) seem desperately irrelevant to the difficulties of the particular circumstances at hand, Anna is always seeking to construct romantic plots out of Clarissa's writings, and projecting such plots into the future through her advice and predictions. This powerful desire for plot, while it initially seems only a form of resistance to the more reprehensible exercises of patriarchal power in the novel, ultimately emerges as a threat to feminine virtue itself.

Anna's interest in plots and narrative is given great prominence in the novel: its opening letter, from her to Clarissa, shows her already conscious of the possibility of a story emerging from the situation in which Clarissa is embroiled, and already casting herself as the potential compiler, interpreter, and disseminator of that story—its master-narrator. She later describes herself as "for ever . . . endeavouring to trace effects to their causes" (356)— that is, constructing explanatory narratives about the past—and prides herself on her sagacity in predicting the outcome of present events. She longs for—and as far as possible, seeks—the power and independence that would enable her to engage in "female knight-errantry," and her advice to Clarissa reflects a pragmatism that judges the worth of an action by its likely effects. These qualities make Anna as close as Richardson ever comes to the positive portrayal of a female "plotter" in all senses of the term. In her frank assessments of Clarissa's family, Clarissa's feelings, and Lovelace's character, in the pragmatic, worldly-wise advice she offers her friend, and particularly in her frequent, astute generalizations about the relative positions of women and men in her society, Anna seems to emerge as a voice of reason, of reality. She is the character most likely to say to Clarissa the things we would like to say to her.

By linking Clarissa with Anna, then, Richardson seems to be presenting possibilities that would be closed out by the model of feminine narration I have put forward. But Anna's penchant for generating plots of every kind is ultimately revealed as suspect, allied with her resistance to properly feminine roles in her relationship with her mother and Hickman. And it is not just in reference to the moral ideal represented by Clarissa that Anna is inadequate: her mannish desire for plot poses practical risks to both herself and Clarissa, because it is necessarily combined with a female incapacity for competing with male plotters like Lovelace on their own ground. Anna's "practical" advice to Clarissa, particularly once the latter is in master-plotter Lovelace's power, is at least as often dangerously miscalculated— precisely because it *is* calculated—as it is sound. Herein lies one problem with reading Anna Howe "straight" as a medium for Richardson's critique of bourgeois patriarchy, as Eagleton and Todd attempt to do. Anna's function in the novel clearly is in part to voice the frustration that readers are

meant to feel at Clarissa's oppression. But if we look at the way her resistance is encoded in the text, the terms of its symbiosis with the novel's more
prominent aim of creating and promoting Clarissa as an "exemplar" of
feminine virtue, it becomes clear that she also serves to debunk one tempting response to that oppression: active, strategic opposition to male power.

A key example is the episode with Miss Partington. Clarissa has refused
Miss Partington's request to sleep with her from a kind of generalized sense
of impropriety: she is alone in the house; Mrs. Sinclair has made too much
"parade in prefacing the request"; "Miss Partington herself is not so bashful
a lady as she was represented to me to be"; and to cap it all, the house is full
of Lovelace's male friends, "avowed supporters of [him] in all matters of
offense" (546). Reflecting to her friend on her refusal, though, Clarissa
finds herself unable to fit it into any coherent interpretation of her current
circumstances: if "nothing were meant by the request," then she was
"uncivil," and she ought to have behaved differently. If, on the other hand,
she believes she has grounds for her refusal, then "I ought to apprehend
everything, and fly the house and the man, as I would an infection." To stay
on after "having entertained suspicions . . . will have an appearance not at
all reputable to myself" (547). Unable to commit herself to the logical consequences of any one interpretation of the episode, Clarissa decides to
downplay the significance of the whole event. Anna, however, insists on a
more consistent and pragmatic view of the matter. She wants both a stable
explanation and a strategic role for her knowledge. Because she herself can
think of no good reason why Lovelace might need Miss Partington to get
sexual access to Clarissa—"if violence were intended, he would not stay
for the night"—she considers it safe to assume no harm was intended.
Consequently, Clarissa's incivility was ill-calculated—it will only alienate
potential allies: "You have brought an inconvenience upon yourself . . . by
your refusal of Miss Partington for your bedfellow. . . . You was overscru-
pulous," she concludes (549).

Both Clarissa's response to Miss Partington and Anna's reflections thereupon are of course to be read in the context of Lovelace's prior confession
to Belford that the whole episode is indeed part of a seduction plot. Anna's
attempt to rely on calculation in dealing with Lovelace is hence revealed as
fatally inadequate. Again and again—as when she later chides Clarissa for
being "impoliticly shy" of Dorcas—Anna's correspondence makes clear
that, much as she longs to take him on, she is no match for Lovelace as a
counterplotter: in the potentially infinite regress of second-guessing, the

"long-sighted" Lovelace is always at least one guess beyond her. Clarissa, by contrast, evades Lovelace's seducing wiles precisely because she does not try to outplot him: unconcerned with being "politic," she steers clear of Dorcas because, as with Miss Partington, she recognizes her immodesty.

Anna's narrative plots have more subtle and, if possible, more dangerous effects. Castle argues that Anna's early "construction" of a romantic plot around Clarissa and Lovelace produces what it purports to describe: her "irresponsible suggestions . . . condition a subtle, but growing emotional entanglement with Lovelace. . . . Clarissa begins to act out her friend's fantasy."[32] Whether or not her romantic plotting has this effect upon Clarissa, who is scrupulously careful about her feelings, it certainly has it upon Anna herself. If Anna's eagerness to outplot Lovelace strategically suggests her vulnerability to his more complex counterplotting, this lust for locating the "plots" of romantic narratives suggests a sexual susceptibility as well. It is not just Lovelace's arrogance that makes him claim that Anna would be easy prey for his schemes for seduction—her own letters reveal it, through her early eagerness to promote in Clarissa a dangerous susceptibility to his charms, and through her elliptical reference to a previous episode in which only Clarissa's intervention sufficed to save her from a similar fate. She clinches the suspicion with her confession that Lovelace is a finer man than the one who tempted her (174).

Anna then, as a "virtuous" woman who nonetheless seeks the power and pleasure of plotting, serves as a way of both including and scapegoating a certain kind of female consciousness. As a trusted and confidential correspondent, Anna is both inside and outside Clarissa's consciousness. On the one hand, she is privy to Clarissa's most private thoughts, while her own reflections thereupon are treated with the utmost seriousness by Clarissa: Clarissa herself writes to her that "your mind and mine were ever *one*" (382); on the other hand, she promotes a pragmatism and a will to power that Clarissa must continually reject as morally impure. Anna can thus bring to consciousness for Clarissa, and for the reader, all the potential "plots" that Clarissa on her own could neither allow herself to think nor (plausibly) fail to notice.[33] These include a retroactive narrative plot of Clarissa's "justification"—the story of a child who suffers because she is too good for her selfish and ambitious family to tolerate; the romantic plot of Clarissa's presumed secret passion for Lovelace; and the various future plots Anna concocts for Clarissa's material salvation: resuming her estate; running away with Anna to London; marrying Lovelace. At the same time, by representing Anna's imposition of these plots as illegitimate and even dangerous, and by glorifying Clarissa's reasoned rejections of them, the novel reaffirms the opposition of feminine virtue to female plotting, however well-intentioned.

Clarissa as Antiplotter

Clarissa's rejections of all such plots continually oppose absolute virtue to Anna's pragmatism, and, as an inevitable consequence, the passive role of the victim to the activity of the "female knight-errantry" Anna longs to espouse. Clarissa spells out the logic of her convictions most clearly in the letter reiterating to Anna her reasons for declining to live on her estate. Anna, with her usual pragmatism, has argued that by taking up the estate, Clarissa would have gained sufficient independence and economic power to insure her against her siblings' ill-wishes, and thus would have prevented all the evils, to herself and them, that have followed therefrom. Clarissa, in her reply, disavows the ability to predict any likely consequences of an act, and hence the right to make a decision based on such predictions: "Who can command or foresee events? To act up to our best judgements at the time is all we can do." If ill-effects were to result from even a well-intentioned act, she argues, she would justly be held responsible, for the arrogance of having "aimed at excelling" by taking on herself, contrary to custom for her sex, the power to act on her own judgment (105). Hence, it is morally purer to disclaim the power and "leave the issue to Providence" (106), for even if the result is suffering, "is it not pleasurable on reflection that the fault is in others, rather than in ourselves?" (105)[34]

Of course, Clarissa does not always act up to such principles: there are several key points in the novel at which she overrides strict propriety in the name of practical necessity, the most important being her early continuation of a forbidden correspondence with Lovelace to prevent injury to her family, and her initial decision to flee her family to escape marriage with Solmes. Significantly, though, Clarissa herself soon repudiates these choices, not merely as tactically miscalculated, but as moral faults sufficiently heinous to go a long way toward justifying her subsequent suffering. Looking back ruefully at the events that led up to her forced flight with Lovelace, Clarissa laments the "presumption" that initially made her think that her good standing with both her family and Lovelace could be wielded for active good: that she could be "the arbitress of the quarrels of unruly spirits." She repudiates the "foolish and busy prescience" that led her to act from "pragmatical motives," suspecting that Lovelace has been too well able to manipulate those: "it is plain to me now . . . that he had as great a confidence in my weakness, as I had in my own strength" (381). That she had been driven to what she did is no consolation, for by her own ethic it is better to suffer at the hands of others than to run the risk of taking matters into one's own hands: "Had I stayed, and had the worst I dreaded happened, my friends would then have been answerable, if any bad consequences had followed" (382). The final drift of Clarissa's moral reasoning, as in Richardson's "Advice to Unmarried Ladies," is that, while morality in general may be reinforced by reflecting on its (frequent) good effects, actual calculations of cause and effect have no place in the moral reasonings of a good woman. If Clarissa sins in corresponding with Lovelace or leaving her family, it is not because she wants anything immoral, but because she tries to *plot* morally.

There are two key occasions on which Clarissa does carry out carefully laid "plots" of her own, involving deception and manipulation of others: both are in her escapes from Lovelace. The latter of these, at least, is highly successful—and in these cases she has no later qualms about the moral purity of her pragmatism, despite her earlier insistence that she would never seek "to *serve* or even to *save,* herself at the expense of her sincerity and by a *studied* deceit!" (336). But these instances, for special reasons, can be considered the exceptions that prove the rule. It has frequently been noted that rape is unique in that its status as crime depends entirely on the state of mind of the victim at the time the act is committed. For Lovelace, and to a large extent for Richardson as well, it depends further on the continued state of mind of the victim *after* the crime: to "turn the other cheek" after being struck may be the perfection of Christian virtue, but to do so after being raped, as Lovelace well knows, suggests a retroactive acquiescence in the initial act. This has to do with the status of feminine virtue as an absolute state rather than as a process in action: any subsequent weakening of opposition to rape can only be the revelation of a flaw that was there all along. Once the threat of physical violation is absolutely clear, then, as it is to Clarissa after Lovelace's first attempt and more obviously after he has actually raped her, protesting passivity ceases to be virtuous—in fact, any opposition that falls short of actual success is grounds for doubt. The peculiarities of rape mean that a static virtue trained to disregard effects can only prove itself by an active, and effective, opposition. It is worth noting, too, that, as Lovelace is quick to reassure himself upon their discovery, even Clarissa's successful "plots" are neither long in the planning nor far-

reaching in their aims. They begin with a chance opportunity and end
when they have succeeded in getting Clarissa out of the house. They hence
do not seriously challenge what Lovelace sees as his exclusive power to
shape the future by "plotting" it.

As Clarissa consciously disowns her rights as a plotter of her own fate, it
is unsurprising that she finds herself, like Pamela, subjected to the plots
of others. From the beginning of the novel, as Castle has demonstrated,
Clarissa is trapped within narrative contexts provided by the people around
her: her family, Lovelace, and to some extent even Anna Howe. I have argued
that, oppressive and unjust as these narrative contexts often prove, Clarissa's virtue consists to a large extent of her refusal to oppose them with plots
of her own construction. Perhaps the most interesting instance of this is the
extent to which she allows the trajectory of her life to be defined by her
father's curse. Clarissa's reaction to the curse is instructive. She appears at
first to believe in it absolutely, writing to Anna: "Think not of corresponding with a wretch who now seems absolutely devoted [i.e., to perdition]!
How can it be otherwise, if a parent's curses have the weight I always attributed to them and have heard so many instances of their being followed
by!" (508). At times, she even seems to feel that it would be almost unduti-
ful to hope that her family's worst expectations will fail to come to pass:
"methinks, I would be glad that the unkindness of my father and uncles,
whose hearts have already been too much wounded by my error, may be
justified in every article," she writes, and though she initially exempts "this
heavy curse" from her self-punishing wish, she quickly amends this to no
more than the hope that her father "will be pleased to withdraw . . . at least
that most dreadful part of it which regards futurity" (566). For the remainder of the novel, Clarissa continually refers to the curse, with a kind of melancholy triumph at its fulfillment "in the very letter of it as to this life"
(899).[35]

Clarissa's relationship to the portion of the curse that regards the afterlife
is more complex. As a good Christian, one of whose most shining virtues is
faith, she ought to know, and at other points apparently *does* know, that her
father's ill-wishes cannot really effect her salvation or damnation. Yet even
on her deathbed, and in the face of the most blissful Divine "assurances" of
her salvation, Clarissa persists with desperate earnestness in her efforts to
get the latter part of the curse revoked. Here, as elsewhere, Richardson
seems to be requiring that Clarissa live a contradiction: that she escape her
father's misguided plotting of her life's trajectory in effect, without herself
ever actively challenging his right to have imposed it, or its power as a shap-

ing force. To put it another way, the reader can only recognize the unsuitableness (and final inefficacy) of Mr. Harlowe's curse because Clarissa demonstrates her dutifulness as a daughter by treating it as deadly serious.

"My Divided Soul": Rape and Narrative Breakdown

Clarissa's relationship to her narrative becomes more complex after the rape. Its most immediate effect upon her is mental disorder, as evidenced in her complaint about "my poor head" (890) in the first "mad paper." This disorientation is of course meant to represent the immediate aftereffects of the overdose of opiates that enabled the rape. But even a month later, Clarissa is still writing of her "disordered" head, which, she says, "I have not indeed enjoyed . . . with any degree of clearness since the violence done" (by the rape) (1022). The recurrent complaint about her "head" can of course be read as a "displacement upwards" of a lament for her lost maidenhead, but it is more significant as an indication of what Castle terms her "hermeneutic fragmentation" after the rape (119).[36] Like Fleur-de-Marie (and for the same reasons), Clarissa can never quite succeed in making her sexual experience "add up" into a coherent narration of her life. On the other hand, though, there is now really nothing left for her to do but to prepare her story for the world and her soul for eternity, both of which tasks entail reflection upon her history.

Clarissa's "mad papers," and the wandering, incoherent letter to Lovelace that follows them, appear in the novel in the midst of a long stretch of otherwise unbroken narration by Lovelace—what is in fact far and away the longest stretch of uncounterpointed narration by any character anywhere in the novel (nearly the whole of the fifth volume in the first edition, and Lovelace has already dominated the last two-thirds of the fourth volume). In other words, the mad papers represent the only textual challenge or alternative to Lovelace's narrative voice in this substantial portion of the novel, as well as our first glimpse of Clarissa's textual response to the rape—and the last for some time.

The mad papers themselves are so fragmented and contradictory that they can hardly be termed a single response at all. They show Clarissa desperately producing and discarding successive conceptual frames that can make coherent what has happened to her. Eagleton is certainly right in chiding critics who take only the third paper—"A Lady took a great fancy to a young lion" (891)—as Clarissa's "recognition" of the "true" shape of her history, but it is also wrong to reject them all as effects of a temporary phase of irrational guilt and disorientation. In fact, the mad papers between them cover the range of often conflicting perspectives on her history that Clarissa will later adopt.

The first paper is addressed to Anna Howe as a continuation of her story, and thus might be said to be written explicitly from the perspective of Clarissa-as-narrator. In it, she attests to a loss of any coherent perspective, which translates into an inability to narrate at all: no longer knowing "what to say first" or how to sort out "thought, and grief, and confusion," Clarissa concludes that she "can write nothing at all" (890). In the remaining papers, she tries out a variety of narrative frames made available by the novel's other "plotters" and interpreters of Clarissa's story. Thus paper 2, addressed to her father, affirms his vision of her as an erring child deservedly punished, who seeks a prodigal daughter's welcome at home, while papers 4 and 5 accept Bella's conviction that she has been motivated solely by vanity, confessing abjectly that "[y]ou knew me better than I knew myself" (891). The third paper, too, with its implicit double standard of virtue and consequent absolution of Lovelace on the grounds that he was only acting in character as a rake, bears a close resemblance to Lovelace's own rationalizations—which may explain the special authority granted it by the novel's more "Lovelacean" critics. On the whole, these four papers (2 through 5) show Clarissa capitulating to her family's and Lovelace's reading of her as responsible—even culpable—for her own fate: they provide a familiar form of narrative coherence for her story by representing her as humbled by the inevitable results of her own pride.

The remaining papers, though, return to a focus on Clarissa's essential innocence and good intentions, insisting on the irreducible guilt of Lovelace's act with prophetic vehemence: "Oh wretch! bethink thee . . . how great must be thy condemnation!" She herself was, at worst, only led astray by her own generosity in interpreting Lovelace's character: "Yet, God knows my heart, I had no culpable inclinations!—I honoured virtue!—I hated vice!—But I knew not that you were vice itself!" (892). In their insistence on her moral integrity and undeserved suffering, these papers may seem closer to what we might term Clarissa's "own" perspective than the self-condemnatory ones that precede them. Yet even these papers, with their emphasis on the public nature of her exemplarity—the audience of "an admiring world, and . . . pleased and rejoicing parents and relations" that is now lost to her, or the "fair leaf of virgin fame" that Lovelace has "destroye[d]" (892), seem to owe as much to Anna Howe's frequently reiterated vision of Clarissa as public role model—and later as exemplary victim of male depravity—as to Clarissa herself, "so desirous," as Anna writes in her first letter, "of sliding through life to the end of it unnoted"(40).

But my essential point here is less to insist on specific external sources for the narrative frames that the "mad papers" provide as to note the coexistence within them of at least two seemingly incompatible models for understanding her story: that of the fallen woman and that of the wronged innocent. This is not to suggest that Clarissa sees herself as a "fallen woman" in quite the Victorian sense of someone who has voluntarily embraced illicit sexuality. Rather, it refers to the way that Clarissa's intermittent belief that the rape was "but the due consequent of my fault" (1117) in seeking to run away from her family merges with her perception of the rape as somehow a moral as well as physical "ruin." It is in this sense, presumably, that she refers to herself in a later letter as Anna's "fallen Clarissa" (1114). These two perspectives—fallen woman and wronged innocent—come together in the poem of paper 10. The first and fifth stanzas, which show her ambiguously longing to "[f]orget myself; and that day's guilt," and later holding forth death as a "relief" from lost "honour" and a "sure retreat from infamy," again seem to represent her as in some sense culpable for her "fall," or at least profoundly morally soiled by it. Others, though, cast her, in opposition to "the bad," as "innocent" and even (again ambiguously) "*Best,*" with death now offering vindication rather than merely the erasure of shame (893). The poem's fragmented and floating verses, and particularly its central appeal to "Miss Howe" to "speak the words of peace to my divided soul," testify to Clarissa's inability to reconcile these two perspectives.

Certainly, as Eagleton notes, the disproportionate sense of shame and guilt that mingles with Clarissa's self-pity can be read as a psychologically astute representation of a common female response to rape. But I want to argue that the construction of Clarissa as a virtuous narrator also demands this self-division. Again, the dual status of sexual experience in relation to feminine virtue is significant here. The whole construction of feminine virtue as founded on sexual purity naturally equates extramarital sexual experience (however acquired) with moral *soilure*. At the same time, virginity's status as merely the physical sign of purity of consciousness and will would be nullified if it were simply equated with a physical state that could be altered by force.

Either perspective is rendered suspect by its potential appropriation as a (retroactive) excuse or a (premeditated) motivation for sexual fall—that is, by its potential within a plot. As usual, Lovelace's own reasoning provides a clear map of the moral pitfalls between which Richardson is steering his heroine, since the logic of *both* perspectives on virtue and sexuality is implicit in Lovelace's inclusion of rape as an (admittedly desperate) strategic move in what remains a *seduction* plot. Initially, the plot turns on what he hopes is Clarissa's absolute equation of virtue and virginity, which makes rape a surefire way of collapsing Clarissa's faith in her own moral superiority. By making her see herself as already fallen, already a whore, he hopes to make her embrace the pleasures that role offers. When Clarissa fails to fall for this ploy, he next shifts to a strategy based on a split between virginity and will: if he can get Clarissa to see the rape as morally a non-event for her ("what will she be the worse for the trial?—No one is to blame for suffering an evil he cannot shun or avoid" [868]) the way is clear for a more subtle process of seduction; perhaps she could be brought to appreciate such guilt-free encounters ("I couldn't stop him"). All Lovelace's plans, of course, are based on the assumption (or hope) that sexual desire for him will influence Clarissa's construction of the rape's significance. Any leaning toward either of the simplifications of her relationship to rape can then be read as evidence that this was the telos she had secretly desired all along. As Lovelace reflects before one interview, "A nice part, after all, has my beloved to act"—since either way, underemphasizing or overemphasizing the rape, provides an excuse for him either to "resume [his] projects" or to resort to "fresh violence" (907).

Clarissa, of course, is not consciously concerned with "acting" a "nice part," any more than she was in the complex maneuverings before the rape: were Clarissa to begin to think strategically about how to deal with Lovelace, she would be lost, trapped in the consequences of his damned-if-you-do, damned-if-you-don't logic.[37] Instead, she resists the implications of any one construction of her story, insisting simultaneously on her absolute innocence and on her need for "severe penitence"(901).

In their contrast with her previously masterful prose, the mad papers testify with eloquent pathos to the traumatic impact of the rape. Their very incoherence seemingly exempts Clarissa from the kind of hermeneutic suspicion (made so explicit in her family's responses to her, and in that of many critics as well) that assumes that any narrative vindication Clarissa can offer really only establishes her insidious skill at constructing such a narrative. Retrieved in scraps by the maid from under her table, the papers clearly have no designs on anyone. The mad papers establish the credibility of Clarissa's genuine resistance to being sexually violated precisely because they are *not* a story to be believed or disbelieved, but the wreckage of a shattered consciousness, which needs to be reconstructed and interpreted by others. In this sense, they could be seen as providing direct access to "Clarissa," without the intervening (potentially calculating) consciousness of Clarissa.[38] But while the "madness" to which they testify eventually subsides, the contradictions in her status the mad papers reveal retain their force: Clarissa will continue to have to live, think, and write within these contradictions to retain the claim to "virtue" that grounds her credibility. She recognizes the impossibility of imposing any form of narrative closure on her adventures other than a devout death, which, since God promises both to absolve the truly penitent sinner and to reward the virtuous, safely evades the question. This comes through most clearly in the debate about marrying her rapist.

For Lovelace, the promise of marriage would retroactively exonerate the rape, as well as all the further "trials" he has in mind: "Am I not in earnest as to marriage? . . . Is not *the catastrophe of every story that ends in wedlock accounted happy*, be the difficulties in the progress to it ever so great?" (944).[39] For Clarissa, this is precisely the problem: marrying Lovelace now would be, in a sense, voluntarily embracing her rape. Hence her arguments against the marriage include not only the obvious points about the new state of her feelings about Lovelace—she could never vow to love a man she now despises, or to obey someone she considers morally depraved (1116)— but the more puzzling suggestion that she would somehow be unworthy to enter his family. Responding to a plea from Lovelace, for example, she argues that, while previously she "could have met the gratulations of a family . . . with a consciousness of *deserving* [them]," the rape has radically changed her status: "thinkest thou that I will give a harlot-niece to thy honourable uncle, and to thy *real* aunts; and a cousin to thy cousins from a brothel?" (909). The argument recurs later in a letter to Lady Betty Lawrance, who has been urging marriage also: "You will judge that I can have no principles that will make me worthy of an alliance with ladies of yours and your noble sister's character, if I could not from my soul declare that such an alliance can never *now* take place" (985). It is hard to believe that Clarissa sees herself as a "harlot" because she has been forcibly raped, or even that she is less deserving of family approval now than she was before the rape (the chief moral error she acknowledges, that of continuing the "prohibited correspondence," having already been made at that point). It is rather that she would *become* a harlot—or rather, be revealed as one—

the moment she could bring herself to redeem her rape within the *telos* of marriage. Even her husband, she later argues, might then "reproach me for having been *capable* of forgiving crimes of *such* a nature" (1116).

The same thing, though, proves true of the choice of a "single life." Here again, Lovelace's exculpatory reasoning anticipates the grounds for Clarissa's refusal. He jokingly argues before the rape that since Clarissa is so penitent already about her dealings with him, and since she claims to prefer the single life to marriage, "ruining" her will only be putting her in a way to be happy:

> Is not this then the result of all, that Miss Clarissa Harlowe, if it be not her own fault, may be as virtuous *after* she has lost her honour, as it is called, as she was *before*? . . . And thus may her *old* nurse and she . . . (for everything will be very old and penitential about her), live very comfortably together; reading *old* sermons, and *old* prayerbooks; and relieving *old* men, and *old* women; and giving *old* lessons, and *old* warnings upon new subjects, as well as *old* ones, to the young ladies of her neighbourhood; and so pass on to a good *old* age, doing a great deal of good, both by precept and example, in her generation.
>
> And is a lady who can live thus prettily without *control;* who ever did prefer, and who *still* prefers, the *single* to the *married life;* and who will be enabled to do everything that the plan she had formed will direct her to do; be said [*sic*] to be ruined, undone, and such sort of stuff? (869)

The answer, it seems, is yes, since, if she can imagine herself satisfied with such a life now, who is to say it was not what she wanted all along? Clarissa anticipates the same kind of shame and merited reproach in embracing the single life as she feels she would deserve for marrying. To choose a life, any life, and to act on the choice, is to construct or "plot" a future of which her "ruin" is a part. It is that, finally, that would constitute her moral ruin.

There is a sense in which Clarissa does construct a future for herself— and even act on it—in anticipating and planning for her death. But as I suggested above, the prospect of a Christian death, because it promises the same end for a penitent sinner as for the truly virtuous (indeed, given human imperfection, the distinction between them is almost meaningless), does not demand that Clarissa determine the precise proportions of guilt and outrage, self-blame and self-justification that her story requires. Richardson is also at some pains to make clear that Clarissa does not so much plan to die as plan for what she recognizes as her inevitably immanent death. Certainly, he is walking a fine line here. Since Clarissa cannot wish for any future in life, she is left, as she says to Anna, with nothing to "wish for but death" (1117), yet actively to embrace death would be a sin. The solution seems to be to transfer to her physical body her principled refusal to choose life, through a play on the physical/emotional meaning of "heart": in an earlier letter suggesting to Anna that she will soon die, Clarissa asks "[w]hat a heart must I have if it not be broken?" Here the broken heart is a physiological state: in breaking her heart, "the blow is given" that will end her life (1018). Yet the "heart" recognizes the same moral logic as the head, which says that it would be morally tainted if it failed to break.

Belford and the Plotted Correspondence

It is no coincidence that the same letter that details Clarissa's grounds for refusing any possible future also contains the first suggestion that she will prove unable to narrate her past (1115). As at Mrs. Moore's, Clarissa cites lack of time and the emotional strain of recalling events as her primary reason for refusing to write her story as promised, but underlying this is what might be termed the logical impossibility, for her, of producing such a narrative. As we have seen, there is no single, noncontradictory position she can adopt about the relationship of her rape to her virtue that would not be appropriable as either evidence of or excuse for a sexual fall—and consequently no narrative she can produce about it.

This time, however, Clarissa believes she has found a way to give her judges privileged access, as she could not at Mrs. Moore's, to her "heart," her "actions," and even her "most secret thoughts" (822): the hint she drops in the letter above eventually develops into her idea of having Belford arrange and edit the correspondence that constitutes the novel. This move displaces narrative authority onto the letters and narrative agency to Belford, exempting her from the moral risk of resolving the contradictions of her position into a coherent account, but also removing the representation of her story from her own direct control.

Critics who are divided on Clarissa's power and status as an epistolary narrator are naturally even more so when it comes to her role in the gathering and editing of the correspondence as a whole into the "story" that bears her name. For Eagleton and Castle, with their focus on Clarissa's victimization and subsequent escape from representation,[40] Clarissa's deathbed concern with arranging for the representation of her story disappears from view. For Warner, by contrast, it looms very large indeed, to the point where Clarissa's managerial hand seems even more insidiously evident in the correspondence Belford edits than it could have been had she produced her own retroactive account of "her" story: "Clarissa shows her daring and intelligence as an author by the way she brings her book into existence. Instead of writing the long first-person narrative she once planned, she chooses to become the dominant member in a collaboration."[41] I would argue that Clarissa's role in the production of her story is important, but not because she assumes in it the exaggerated dominance Warner attributes to her. The planning of her story, like the writing of her will, represents Richardson's testing of the limits of feminine narration. In naming her as "the dominant member in a collaboration," Warner grossly overstates the extent of her control over the shaping of multiple correspondences into "her" story: Clarissa never even sees the letters between Lovelace and Belford, with the exception of a few extracts made by the latter, nor does she have (or seek) any opportunity to edit her own letters to Anna, or to determine the range or order of the documents to be included. The desire to have the story produced, and the perception that that story will constitute her justification with regard to the rape, remains, but she herself abdicates the right to give it any particular shape, either by narrating it herself or by becoming the master-narrator of an edited and shaped collection. Turning this task over to Belford, to be carried out without her supervision, is a final gesture of faith that this simply *is* the shape of her story, that her letters, with the others, will provide a self-evident "witness" to her good intentions and sexual innocence (though to judge from *Clarissa's* critical history, this faith is clearly misplaced).

Clarissa's decision casts Belford in the role of the master-narrator: he will to a limited extent determine the shape of her story. But it also makes him the "executor" of her narrative as well as her material "will." He is both a figure of power—the only character with privileged access to both Clarissa and Lovelace during her life, the arbiter among Anna Howe, the Harlowes, and Lovelace after her death—and an acquiescent tool of her wishes. This ambivalent position enables him to mediate between the novel's gendered oppositions.

As Eagleton argues, the moral opposition Clarissa/Lovelace finally leaves us with a seemingly impossible choice: between a concept of virtue and truthfulness that, in an imperfect world, is a recipe for self-destruction, and the amoral pragmatism of a Lovelace, which is indifferent to the oppression of others. Richardson cannot reject Lovelace and all he stands for out of hand, because his activities are uncomfortably close to his own.[42] *Clarissa* as a novel depends on the same kind of manipulation of audience response—the canny withholding of information, the ironic juxtapositions—in which Lovelace takes such pleasure in both his material and literary plots: the novelist by definition must be, like Lovelace, "a great plotter and a great writer"—though he may also wish to be, like Clarissa, a great moralist.

While noting offhand that she is "no feminist paradigm," Eagleton seems to put forward Anna Howe as a tentative figure of compromise: "Caustic, humorous and debunking, unswerving in sisterly solidarity yet astringently critical," Anna seems to combine ethical commitment with political/linguistic astuteness: "Anna shrewdly recognizes that [truth and justice] are indissociable from the shifting power strategies in which they are embedded. To be false or unjust, in conditions where the other has the power advantage, may be a productive error, as near to 'genuine' truth and justice as one can get."[43]

But as we have seen, there are problems with reading Anna's rebelliousness straight: her "pragmatism" makes her yet more vulnerable to rakes than Clarissa's rectitude, and generally proves more misguided when put to the test. However bright or insightful she may (sometimes) be, Anna is no model for combining rectitude of heart with effective action. Richardson's supposed "feminism," here and in general, is undercut by his conviction that, however ambivalent male protection may prove in practice, female weakness still requires it. His compromise between Clarissan commitment and Lovelacean power lies rather in the reformed rake Belford, whose masculine prerogatives as a plotter better suit him to mediate between a (feminine) moral "will" and (masculine) action in the world. Indeed, the rejection of Anna Howe as a mediating figure in favor of Belford is made more conspicuous by the fact that Anna had explicitly requested this role in the novel's opening letter.

Belford has generally proved an unappealing figure for critical analysis: for the most part, he lacks Lovelace's or Anna's wit and liveliness, and Clarissa's tragic earnestness. Furthermore, he does not really come into his own as an influential actor in the story until the period after Clarissa's escape from Lovelace—easily the heaviest and flattest portion of the novel. Nonetheless, his apparent drabness may be a necessary by-product of his role as a facilitator, a kind of ideological bridge: Belford by definition cannot provoke the kind of impassioned responses, pro or con, that Lovelace and Clarissa do. To put it another way, his flatness gives us an early intimation of "the Grandison problem."[44]

Belford's status is also reduced by his role as "straight man" for Lovelace's narrative and argumentative games through most of the novel. Belford often resists Lovelace's construction of his situation with Clarissa with telling force, but his letters do little to counter his friend's construction of Belford himself as an awkward and comparatively uninteresting fellow. Though his position as Lovelace's closest confidant and fellow rake suggests that he shares at least some of the properties that make Lovelace "a great plotter and a great writer," we get little intimation of them in the first two-thirds of the novel. But once Belford has the access to Clarissa that Lovelace is denied, the power relations of their correspondence alter dramatically. And Belford is far from passing up the advantage offered thereby, though he uses it for moral rather than egotistical ends. He tantalizes his friend with a self-conscious narrative sadism worthy of Lovelace himself. Writing an account of his mission to free Clarissa from prison, for example, he deliberately ends his letter in the middle of the story, in terms that suggest his astute assessment of his effect on his reader: "I will make thee taste a little in thy turn of the plague of suspense; and break off, without giving thee the least hint of the issue of my further proceedings. I know that those least bear disappointment who love most to give it. In twenty instances hast thou afforded me proof of the truth of this observation. And I matter not thy raving" (1068).

This deliberate narrative "torture" (as Lovelace will call it) is not, like Lovelace's, purely a way of wallowing in his own power of superior knowledge (though there is undoubtedly an element of personal revenge in it), but it is also qualitatively different from the kind of suspense often generated by Clarissa's actual ignorance of what will become of her next. Belford is whipping up remorse with a skillful hand. Lovelacean narrative skill has been turned to "ethical" ends—just as he later turns the Lovelacean weapon of parodic deflation toward more "proper" targets in his grotesque account of Mrs. Sinclair's death.

In one sense, Belford acts largely as a conduit for Clarissa's desires. If he is merely the extension of Clarissa's will (in every sense of the word), then she remains the active plotter of all that is carried out in her name. Yet it is significant that Clarissa requires such a conduit to put her will—hitherto so painfully ineffectual—into action. It is notable, for example, that among all of Clarissa's posthumous expressions of her wishes—the will itself, her instructions to Belford about her correspondence, and the posthumous letters—only those that are explicitly backed by Belford's authority actually take effect. The accounts of family resistance to the carrying out of the will, as well as Lovelace's threats, seem designed to indicate just how necessary this masculine backing is. More telling evidence is provided by the "posthumous letters," which are sometimes read as the ultimate example of Clarissa's influence.[45] The letters, touching as they may be to their readers, are curiously ineffectual in practical terms: her brother, advised to learn to control his anger, posts off provocative threats to Belford about the executorship apparently within hours of receiving it; Morden, exhorted not to challenge Lovelace, does just that; even her beloved Anna Howe, encouraged to hasten her marriage to Hickman, instead uses mourning for her friend as another excuse to delay it.

Thus the efficacy of Clarissa's will finally depends upon its congruence with, and validation by, Belford's will to act on her behalf, just as the organization of the letters into a story with a particular shape depends on his conviction that this is the "true" shape of this story. That this validation must be provided by Belford, in particular, (as against Anna Howe) shifts the locus of Clarissa's credibility and moral authority away from her own narration and her own self-conscious agency—that is, away from Clarissa the acting, writing character and toward the image of "Clarissa." For Belford's loyalty to Clarissa, the conviction of her innocence that motivates his willingness to carry out her narrative and material will, does not come about through a process of *believing what she says,* but rather through his critical reading of *Lovelace's* narrative. It is entirely a product of "Clarissa" rather than Clarissa. In fact, Belford's first real exposure to Clarissa's textual voice, except for a few short and irritated notes from her to Lovelace, comes from Lovelace's transcription of her mad papers. (Imagine how different this novel would feel if our textual experience of it mirrored Belford's!) Belford is able to underwrite Clarissa's credibility because he has already constructed "her" version of events as the "true" one—without ever having to grant her the authority to *tell* a true story. He is needed to underwrite it because Clarissa's vindication, within the terms of the novel, can only be founded on her abdication of narrative authority. To the extent that Clarissa triumphs morally, she does so because she willingly resigns herself to having no story to tell, resigns herself to the benevolent male authority who will tell it for her. Clarissa's use of Belford as "executor" of her material and narrative "will" thus partially circumvents the masculine monopoly on plotting only by underlining her own exclusion from it.

Clarissa is in many ways an excessive novel: excessive in its length, in the suffering it heaps upon its heroine, and, not least, in the moral standards to which that heroine is expected to adhere. This excess is in part a product of Richardson's effort to push his ideology to its logical limits. Eagleton argues that in doing so he exposes its contradictions: Clarissa's suffering and death ultimately emerge as a profound critique of the bourgeois patriarchal society whose values she dies for. But Clarissa herself remained an admired "exemplar" of those values—one that profoundly influenced the representation of female heroines, and female narrators, long after the novel's publication. While subsequent authors might never demand so much from, or grant so much to, their heroines, the logical opposition Richardson elaborated between feminine virtue and material plotting, and between female narrative credibility and active narrative shaping, remained powerfully in force.

Two

COMIC FEMININITY
The Uses of Convention in
Humphrey Clinker and *Redgauntlet*

This chapter will consider two epistolary or partially epistolary novels written between the publication of *Clarissa* and *Jane Eyre*—the next crucially influential text in the evolution of female narrative voice in the British novel. The gender dynamics of narration in both novels are shaped, in different ways, by the convention of feminine narration that Richardson's novels had helped to put in place. In both, feminine narration is largely a comic resource, though more ambiguously so in *Redgauntlet,* and both novels depend for their effects on their readers' acceptance of a conventional split between masculine and feminine narrative roles. At the same time, they begin to show a broadening range of fictional uses for the convention.

Humphrey Clinker offers a mix of male and female epistolary voices whose authority and narrative functions diverge markedly along gender lines, with the women unconsciously embodying or witnessing to the satiric and sentimental truths the men's letters explicitly preach. In *Redgauntlet,* there is no female narrator per se, but the epistolary and then diary narration of the "hero," Darsie Latimer, closely associates him with femininity, an association that is confirmed when he is also compelled to dress as a woman. But Scott employs the gendering of narrative status only to trouble it, calling into question the power of *any* figure to "master" the narrative of history.

Humphrey Clinker

In *Humphrey Clinker,* the narrative is carried forward by a number of letter writers of both sexes. Since they write frequently along the course of their journey, none of them knows what will happen next, or the shape their story will finally take—or even that they are *in* a story with a recognizable end (other than the predictable end of the journey). And in fact, unlike *Pamela* and *Clarissa,* the novel has no clear plot, no single unified story to which these voices, consciously or unconsciously, contribute. Certain story threads recur—Tabitha Bramble's desperate search for a husband, Lydia's love for the mysterious "Wilson," and the gradual unfolding of the character and identity of Humphrey Clinker—and these are resolved and at least perfunctorily linked in the triple marriage that provides the novel's closure, but they can hardly be said to dominate the novel, which devotes at least as much energy to local comic or sentimental episodes and satirical or admiring commentaries on well-known people and places. *Clinker* is sometimes viewed as an early exercise in perspectivism: there is no stable, authoritative perspective from which to see the world of the novel; it is a different place depending on whose eyes you see it through.[1] Certainly, the sometimes radically contrasting views of the various correspondents provide much of the novel's humor. But even in *Clinker* not all correspondents are created equal, and the differences in tone and function between the men's letters and the women's provide a telling illustration of the linkages of gender and narrative authority.

What narrative movement and coherence there is in the story is provided by the letters of Matthew Bramble and Jery Melford, with the letters of the three women being interpolated largely for comic relief or to fill in minor details.[2] While the men's letters would make perfect sense without the interpolated letters from the women, those of the women would be confusing and at times completely incomprehensible without the men's. Win Jenkyn's grateful account of Clinker's deliverance from prison by a five-hundred-year-old magician named Apias Korkus,[3] for example, makes sense only in the light of Bramble's preceding letter detailing the legal measures taken for his release on a writ of habeas corpus. Win's letter tells us nothing concrete about that episode that we have not already learned from Bramble, and serves largely to contribute to the comic portrait of Win, while Bramble's account not only fills in the story and contextualizes Win's, but also offers a pointed critical commentary on the legal system more generally.

In the case of Tabitha Bramble's abortive flirtation with Sir Ulic Mackilligut in Bath, the men's letters not only contextualize the women's, they reveal the self-conscious "plotting" on Bramble's part behind what remains to the women an unexplained development. Bramble's letter of May 5 announces that he has let Mackilligut know the real (modest) size of Tabitha's fortune, and anticipates that this will "cool the ardour of his addresses. Then her pride will take the alarm; and the rancour of stale maidenhood being chafed, we shall hear nothing but slander and abuse of Sir Ulic Mackilligut—This rupture, I foresee, will facilitate our departure from Bath" (54). Subsequent letters from Jery, Lydia, and Win reveal that this is exactly what happens. This sets the pattern for Bramble's subsequent relationship to Tabitha's comical plots to catch herself a husband.

Lydia's efforts to put herself in the center of a plot also prove comically ineffectual. About Mr. Barton's proposal, for example, she writes, "What will be the result of this consultation, Heaven knows; but I am afraid it will produce an explanation with Mr. Barton, who will, no doubt, avow his passion, and solicit their consent to a union which my soul abhors; for, my dearest Letty, it is not in my power to love Mr. Barton, even if my soul was untouched by any other tenderness. . . . No, my dear Willis, I may be involved in fresh troubles, and I believe I shall, from the importunities of this gentleman and the violence of my relations, but my heart is incapable of change" (135).

It is pretty clear what plot Lydia has in mind for her story here—one obviously derived, like her writing style, from her boarding-school reading habits ("truly, she has got a languishing eye, and reads romances," writes Bramble in introducing her [12]), but her efforts here to cast herself as Clarissa are undercut by the obvious good sense and good intentions of her male relatives. Not only do Lydia's fearful anticipations of violent compulsion by her relations prove unfounded, but she never even has to try to assert her will or judgment in convincing them to abandon the match, since they can read her feelings without her active assistance and already accede to the sentimental values she imagines herself clinging to in their despite. This pattern of comically deflating Lydia's self-positioning as a potentially tragic romantic heroine is also carried out in the conclusion of her romance with the mysterious "Wilson," the relevant parents and guardians cheerfully arranging the match themselves without much need even to consult with Liddy (whose feelings, again, are already obvious to all).

Thus, while the narrative position of each of the five correspondents in *Clinker*—that of epistolary witness to mutually experienced events— seems roughly equivalent, the authority each acquires varies enormously according to their gender. Bramble (and to a lesser extent Jery) becomes the controlling consciousness of the narrative, not only in the greater comprehensiveness and reliability of his letters, but in the shaping influence his various benevolencies have on the story as they begin to bear fruit. His influence and actions pull all the characters toward the restrained, productive, rural life that has been his center of value from the start.

More central gender differences emerge in the correspondents' relationships to two of the novel's dominant impulses: to comedy and to social satire. While Jery and Matthew are consistently the conscious purveyors of comedy and satire, the women are equally consistently its unconscious objects. Jery's and Matthew's letters contribute to the humor of the novel mostly by retailing scenes or events they themselves find funny. Even when the joke is at their expense—as when Matthew's long-lost friend steps on his gouty toe while greeting him, causing him to "shed tears in sad earnest" at the reunion (55)—the reader is being asked to *share* in a laugh, rather than to laugh *at* him. The humor of the men's letters, in other words, generally depends on our accepting the letter writer's vision of what is funny, just as the humor of *Humphrey Clinker* as a whole depends on our accepting Smollett's concept of the humorous.

The same is true of the men's roles as the vehicles of social satire, roles that also grant them a certain authority as judges of what in society is deserving of ridicule or critique. Since the novel offers us two very different satirical voices rather than one clearly-defined master-narrator, we might expect them to undercut each other's authority. But while Jery's and Matthew's critical perspectives on the people and places they encounter often conflict, ultimately they are complementary rather than contradictory. Jery sees with the forgiving eyes of youth, Matthew with the more jaundiced eye of experience, but their fundamental values are in accordance, and both occasionally express respect for the other's opinions.

Perhaps more important than their complementarity is the fact that each writer explicitly recognizes the limitations of his own perspective, and provides the clues for reading through the idiosyncrasies of his own as well as his fellow travelers' letters. This is especially true of Matthew Bramble. Upon announcing in one letter, "I find nothing but disappointment at Bath," for example, he goes on to analyze his own impressions, taking into account the distortions his physical discomforts put on his perceptions: "Methinks I hear you say, 'Altered it is, without all doubt; but then it is altered for the better; a truth which, perhaps, you would own without hesitation, if you yourself was not altered for the worse.' The reflection may, for aught I know, be just. The inconveniences which I overlooked in the high-day of health will naturally strike with exaggerated impression on the irritable nerves of an invalid. . . . But, I believe, you will not deny, that this place . . . is become the very center of racket and dissipation" (34).

This kind of self-reading—which occurs frequently in Bramble's letters —serves not so much to warn us of his idiosyncrasies, which are obvious enough, but to increase his reliability by assuring us that Bramble himself recognizes and to some degree compensates for his own limitations as an observer. It also provides a framework for reconciling his views with Jery's. Jery is young and healthy, and hence more tolerant of social absurdities and inconveniences. Jery himself later confirms this view, writing to his friend of the Bath public rooms that "this is what my uncle reprobates, as a monstrous jumble of heterogeneous principles; a vile mob of noise and impertinence, without decency or subordination. But this chaos is to me a source of infinite amusement. . . . Those follies, that move my uncle's spleen, excite my laughter. He is as tender as a man without a skin; who cannot bear the slightest touch without flinching" (49).

While acknowledging the seemingly drastic difference in their impressions—what outrages Bramble delights Jery—Jery here recognizes the fundamental similarity in their values, the difference lying only in a skin-deep, almost physically conditioned reaction to a situation both find equally absurd. Furthermore, Jery early on begins to adopt Bramble as a role model. Bramble's secretive charity to the poor widow (21) gives Jery "a strong inclination to follow my uncle's example" (though the inclination is squelched from anxiety about his peer image), and from Bath he entertains his friend with "an incident that seems to confirm the judgement of those two cynic philosophers [Bramble and his friend]" (51). By the time they get to the highwayman's plea for help, Jery and Bramble can discover their identical sympathetic responses to the situation by the "sparkling" in each others eyes. As the novel progresses, the viewpoints of the two correspondents begin to merge, to the point where, near the end of the novel, it becomes difficult without a conscious effort to keep track of which of them is narrating at any time.

The role of the women correspondents is again completely different. Where Bramble and Jery analyze their own and everybody else's characters, the women reveal theirs in spite of themselves. And while the men's letters are rarely unconsciously funny, this is the only kind of humor in the women's; in the case of Tabitha and Win, in fact, it is practically the sole function of their correspondence. Liddy is a slightly more serious character, but her letters, too, are to be read 'against the grain' rather than with it. Her accounts from the various resorts read like promotional literature, or at best like the fantastically heightened descriptions of romance, which makes one suspect her impressions even without the deflating parallel accounts by Bramble or Jery. Ranleigh, for example, "looks like the inchanted palace of a genie . . . enlightened with a thousand golden lamps, that emulate the noonday sun; crowded with the great, the rich, the gay, the happy, the fair [etc.]" (92). Later, she says, "I had the happiness to hear the celebrated Mrs.———, whose voice was so loud and so shrill, that it made my head ake through excess of pleasure" (93)—here, clearly, Lydia's prose is conveying something comically at odds with what she believes she is saying.

This gendered split in the relationship of the various correspondents to the novel's comic and satiric effects forms an important part of what makes *Humphrey Clinker* a pleasure to read. The women's letters offer a form of "comic relief"—not in the sense that they are funny while the men's are not, but in the sense that they put the reader in a different relationship to their comedy. While the men's letters ask (or in the case of some of Bramble's harsher satires, demand) only that the reader acquiesce in their writers' vision, the women's allow us to train our own comic or satiric judgment on their contents; as audience, we occupy a privileged position of superior judgment vis-à-vis writer and addressee both. We are hence made active partners in the men's comic and satiric vision, rather than simply sharing in the largely passive role of their addressees. In other words, the reader is invited to occupy the same interpretive relationship to the female correspondents' *discourse* that the male correspondents have toward the *story*.[4]

Liddy's socially determined discourse, the product of romances and young-ladies'-boarding-school values—through which rather more negative impressions of her surroundings sometimes unconsciously emerge—serves another function besides that of comic relief, one that recalls the resistance to "preaching" in *Pamela*. It is a way for Smollett to portray Liddy as good-humored, impressionable, and easily pleased (important elements in a young lady's attractiveness), while suggesting that she will prove susceptible to her uncle's—and later her husband's—more austere rural values. For Liddy to turn up her nose at London's pleasures would make her too priggish—another way of saying that it would endow her with an inappropriately "preachy" authority—but for her to enjoy them thoroughly would implicate her in the suspect social values of the town. The solution is to have her reveal her exhaustion unconsciously between the lines of her "girlish" enthusiasm, to have her head "ake through excess of pleasure." Liddy's letters thus witness to the same social values the men's letters preach. She becomes an embodiment of the novel's values rather than a self-conscious and authoritative expositor of them.

Humphrey Clinker differs from *Pamela* and *Clarissa* in that it employs the conventions of feminine narration largely for comic purposes. But in both cases, feminine narration acts to define authority, of whatever kind, in opposition to femininity. *Humphrey Clinker* constructs a feminine relationship to comedy and satire in ways analogous to that in which Clarissa defines a feminine relationship to virtue under duress.

Redgauntlet

Hitherto I have been examining texts that work to instate or reinforce—however problematically—a gendered split in the use of autodiegetic narrators. Where *Pamela* and *Clarissa* can be seen as engaging directly with the heroine-narrator's relationship to narrative and material agency, as actively constructing the conventions of feminine narration, *Humphrey Clinker* uses the opposition between male and female narrative voices as a largely unproblematic resource to heighten its comic, satiric, and sentimental effects.

Redgauntlet makes use of the convention of feminine narration in a very different way. The feminine narrator of the epistolary portion of *Redgauntlet* is actually a man, but one compelled, in literal as well as literary terms, to adopt a "feminine dress."[5] Scott uses his feminized hero to explore the role of individual agency and will in the making of history—both history-as-narrative, the construction and dissemination of stories of the past, and history-as-event, the human acts that form the raw material of those stories. Darsie Latimer's female disguise suggests, predictably enough, that his relationship to both will be largely passive, while the most powerfully masculine figure in the novel, Hugh Redgauntlet, equally predictably associates manliness with the power both to deploy historical narratives effectively and to act on history. Scott himself, though, undercuts this polarization by suggesting that the masculine position is in fact unavailable or merely illusory—that the power of history resides in a broader process of social change that supersedes individual human agency altogether.

Redgauntlet, published in 1824, is the only one of Scott's novels to make extensive use of epistolary and diary narration, which make up most of the first half of the novel before being abandoned in favor of what the author calls "direct narrative." The novel opens with the correspondence between its two male protagonists Alan Fairford and Darsie Latimer, which modulates, after two short chapters of authorial narrative, into Darsie's journal of captivity, nominally still addressed to Alan. This section thus mirrors the narrative shape of *Pamela,* which also shifts from direct correspondence with her parents, via a brief authorial transition, to a journal of captivity written (at least initially) for their eyes. As Kathryn Sutherland notes, the similarities between the novels extend further, appearing also in the subjection of the hero/heroine to "a man whose lawless behavior is apparently sanctioned by the law and by a network of conventional relations"— primarily those of master and servant in *Pamela,* and of guardian and ward in *Redgauntlet;* and in their almost obsessive focus on the act of writing and its "material requirements": "privacy . . . pen, ink, and paper," and so on.[6]—Darsie, like Pamela, even resorts to secreting the sheets of his journal in his clothes. The effect of these parallels is comically heightened, of course, when Darsie is compelled to wear women's clothes and a mask when he appears in public. The association with *Pamela* is in keeping with Scott's persistent focus on both plotting and storytelling, which are obsessive concerns for nearly all the novel's characters, as well as its narrator.[7] In this context, Darsie's Pamela-esque position indicates his subjection to the plots of others—most obviously those of his uncle.[8]

The Darsie we are introduced to in the novel's epistolary first one-third is not quite so passive. He is represented as someone constantly *trying* to generate plots for himself—both in the sense of coherent narratives and of plans for action—and even compares himself and Alan to Lovelace and Belford (26). Alan repeatedly warns him about his tendency to make himself "the hero of some romantic history" (24) or to "mak[e] histories out of nothing" (46), and Darsie himself confesses to the tendency: "truly, I think, writing history (one's self being the subject) is as amusing as reading that of foreign countries, at any time" (76). Such adventures as his evening jaunt with Wandering Willie are the result of the romantic plot Darsie quickly conceives around the mysterious "Green Mantle," for example.

But even here, an element of passivity creeps in. Alan suggests that Darsie is not so much a plotter in his own right as someone hungry to find himself *in* a plot, hoping that "the mystery . . . which at present overclouds your birth and connections, will clear up into something inexpressibly and inconceivably brilliant, and this without any effort or exertion of your own, but purely by the good-will of Fortune" (24). He also suggests that Darsie is "not naturally courageous," lacking the "strength of nerves" and "self-possession" to work his way confidently out of the situations his superficially "daring spirit" gets him into (25). Darsie, much as he objects to his friend's characterization, nonetheless shows himself eager to turn over the shaping of both his history and his future to other hands. He asks Alan to "turn . . . thy sharp, wire-drawing, lawyer-like ingenuity to . . . make up my history as though thou wert shaping the blundering allegations of some blue-bonneted, hard-headed client" (17). He tells Lilias, when they have barely met, "I will be what you wish me to be . . . you have but to choose my path, and you shall see if I do not pursue it with energy, were it only because you command me" (126). Later, in detailing the circumstances that led to his captivity, he acknowledges the "facility with which I have, in moments of indolence, suffered my motions to be directed by any person who chanced to be near me, instead of taking the labour of thinking or deciding for myself" (162–63).

Once the shift to journal narration takes place, Darsie becomes more conspicuously feminized as both narrator and character. No longer do we have the jocular epistolary struggle with Alan about the real shape and meaning of their own and each other's narratives. Instead, the opening words of the journal stress its status as raw data to be interpreted by others presumed to have more power to affect his situation than he has himself:

> I will endeavor to pour my thoughts out, as fully and freely as of old, though probably without the same gay and happy levity. If the papers should reach other hands than yours, still I will not regret this exposure of my feelings; for, allowing for an ample share of the folly incidental to youth and inexperience, I fear not that I have much to be ashamed of in my narrative; nay, I even hope, that the open simplicity and frankness with which I am about to relate every singular and distressing circumstance, may prepossess even a stranger in my favour; and that, amid the multitude of seemingly trivial circumstances which I detail at length, a clew may be found to effect my liberation. (161–62)

This opening casts Darsie squarely in the role of the feminine narrator. Like Clarissa, he trusts that the honest exposure of his feelings—even those that may be subject to censure as "folly"—will establish his innocence better than a more self-consciously edited and shaped effort could. And he imagines a reader deriving from the journal a practical significance—the "clew . . . to effect my liberation" that he himself is unable to find amid the "seemingly trivial circumstances" he relates.

Whatever hunger for plotting Darsie had to begin with diminishes considerably during his captivity: "there has stolen on me insensibly an indifference to my freedom—a carelessness about my situation, for which I am unable to account" (181). Darsie himself recognizes something disturbingly "unmanly" in this "passive acquiescence," when compared to the "men" he has "read of . . . who, immured as I am, have surprised the world by the address with which they have successfully overcome the formidable obstacles to their escape" (181).

Darsie has, in fact, become the quintessential damsel in distress, reduced to scribbling furtive complaints about his treatment, trying to smuggle out pleas for rescue, and analyzing the mixture of fear and awed attraction that his Gothic captor provokes. Redgauntlet, like Mr. B., seeks to threaten or force his captive into a form of liaison—in this case political rather than sexual—that he nonetheless needs to see as voluntary. In other words, as for Pamela, the moral weight for Darsie rests more on what he will not do—commit himself to the Pretender's cause, and thereby, he firmly believes, be "ruined"—than on what he does. As Judith Wilt writes, "the only self-assertion open to him/her is to say no."[9] Redgauntlet, meanwhile, pressures Darsie by constituting himself as the only authorized narrator or plotter of Darsie's past and future, constructing for him a family and national history whose structure will compel his compliance with Redgauntlet's plot for the future.

Redgauntlet calls himself a fatalist, telling Darsie, "The line of conduct which I am pursuing towards you, is dictated not by choice, but by necessity. . . . The privilege of free action belongs to no mortal" (212). In pressuring Darsie to fall in with his plans, he claims to be submitting himself as well to external compulsion: "Beware, therefore, of struggling with a force sufficient to crush you, but abandon yourself to that train of events by which we are *both* swept along, and which it is impossible that *either of us* can resist" (186, emphasis added).[10] But other characters stress Redgauntlet's power to bring about almost singlehandedly the "train of events"— the secret return of Charles to England and gathering of old Jacobites for a new rebellion—to which he claims to be abandoning himself. Nanty Ewart, for example, describes him as "a firebrand in the country [who] is stirring up all the honest fellows who should be drinking their brandy quietly, by telling them stories about their ancestors and the forty-five; . . . he is trying to turn all waters into his own mill-dam, and to set his sails to all winds" (281). Nanty's account stresses both the power of Redgauntlet's narrative constructions and his capacity to put material forces—"all waters" and "all winds"—to his own uses. Lilias calls him "a political enthusiast of the most dangerous character [who] proceeds in his agency with as much confidence, as if he felt himself the very Atlas, who is alone capable of supporting a sinking cause" (323). Even Redgauntlet himself talks of the projected uprising as largely the product of his own efforts: "Is there an art I have not practised—a privation to which I have not submitted, to bring on the crisis which I now behold arrived?—Have I not been a vowed and devoted man, foregoing every comfort of social life . . . submitting to every thing to make converts to this noble cause?—Have I done all this, and shall I now stop short?" (339).

Redgauntlet's "fatalism," then, which in tone is reminiscent of Lovelace's equation of his own plans with Clarissa's "fate," is in substance more like B.'s capitulation to the providential plot of virtue rewarded—it is a belief system that (he thinks) underwrites his own power as a plotter of others' lives, and indeed of British history, by making him the spokesman for destiny.

In fact, of course, Redgauntlet has the plot of history all wrong, and far from being "swept along" by it into the rebellion he seeks, he is ultimately revealed as someone heroically but futilely swimming against the tide. Even the multiple histories of the Redgauntlets potentially compel any number of different conclusions: murder of the younger generation by the older, inevitable defeat for all Redgauntlets, and so forth. Sutherland suggests that only one of these—the rebellion of each generation against the preceding—proves to be determinative,[11] but really none does. Darsie never actively rebels against Redgauntlet, cautiously drifting along to the end in the hopes of getting out without a showdown. When circumstances finally do permit him to break officially with his uncle, it is with the latter's reluctant blessing.

But when Redgauntlet is dislodged from his would-be position as the master-narrator, no one else steps up to fill the gap. While Pamela's paper endurance eventually succeeds through the generation of a story/plot that B. takes it upon himself to complete, Darsie's journal has no impact on anyone—in fact no one within the narrative ever sees it. The various potential plots and stories Darsie's letters and journal suggest never come to pass either. After his coded musical conversation with Wandering Willie, for example, Darsie has it "deeply impressed on my mind, that his services may be both useful and necessary" (223)—but in fact Willie's later efforts prove materially irrelevant to his fate.

Nor is this disruption of narrative expectations limited to Darsie and Redgauntlet, being in fact characteristic of the novel as a whole. When Scott draws all the threads of his plot together with the comic convergence of characters at Father Crackenthorpe's inn, we naturally expect that this convergence will have concrete results that will tell on the outcome of the story: that the meeting between Nanty Ewart and Peter Peebles will affect either the former's unresolved self-hatred or the latter's lawsuit; that either Alan or Nanty or Joshua or Willie or the Chevalier—or a newly remasculinized and defiant Darsie himself—will be the catalyst that frees Darsie from his uncle's imprisonment; and so on. In fact, the novel's conclusion renders all of their efforts beside the point. Critics often find it difficult to resist elevating one strain of the story or another to causative status: hence, Sutherland privileges the Redgauntlet history of generational rebellion, while Kerr suggests that "the rescue of Darsie and his eventual restoration to his patrimony . . . lead to the destruction of his uncle's dream of rebellion."[12] But such readings have the same status as the legend mentioned by Dr. Dryasdust, that it was Wandering Willie playing "The Campbells Are Coming" that saved the Chevalier and his adherents from arrest and execution. In fact, Scott makes each of his various interwoven private plots irrelevant to the novel's main outcome with the same care and precision that a novelist like Dickens would have striven to make them all relevant.

If there is a master-plotter in *Redgauntlet,* it is the historical process itself. This, finally, is where agency resides. The emphasis on history as *process* is what prevents the novel from being simply about all-powerful interpretation, or history as narrative. The laurels do not go to the most compelling, charismatic, or consistent interpreter and plotter (surely Redgauntlet); the grounds of his plots slip out from under him because the people whose identities and loyalties he tries to shape have already been irrevocably shaped—in some cases more than they themselves realize— by historical forces beyond the control of any of them. Most of Charles's "Jacobite" supporters are Jacobite by sentimental attachment only: their most basic political principles, as Charles himself vaguely realizes, have become Hanoverian.[13] "The cause is lost forever," as Redgauntlet laments, not because it is outmanned or outplotted by individuals, but because the broader movements of social history mean that it no longer has either a coherent identity of its own or an enemy against which to define itself.

History as master-plotter thus transcends and supersedes all the human plots the novel generates. If Darsie is the damsel in distress, history acts like the beloved hero of melodrama who fights his way in, unbeknownst to the heroine, to rescue her from the forced marriage against which she has hitherto struggled in vain—and then happily marries her himself: history intercedes to rescue Darsie from the political identity his uncle would compel him to, and provides for him a secure social identity.

For Scott, the convention of feminine narration is a resource by which he can foreground his protagonist's problematic relationship to narrative and material plotting. Darsie's increasingly feminized narrative voice invites us to look for the masculine force that can reclaim and redeem his words for a master-narrative—be it Hugh Redgauntlet, voice of his unknown heritage and archplotter on behalf of "destiny," Alan Fairford, the legal constructor of narrative sense from tangled nonsense, or a revitalized Darsie himself. But as with every other conventional narrative expectation Scott evokes, we are deflected instead into an awareness of even the most hypermasculine characters' inadequacy to "master" their own and others' narratives or to "plot" their outcomes effectively.

When Redgauntlet finally removes the female disguise to which he has consigned Darsie, he tells him: "I restore you to yourself, and trust you will lay aside all effeminate thoughts with this feminine dress. Do not blush at having worn a disguise to which kings and heroes have been reduced. It is when female craft or female cowardice find their way into a manly bosom, that he who entertains these sentiments should take eternal shame to himself for having thus resembled womankind" (367).

Redgauntlet here seeks to reinstate the clear gender divisions he has helped to disrupt. Cowardice and craft—fainting Pamela and cunning Shamela—should belong only to "womankind." He makes the same move in responding to the Chevalier's commands, agreeing that "a female influence predominates" when they prove too cautious for his liking (315). But we have already seen the Chevalier refuse his mistress's advice, saying his plans "do not admit of female criticism" (307), so the "cowardice," if it is that, is clearly his own.[14] And no figure in the novel is more shamelessly crafty than Redgauntlet himself, who readily stoops to the role of "a mere vulgar conspirator" (329), as Lilias calls him. In fact, Lilias herself, the only major female character in the novel, has consistently proved not only more honest than her uncle, but braver than her brother. Redgauntlet's versions of manhood and womanhood prove as materially irrelevant in the actual world of the novel as his Jacobitism.

This is not to say that Scott is interested in questioning or disrupting the conventional social relations of men and women. The ease with which he subsides into cliché—writing of Lilias and Alan that "the relative situation of adviser and advised, of protector and protected, is . . . peculiarly suited to the respective condition of man and woman" (389), despite the fact that it is Lilias who has more often played the role of adviser and protector— would belie any such aim. The point is rather that because both men and women are portrayed as subject to the shaping forces of history, gender polarities are not needed to prop up the anxious construction of a model "man" as authoritative voice, actor, shaper of destiny.[15] Narrative authority, if it resides anywhere, belongs to the disembodied voice of the historian-narrator, whose authority derives in part from his disinterested stance as one to whom the comprehension of these competing plots and interpretations conveys no personal power.[16]

Three

REDEEMING THE PLOTTING WOMAN
Charlotte Brontë and the Feminine Narrator

*F*or Charlotte Brontë, adopting an explicitly male first-person narrative voice in *The Professor,* her first novel written for publication, was clearly at least in part an effort to evade the particular problems of writing "as a woman." The male voice, combined with a male pseudonym as author, could assure her a reading untroubled by prejudices about what was appropriate to women as either narrators or authors, while screening herself as well as her readers from the more painfully autobiographical aspects of the story.[1] The result was not particularly successful: *The Professor* was the only one of the three manuscripts submitted by the sisters to be rejected, remaining unpublished until after Brontë's death, when her fame was sufficiently established to make almost any product of her pen marketable. As a work of art, it has found few advocates since, being considered of interest primarily as apprentice-work for *Jane Eyre* and later *Villette.*[2] This is also the context in which I would like to consider it, but less in psychological than in formal terms, by looking at its narrative voice in relation to the tradition of feminine narration.

The Professor

The Professor opens like an epistolary novel, with a letter sent from Crimsworth to an old schoolfriend, detailing his family history and the events that lead up to his arrival at his brother's house. In this letter, we see Crimsworth positioning himself in a role like that of the epistolary heroine: he is looking for a confidant, someone to take an interest in his story as it unfolds, and to respond with sympathy and advice—someone, in other words, whose concern for and engagement with his life can motivate the continued telling of the story.

Such a relation, as we have seen, is inevitably to some degree one of vulnerability and dependence. The most self-confident of epistolary heroines will become anxious and self-doubtful if her correspondent's sympathy and

85

approval are withdrawn; she can become paralyzed into inaction at crucial moments when awaited advice fails to arrive. (Even when responses are not included, the heroine's anticipation of them is a crucial part of her consciousness.) Such a heroine is also likely to be caught out by readings she is unaware of, or by later unforeseen events that reveal mistakes of judgment or failures of self-understanding.

It is difficult to imagine the Crimsworth of the opening letter inviting, let alone sustaining, such a relationship. Throughout the letter, he stresses with unpleasant insistence his independence of such claims. In his first paragraph, he admits to feeling neither affection nor respect for his old school companion: he sees their relationship as devoid on both sides of any "romantic regard," and feels himself "superior" to any "check" his friend may offer to his judgment or feelings.[3] Small wonder the "friend" failed to reply: Crimsworth has rejected in advance any possibilities the correspondence might offer.

As a device for introducing the hero's background, the letter is worse than useless: in effect, Brontë has Crimsworth recounting his past to the only person in the novel or out of it who can be presumed to know a large portion of it already—hence, he must frequently preface his accounts with "you know," or "you are aware that." Such a device is common enough in epistolary fiction as a way of introducing background information without breaking the convention of epistolarity, but it is not, generally speaking, one of the things the form can handle most gracefully. Such moments of epistolary retrospection, in fact, are precisely the points where the fiction of documentary verisimilitude is most likely to erode or break down altogether: even if they are skillfully handled, the reader cannot help but be conscious of their status as a necessary authorial device, a compromise between the fiction of a "found" correspondence and the requirements of the storyteller who in fact constructs it.

But if the novel's opening letter is less than ideal as an introduction, the epistolary form would have come into its own at the point where the hero-narrator began recounting his experiences and reflections day to day. Yet this is precisely the point at which the correspondence stops, halted for want of a correspondent. The letter remains isolated as an introductory device, a brief intrusion of epistolary form put to the one use for which it is most ill-suited.

In posing as a "real" document, the letter calls to mind, in the way an unframed narrative does not, the implicit presence of an editor, a controlling consciousness who has chosen, for whatever reason, to integrate this document into a narrative—whether the narrative is composed entirely of such documents or not. What is unusual about *The Professor* is that this controlling consciousness, or master-narrator, should be identical with the author of the letter. Normally a letter is interpolated into a narrative to provide access to something—a consciousness, a state of affairs—that would otherwise remain closed to the narrator, or on which the narrator might not be supposed to speak with authority. To have a first-person narrator include his own letter as evidence of his own state of mind seems as gratuitous a literary gesture as having him explain his background to someone who already knows it.[4]

But I do not wish to dismiss the novel's opening as a simple piece of literary ineptitude. Precisely because of its awkwardness, the opening letter advertises its status as a literary device, and foregrounds the issue of literary control by both author and narrator. Ultimately, it has more significance as a formal statement than as a device for introducing Crimsworth's past. In both the failed correspondence it represents and in its formal position within the narrative, the letter acts as a public rejection of the epistolary form and, more specifically, the passive, dependent role of the epistolary heroine. In opening his narrative with his own unanswered letter, Crimsworth not only signals his refusal of the epistolary heroine's day-to-day dependence on the responses of others, he also proclaims himself his own master-narrator. Significantly, the failure of his correspondent drives Crimsworth, not to a private journal, but to a retrospective narrative begun a year after the letter was written, the form that offers the greatest knowledge and, hence, control of the shape of his story.

And control, of others as well as himself, seems to be Crimsworth's highest priority. Within the story, he is preoccupied with power relations, representing nearly every character with whom he is in contact as seeking power over him. His chief defensive weapon is his own power to withhold information about himself. His brother, for example, he keeps at bay by maintaining "the padlock of silence on mental wealth in which he was no sharer" (31). In the more sympathetic Hundsen, he still detects "a tone of despotism" (37) and takes pleasure in making him falsely believe him aggrieved over his dismissal (49); when they meet later in Brussels, he gains a perceived edge by leaving undisturbed his friend's misperceptions about his impending marriage (203). With Zoraide Reuter, and to a lesser degree with Pelet, he carries on an extended hostile "game" in which she tries to worm out the knowledge that would make her "mistress of my character" while Crimsworth enjoys tempting her with the promise of revealed vulnerability (89–90), only to offer in the end "a smooth and bare precipice, which offered neither jutting stone nor tree root, nor tuft of grass to aid the climber" (105). The challenge, in each case, is not only to escape vulnerability himself but to acquire the power others seek by reading their characters without allowing his own to be read. Thus of Pelet, he says "I felt half his master, because the reality of his nature was now known to me" (113), while Zoraide Reuter, when she knows she has been seen through, becomes almost "slavish" (129) in her submissiveness. Crimsworth's anxiety about relative power extends even toward those who are unambiguously friendly toward him: he is not comfortable receiving assistance from the rich and influential M. Vandenhuten, whose son he saved from drowning, until he is able to convince himself that "my mind having more fire and action than his, instinctively assumed and kept the predominance" (211).

This preoccupation with the power to manipulate others is what renders Crimsworth's romance with Frances Henri so often unappealing: he savors his power to play on her feelings—negatively as well as positively—with an almost Lovelacean connoisseurship:

> The reproofs suited her best of all: while I scolded she would chip away with her pen-knife at a pencil or pen, fidgetting a little, pouting a little, defending herself by monosyllables, and when I deprived her of pen or pencil, fearing it would be all cut away, and when I interdicted even the monosyllabic defense, for the purpose of working up the subdued excitement a little higher, she would at last raise her eyes and give me a certain glance, sweetened with gaiety, and pointed with defiance, which, to speak truth, thrilled me as nothing had ever done, and made me, in a fashion, (though happily she did not know it), her subject if not her slave. (177)

Crimsworth assures us that his manipulations are as delightful to Frances as to himself, and suggests at least a buried reciprocity in subjection (though Frances is unconscious of his, and therefore unable to act on it), but his descriptions of his pleasure in her company continue to stress his power over her: "You have the secret of awakening what expression you will. . . . You can hold her under a potent spell . . . you can seal her lips . . . you know that few could rule her as you do" (198–99). When he describes Frances, upon his proposal of marriage, as "stirless in her happiness as a mouse in its terror" (224), it is hard not to see an element of sadism in his pleasure.

Crimsworth's approach as a narrator exhibits a similar preoccupation with power. The narrative confidence, competence, and control that characterize an authoritative narrator are not so much assumed as loudly insisted upon, in ways that often mirror his relations to characters. His assertion in introducing Hundsen, for example, that he is not yet "disposed to paint his portrait in detail" (24), is echoed later when he informs us he was "not disposed to show" Hundsen the satisfaction he felt on being dismissed by his brother (49). He clearly relishes his power to withhold or ration narrative information: in describing the scenes on the "four walls" of his memory, for example, he says of the fourth, "a curtain covers it, which I may hereafter withdraw, or may not, as it suits my convenience and capacity" (55). He seems to take the same pleasure in manipulating our experience of Frances Henri as he does in manipulating hers of him, gloating over the inadequacy of his portrait of her: "Now reader, though I have spent more than a page in describing Mdlle Henri, I know well enough that I have left on your mind's eye no distinct picture of her; I have not painted her complexion, nor her eyes, nor her hair, nor even drawn the outline of her shape. You cannot tell whether her nose was aquiline or retroussé, whether her chin was long or short, her face square or oval; nor could I the first day, and it is not my intention to communicate to you at once a knowledge I myself gained by little and little" (123).

The point here is not that Crimsworth withholds information to heighten certain narrative effects—any competent retrospective narrator must do that—but that he signals so insistently, and at times so unpleasantly, that he is doing so. Asserting his claim to narrative authority seems at least as important as actually exercising it. Here, too, he comes across as a rather charmless (if also comparatively harmless) version of Lovelace: as both character and narrator, he exhibits a Lovelacean sadism without the excitement of Lovelace's transgressive exuberance, or the compensatory readerly satisfaction of Lovelace's eventual self-punishment.

But Crimsworth, like Lovelace, protests too much. His excessive assertions of narrative and personal mastery attest to a profound anxiety about the extent to which he can really claim them, while his grim refusal of any vulnerability whatsoever denies him the readerly sympathy needed to underwrite his authority. Brontë's adoption of a male voice in her first novel does not so much bypass the problem of narrative authority as call attention to it. Perhaps recognizing this, in her subsequent novels, Brontë tackled the authorizing of a female voice more frontally.[5] Crimsworth's obsession with control reappears with Jane Eyre and Lucy Snowe, but there it is inevitably set against the forms of enforced vulnerability and lack of control inherent in being a female in Brontë's culture. In *Jane Eyre,* Brontë crossbreeds

Crimsworth's hunger for narrative mastery, a hunger she initially construed as masculine, with a feminine romance-plot structure that had traditionally —as in *Pamela*—put its heroine in a more passive role. In that context, the heroine's conflicted efforts to retain or reclaim control over her narrative and her life are more heroically engaging, or at least (as in Lucy Snowe's case) more psychologically compelling, than Crimsworth's.

Jane Eyre

In the history of female narrative voice in the English novel, *Jane Eyre* stands out as a unique and startling moment. As Lanser notes, the novel conspicuously lacks the deferential, apologetic, and moralizing frames that had been used to downplay the presumption of earlier autodiegetic female narrators by stressing the subordination of their story to moral and religious authorities and purposes.[6] Instead, the narrator plunges us directly into her story, presuming and indeed compelling our interest in its heroine on her own terms. While some reviewers clearly noticed (and duly chastised) its subversive potential, the book's massive popularity and subsequent literary influence indicate that its strategies for authorizing its female narrator were largely effective. But Jane Eyre's self-authorization does not occur in a literary vacuum. Throughout the novel, Brontë engages directly and indirectly with the conventions of feminine narration, particularly as figured by Pamela and her narratorial alter ego, the plotting woman.

Pamela makes her overt appearance in the first pages of the novel, as one of the sources of the nurse Bessie's stories, along with "old fairy tales and older ballads . . . and Henry, Earl of Moreland."[7] That *Pamela* is keeping company with *Henry, Earl of Moreland,* a didactic novel, suggests that the former, too, has been mined as much for didactic as for entertaining purposes, and in fact we soon see the fairy stories, too, being used to enforce social control, as Abbot warns Jane that if she fails to "repent, something bad might be permitted to come down the chimney, and fetch [her] away" (13). (Similarly, Bessie later evokes the supernatural in conversation with her fellow servant Sarah, describing a figure "'all dressed in white . . . a light in the churchyard just over his grave'—&c. &c." (20) to manage her own guilty perception that "Missis was rather too hard" on Jane (19). Nonetheless, even after her rebellion has made Jane more skeptical of the narratives other adults use to attempt to control her—like the "account of the awfully sudden death of Martha G—, a naughty child addicted to falsehood and deceit" that Mr. Brocklehurst proffers (35)—she continues to find Bessie's tales "enchanting" (40), and throughout she has found them "as interest-ing" as anything in even her most beloved books (9).

Lanser suggests that Jane Eyre's self-authorization as a narrator occurs at the expense not just of Bertha Mason, but of every other female voice in the novel—particularly those of lower-class women like Mrs. Fairfax. But this critique overlooks Bessie's crucial function as narrative role model. Bessie's narratives shape Jane's perceptions and the narrator's presentation throughout the novel,[8] in the frequent references to fairies, sprites, and goblins as images for herself, Rochester, and Bertha, for example, or in the use of Bessie's ballad about the "poor orphan child" (22) to prefigure Jane's starved wanderings after her flight from Thornfield. Unlike Mrs. Fairfax, who has "no notion of sketching a character" (106), Bessie is described as "a girl of good natural capacity . . . smart in all she did, [with] a remarkable knack of narrative" (29). But with her "capricious and hasty temper, and indifferent ideas of principle or justice" (29), Bessie lacks the analytic power to test the value of the old stories and the received opinions they embody against real-life circumstances. Faced with the daily evidence of the Reeds' mistreatment of Jane, she can offer only the Pamela-esque injunction to "try to be useful and pleasant" (13) and concur in Abbot's judgement that the conventionally pretty Georgiana would be "more moving in the same con-dition" (26). As both her first mother-figure and her role model for story-telling, then, Bessie offers the option of uncritically retelling stories "from the pages of *Pamela*"—with all their submissiveness to patriarchal authority and uncomplaining acceptance of a lower social position. Indeed, Bessie even starts to initiate Jane into such a position, employing her "as a sort of under nursery-maid, to tidy the room, dust the chairs, &c." (30).[9]

In one sense, *Jane Eyre* does retell a story "from the pages of *Pamela*"— critics have often noted the ways Brontë's plot echoes Richardson's[10]—but its defiantly authoritative retrospective narrator is anything but Pamela-esque. As we shall see, the novel's specific engagements with *Pamela* serve to underscore the necessity for Jane to reclaim the kinds of narrative and personal agency Richardson's heroine so insistently disavowed. At the same time, though, the narrator must continually counteract the sinister image of the plotting woman that threatens to take over when a female figure claims such agency.

An "Infantine Guy Fawkes": Gateshead and Lowood

Right from the beginning, the narrator has to position her childhood self in relation to persistently suspicious readings of her voice and actions. The

problem Jane faces at Gateshead is not just that she is disliked and disbelieved, but that she is consistently assumed to be up to no good: "an underhand little thing" (12), "sullen and sneaking" (15). Like Clarissa within her
family, Jane finds her most heartfelt appeals for consideration discounted
as self-conscious strategies of manipulation: "She has screamed out on purpose," the maid Abbot declares. "If she had been in great pain one would
have excused it, but she only wanted to bring us all here: I know her naughty
tricks" (17). When she pleads desperately with Mrs. Reed, she is perceived
only as a "precocious actress" displaying a "dangerous duplicity" (18). In
other words, Jane confronts a situation in which not only is she denied an
authoritative voice,[11] but she finds herself treated with distrust specifically
as a *plotter:* "a tiresome, ill-conditioned child, who always looked as if she
were watching everybody, and scheming plots underhand" (25): her image
within the household, she suggests, is that of "a sort of infantine Guy
Fawkes" (25)—the most notorious plotter of English history. Jane understands all too well the bind this presumption puts her in: asked by Mr.
Brocklehurst if she is "a good child," she finds it "[i]mpossible to reply to
this in the affirmative; my little world held a contrary opinion: I was silent"
(32). Once she has been branded as an "artful, noxious child" with a "tendency to deceit," she feels helpless to make a good impression even on new
people or in a new setting: any effort to do so will only be understood as
further duplicity, an "attempt to impose on Mr. Brocklehurst" (33–34).

In countering this image of herself as an artful plotter, the narrator unsurprisingly stresses her childhood artlessness, continually calling attention
to the unpremeditated, even involuntary, quality of her acts of self-assertion.
Her outburst to John Reed consists of observations "which I never thought
thus to have declared aloud," and in defending herself she "received him in
frantic sort. I don't very well know what I did with my hands" (11). This
emphasis on the involuntary persists throughout the Gateshead section: "I
was a trifle beside myself; or rather *out* of myself, as the French would say"
(12); "I was oppressed, suffocated: endurance broke down—I uttered a
wild, involuntary cry" (17); "I cried out suddenly and without at all deliber-
ating on my words" (27); "it seemed as if my tongue pronounced words
without my will consenting to their utterance: something spoke out of me
over which I had no control" (27).

On one of the rare occasions when speech is likely to be of service to her,
in her exchange with the apothecary Mr. Lloyd, the narrator is at pains to
make clear that Jane is not deliberately seeking to deploy him as an ally
against the Reeds. Her initial account of how she fell ill is "jerked out of

me" by "pang[s] of mortified pride" (23) at the demeaning explanations Bessie offers for her, and in the subsequent conversation, the narrator stresses Jane's trouble in articulating what she feels: "How much I wished to reply fully to this question! How difficult it was to frame any answer! Children can feel, but they cannot analyze their feelings; and if the analysis is partially effected in thought, they know not how to express the result of the process in words" (23–24). Jane's responses, consequently, are portrayed as barely intelligible: they are "meagre, though as far as it went, true," or "bunglingly enounced" (24). By claiming that children are by nature unable to analyze their experience or organize it effectively for presentation to others, the narrator makes Jane's youth itself a guarantee of her artlessness. In such a context, an "infantine Guy Fawkes" would be a contradiction in terms. In this case, the move casts Mr. Lloyd in the role of potential master-narrator: a benevolent male authority who can interpret her "meagre" and "bungling" words in the context of other data—Bessie's evasiveness, the marks of illness and ill-use on Jane's own body, and so forth—to arrive at a coherent account of her situation and a viable strategy for improving it by removing her from the house. (Lloyd briefly reprises this role when Miss Temple writes to him to validate Jane's account of her childhood before vindicating her to the school.)

But as we have seen, artlessness is a mixed blessing. Emphasis on the involuntary quality of Jane's acts of self-assertion props up her credibility at the expense of her self-control, planting the seeds for her later anxious relationship to the madwoman Bertha Mason.[12] Her lack of self-knowledge also renders her psychologically vulnerable to the constructions of others: hence Jane's "habitual mood of humiliation [and] self-doubt": "All said I was wicked, and perhaps I might be so" (16); or "Bessie . . . proved beyond a doubt that I was the most wicked and abandoned child ever reared under a roof. I half believed her; for I felt indeed only bad feelings surging in my breast" (28). Countering the image of her as artful plotter with proof of her artlessness converts Jane from an "infantine Guy Fawkes" to an object of sympathy—or from Shamela to Pamela—but in itself it can do little to move her toward the mastery of self and narrative implied in the narrator's own ability to "see . . . clearly" (15) *now* what was so painfully incomprehensible to Jane *then*.

Hence the stress on Jane's artlessness and self-interpretive incompetence is mitigated by other strains in this section that suggest the image of Jane as interpreter and judge rather than simply victim. The most significant of these is in the narrator's account of why she is hated by the Reeds. The explanation is introduced in terms that again emphasize both the loss of control that fuels Jane's defiance and her interpretive helplessness: "How all my brain was in tumult, and all my heart in insurrection! Yet in what darkness, what dense ignorance, was the mental battle fought! I could not answer the ceaseless inward question—*why* I thus suffered" (15). Only the mature narrative voice, writing "at the distance of—I will not say how many years" (15), can intervene to provide the analysis her childhood self cannot: "I was a discord in Gateshead Hall: I was like nobody there: I had nothing in harmony with Mrs. Reed or her children, or her chosen vasselage. If they did not love me, in fact, as little did I love them. They were not bound to regard with affection a thing that could not sympathize with one amongst them; a heterogeneous thing, opposed to them in temperament, in capacity, in propensities; a useless thing, incapable of serving their interest, or adding to their pleasure; a noxious thing, cherishing the germs of indignation at their treatment, of contempt of their judgement" (15–16).

At first glance, this statement is disarmingly generous to the Reeds. To say that their inability to love Jane is matched by her inability to love them is to ignore the real power differential in the relationship created by their greater age and wealth and by Mrs. Reed's quasi-parental authority—thus absolving them of culpability in her oppression. But the equivalence set up here between Jane and the Reeds is double-edged, as it also has the effect of subtly empowering Jane. Rather than being simply the victim of inexplicable malice, she is the (albeit unconscious) agent of "discord" and discomfort. She gives as good as she gets. And in the ascending scale of her negative qualities, ("a heterogeneous thing . . . a useless thing . . . a noxious thing"), her powers of judgment are at the peak. If "indignation at their treatment" could refer simply to Jane's incoherent rage, "contempt of their judgement" implies an analysis carried out from a position of presumed superiority. And in fact it is precisely such an analysis that has gotten Jane into trouble in the first place, as she articulates out loud (though involuntarily) the "parallels" she has drawn in silence between John Reed and the Roman emperors.

The Gateshead portion of Jane Eyre, then, seeks to appropriate for Jane the credibility and sympathy associated with the "artless" feminine narrator. At the same time, unlike *Pamela,* it resists instating a radical gap between the young Jane who "involuntarily" spews forth the evidence of her oppression and misery and the reader or master-narrator who comprehends and contextualizes that evidence in a coherent narrative of her vindication.

Instead, the lack of control implied in such a position is associated with madness. While the pathos of her "fit" in the "red-room" wins the reader's sympathy and credence, much as Pamela's "fits" win B.'s, her emphasis on the "shock" to her "nerves . . . of which I feel the reverberation to this day" (20) suggests that her own achievement of rational control and distance from such events will prove more important than simply gaining credibility with a powerful external authority.

This is the achievement of her years at Lowood. There, in moving beyond Pamela's model of unselfconscious artlessness, she engages with the more self-conscious ethic of passive virtue represented by Clarissa— embodied at Lowood in Helen Burns. There, too, Jane finally overcomes the image of her as an "artful, noxious" child when she produces a "credible" narrative of her Gateshead years to replace the one underwritten by Mrs. Reed's and Mr. Brocklehurst's authority.

Helen Burns's role as a Christ-figure (and as a reminiscence of Brontë's sister Maria) is well established, but she also echoes *Clarissa* in her role as the perfect exemplar of feminine virtue: this is apparent in her willingness to be held by others—and to hold herself—to more exacting moral and intellectual standards than her peers, in her reluctance to accuse those in authority over her of unjustified oppression of her, and, most notably, in her advocacy of passive suffering under injustice over any form of purposive resistance: "It is far better to endure patiently a smart which nobody feels but yourself, than to commit a hasty action whose evil consequences will extend to all connected with you" (56) (cf. *Clarissa* 105, 382). In both admiring Helen and declining to follow her example—indeed, passionately advocating to her her own version of justice—Jane echoes the position of Anna Howe. She finds Helen's quiescence morally inspiring but also practically ill-judged: like Anna, she argues that actions should be judged in part upon their likely effects. Just as Anna points out that "[t]he person who will bear much shall have much to bear all the world through" (*Clarissa*, 69)—adding that no one would dare to treat *her* the way Clarissa has been treated by her relations—Jane argues that "if people were always kind and obedient to those who are cruel and unjust, the wicked people would have it all their own way: they would never feel afraid, and so they would never alter, but would grow worse and worse" (58). But whereas Anna's advocacy of practical resistance is subtly undercut by the inadequacy, and even danger, of the alternative "plots" she proposes for Clarissa (see chapter 2), the narrator does nothing to distance us from Jane's advocacy of resistance,[13] which has indeed already won her freedom from her oppressions at Gateshead. (By contrast, Helen's patience under Miss Scatcherd's exactions seems only to provoke her further.)

Although the Christ-imagery surrounding Helen suggests that Jane's friendship with her constitutes a conversion experience, moving Jane from the revenge orientation of her early years—"When we are struck at without a reason, we should strike back again very hard" (58)—to a capacity for forgiveness, Jane never disclaims the right, or even the moral necessity, of active resistance to oppression. Though Jane does eventually "forgive" Mrs. Reed, she does so from a position of superior power: her aunt is on her deathbed, weak, and obviously haunted by guilt—indeed, Jane's display of Christian goodness is probably considerably more painful to her than a display of peevish resentment would have been, since the later would at least have vindicated her continuing hatred of Jane. Similarly, while Jane is "forbearing" afterwards with Georgiana's selfish demands, she makes clear that "it is only because our connection happens to be very transitory . . . that I consent thus to render it so patient and compliant on my part" (243); in longer association with her, she suggests, she would have "compelled" a more equal relation.

The effect of Helen's example is made evident in Jane's experience of retelling the story of her Gateshead years to "clear" herself to Miss Temple. She takes to heart "Helen's warnings against the indulgence of resentment," not by relinquishing the impulse to self-justification (as Helen does), but as a strategy for achieving it more effectively, by producing a more "credible" narrative. Though we might see this (as Lanser does) as an indication that Jane is learning to discipline her voice to fit with socially constructed notions of "credibility," there are other factors at work here in producing a new orientation toward her story. She is also "exhausted by emotion" and therefore has a calmer attitude in her own right. Credibility is thus a product not of immediacy—temporal or emotional—but of distance: "having reflected a few minutes in order to arrange coherently what I had to say" (71). That she resolves to be at the same time "most moderate" and "most correct" suggests that the immediacy of strong emotion, with the "gall and wormwood" it ordinarily "infused into the narrative," has threatened its accuracy as well as its credibility (71). Just as it had earlier taken all the distance of adulthood to comprehend "*why* I thus suffered" at Gateshead, here it takes the combined factors of time to reflect, the emotional distance of "exhaustion," and the self-conscious self-restraint produced by Helen's comments, to generate a narrative that sounds "credible" to herself as well as to Miss Temple. This last point is important, for the very vehemence of Jane's violent feelings in her outbursts at Gateshead, as we have seen, undercut her own confidence in the rightness of her position.

We can see Jane's narrative at Lowood as a kind of intermediate point in the journey from the "artless"—and thus often incoherent—Jane of Gateshead to the confidently authoritative narrator of *Jane Eyre*. Though she has succeeded in gaining some control over her story, she suggests that her emotion still "break[s] bounds" in describing the red-room scene, when she is overwhelmed again by the "spasm of agony" at her abandonment in the "dark and haunted chamber" (72). The immediacy of her pain in narrating that episode doubtless contributes as much as her previous restraint to the impression the narrative makes on Miss Temple, who is silent "a few minutes" on its conclusion before pronouncing Jane "clear" in her mind. Furthermore, whatever the impact of the tale on Miss Temple herself, she is unwilling to grant *public* authority to Jane's narrative without having its credibility underwritten explicitly by a male authority, Mr. Lloyd.

Whereas Jane's escape from Gateshead had been engineered by Mr. Lloyd, her departure from Lowood is the product of her own deliberate planning and forethought. In fact, her descriptions of the circumstances that lead to her hiring at Thornfield put an unusual degree of emphasis on the planning and imaginative projection—the plotting—needed to bring her first vague dissatisfaction to practical fruition. While Jane's self-suppression of her initial longing for "liberty," or even "change, stimulus," in favor of settling for "a new servitude" (86) has been much commented upon—and for obvious reasons—the narrator's equally detailed depiction of the surely rather unremarkable thought processes that get her from that point to the plan to advertise for a position in the ——shire Herald is also worth noting. The account of the process emphasizes the need for foresight and planning, for a deliberate, projective effort of the "brain," to bring her "will" to fruition: "Can I not get so much of my own will? Is not the thing feasible? Yes—yes—the end is not so difficult; if I had only a brain active enough to ferret out the means of attaining it" (86–87). She gives in considerable detail the process of interior dialogue, the self-questioning about means, and the determined "order" to the brain to "find a response" to her problem. When the response from her exhausted brain at last arrives, the narrator is equally detailed in showing how Jane works through and refines her plan of action: "'You must inclose the advertisement and the money to pay for it under a cover directed to the Editor of the Herald; you must put it, the first opportunity you have, into the post at Lowton; answers must be addressed to J.E. at the post-office there: you can go and inquire in about a week after you send your letter, if any are come, and act accordingly.' This scheme I went over twice, thrice; it was then digested in my mind: I had it in a clear practical form; I felt satisfied, and fell asleep" (87).

The account of the actual writing, sending, and response to the advertisement that immediately follows closely matches the plan the narrator has just described, almost to the point of redundancy. The close juxtaposition of Jane's imaginative projection of everything she will do to obtain a position with the fulfillment of that projection to the letter suggests that what is at issue here is precisely Jane's power to put her projective constructions—her plots—into action. The result brings her to Thornfield, the site of the novel's most explicit engagements both with *Pamela* as pre-text and with the figure of the plotting woman.

"Somebody Has Plotted Something": Thornfield

Jane Eyre's plot echoes Richardson's novel both in its broad shape—the master who desires a servant and seeks to pressure or trick her into becoming his mistress, but eventually repents and marries her—and in many major and minor details of its development.[14] Brontë's rewriting of *Pamela* can be pointed in any of a number of thematic directions: toward the representation of class boundaries and the means and motives for crossing them; the account of female desire; the representation of the heroine's development, or lack thereof, and so on. But for my purposes, the most obviously significant revision of *Pamela* lies in its narration: Jane as narrator is empowered to shape her tale retroactively in a way that, as we have seen, Pamela is unable to without undercutting the very grounds of her famous "virtue." There are features in the text that work to de-emphasize this break: Kaufman argues that *Jane Eyre* still recognizably falls within the tradition of the "amorous epistle," with its narrator seeking to reawaken and relive in the present the vitality of her past tormented passions,[15] and Lanser points out that the novel's narrative strategies—specifically the "suppression of retrospectivity" apparent in moments of present-tense narration and other erasures of the distance between narrating and narrated self, and the many direct addresses to a single "Reader"—seek to evoke the "immediacy" and "intimacy" of epistolary fiction, to promote "the narrator's wish to be accepted despite her unconventional assertiveness."[16]

But while the effects of intimacy and immediacy produced by self-conscious narrative techniques like these may partially elide the differences between the powerlessness that accompanies and enables Pamela's actual immediacy and the control and "assertiveness" that in fact characterize *Jane Eyre*'s narrator—much as Lovelace's carefully-constructed "lively *present-tense* manner" mirrors the effects that Clarissa authentically produces—the differences remain, and the masks of passionate vulnerability or epistolary immediacy are not sufficiently prominent to do away with the tensions between narrative authority and feminine virtue. The novel addresses these tensions in two ways that I will discuss in detail: first, by using the parallels with *Pamela* pointedly to reclaim forms of narrative and material agency for Jane that Pamela persistently disavowed; and second, by projecting the image of the sinister plotting woman onto Bertha Mason.

One of the most important things *Jane Eyre* picks up from *Pamela* is the sexual energy of the heroine's verbal resistance to her employer. While the influence of Pamela's pretty face and, increasingly, her eloquent letters, on her attractiveness to B. should not be underestimated, her ready wit in defying and denouncing him to his face clearly also feeds the flames of his desire. He calls her "Sawcebox," "Boldface," and "Impudent," terms of affectionate abuse that suggest he finds her more piquant than irritating. Jane, too, first catches Rochester's interest by resisting him—refusing to leave him injured in the lane, to flatter him on his looks, or to speak for his pleasure, and critiquing the ethics of his remarks and resolutions in a way that prompts him to tell her, "You have no right to preach to me" (137). She, too, eventually earns the epithets "provoking puppet" and "malicious elf" from a Rochester who is nonetheless "excellently entertained" (276).

But what begins as simple resistance to encroachments on her dignity or sense of what is right (and remains so for Pamela) soon becomes a more deliberate strategy on Jane's part: "I knew the pleasure of vexing and soothing him by turns; it was one I chiefly delighted in, and a sure instinct always prevented me from going too far: beyond the verge of provocation I never ventured; on the extreme brink I liked well to try my skill. Retaining every minute form of respect, every propriety of my station, I could still meet him in argument without fear or uneasy restraint: this suited both him and me" (160). Jane has become an artful manipulator, who self-consciously reproduces the effects of Pamela's uncalculated alternation (according to circumstances) between outraged resistance and dutiful subordination. But rather than aligning her with Shamela's sinister manipulations, Jane's actions are represented as part of a mutual pact of pleasure: "this suited both him and me." In effect, Jane moves beyond the opposition between sinister artfulness and virtuous artlessness to the practice of a mutually acknowledged artistry. Both her pleasure and, it seems, his, derives from the exercise of her "skill." It is no coincidence, then, that the narrator's account of how Jane gives pleasure in conversation with Rochester also describes perfectly the pact of pleasure between a reader and a conventionally authoritative retrospective narrator, like that of *Jane Eyre,* who also exercises her skill by "vexing and soothing [us] by turns."

After Rochester and Jane become engaged, her skill at manipulating his responses becomes valuable for reasons other than just pleasure, being put to use to resist his inclinations to despotism and passionate excess: "with this needle of repartee I'll keep you from the edge of the gulph too," she reflects, "and, moreover, maintain by its pungent aid that distance between you and myself most conducive to our real mutual advantage" (276). Jane pursues "the system thus entered on" not just to defend herself and please them both, then, but to protect Rochester from his own more destructive inclinations: he may believe that he wants a "lamb-like submission and turtle-dove sensibility," but she knows that her skillful manipulations, while not "fostering his despotism" in fact "pleased his judgement, satisfied his common-sense, and even suited his taste" more than her acquiescence would (276).

Jane's use of "repartee" both to defend herself and to recall her "master" to the more virtuous side of his conflicting inclinations is in some respects reminiscent of Pamela's, but it is significant that this use of her "skill" comes about after their engagement, a point at which Pamela herself has begun nurturing a "lamb-like submission" to B.'s now socially authorized despotism. *Jane Eyre* thus rewrites *Pamela* both by allowing Jane to be self-conscious and deliberate about the effects of her resistance—both pleasurable and disciplinary—on her lover, and by having her exercise her power even more strenuously when he has stepped into the position of social authority as her future husband. Jane proves herself both more skillful than Rochester at setting the tone of their interactions and a better judge of what *he* needs and wants morally and emotionally. The potential for female power that the depressing final one-third of *Pamela* is concerned to defuse, and that *Shamela* renders a threatening reality, is reshaped here. Jane congratulating herself on her resourcefulness in manipulating her lover could well be Shamela anticipating further deception of the unfortunate Booby: "I laughed in my sleeve at his menaces: 'I can keep you in reasonable check now,' I reflected; 'and I don't doubt to be able to do it hereafter: if one expedient loses its virtue, another must be devised'" (277). But the power of the plotting woman has become associated with the power of virtuous *self-*

control: not only does Jane need to supply the deficiencies in Rochester's self-restraint, she must resist her own inclinations toward a "turtle-dove sensibility" that threatens her spiritual virtue: "Yet after all my task was not an easy one: often I would rather have pleased than teased him. My future husband was becoming to me my whole world. . . . He stood between me and every thought of religion" (277).

But the figure of the sinister plotting woman is not so readily overcome. The reference, above, to vexing and soothing by turns occurs immediately after the nighttime fire in Rochester's bedroom, the product of a very different kind of female plotting. This scene, which moves their relationship to a new level of intimacy—indeed, Jane has to exercise some resourcefulness to escape from Rochester's bedroom—recalls an episode in *Clarissa* in which Lovelace plots to set a fire in the middle of the night, hoping to frighten Clarissa from her locked room in a state of physical and emotional vulnerability to his advances in the guise of her rescuer. In *Clarissa,* the fire both symbolizes Lovelace's passion and operates as part of a practical plot for acting upon it. The fire in *Jane Eyre* operates similarly, though in this case it is Jane who acts as rescuer and Rochester who is surprised in a state of undress and brought to the brink of acknowledging his passion. But whose plot is it? On awakening, Rochester accuses Jane: "Have you plotted to drown me?" "Somebody has plotted something," she replies (150).

The plot, of course, will turn out to be Bertha's. Bertha can be read here—as Gilbert and Gubar read her throughout—as Jane's repressed double, acting out the rage and sexual passion (the fire may express either or both) Jane denies in herself, but I want to stress the representation of Bertha specifically as a *plotter.* When Jane still identifies the mysterious plotter with Grace Poole, she is unnerved by her "scrutinizing and conscious eye," and when Grace asks her if she locks her door, she assumes that "she wants to know my habits that she may lay her plans accordingly!" She marvels, too, at Grace's "miraculous self-possession and most inscrutable hypocrisy," (157) much as the Gateshead servants thought Jane "looked as if she were watching everybody, and scheming plots underhand." Even when the author of these plots is revealed not as Grace but as Bertha Mason, the madwoman, emphasis remains on her capacities as a plotter: "she is so cunning: it is not in mortal discretion to fathom her craft" (296). If Bertha on the one hand represents Jane's fear of losing control, of going "mad" with fear, or love, or rage, she is also a projection of the most sinister aspects of the plotting woman—the aspects Jane had had projected onto her at

Gateshead. First setting fire to Rochester's bed, and eventually burning down all of Thornfield, Bertha is as an "infantine Guy Fawkes" grown up.

St. John Rivers: "Assuming the Narrator's Part"

Both *Pamela* and *Jane Eyre* portray power struggles in which men seek to subordinate women to their own narrative constructions as well as their material plots. I have suggested that Mr. B. succeeds, in the end, by shifting positions, by abandoning his seduction plot in favor of the role of the providential plotter, a role from which he can fully reclaim moral and social authority over Pamela's voice and actions. *Jane Eyre* splits B.'s role in two, with Rochester acting as the plotting seducer and St. John Rivers claiming the role of providential authority. For both men, narrative and material plots intertwine, in that, like Redgauntlet with Darsie, each seeks to provide a narrative of the past—his own and Jane's—that will compel her subordination to his plot for the future. Hence, Rochester constructs Jane as the (unconscious) agent of his own reformation, his salvation from despair and degradation. He constitutes her life before meeting him as almost a blank, a "memory without blot or contamination"—though we have seen that Jane's past has memories that are far from being "an inexhaustible source of pure refreshment" (136). He tells her, "it is not your forte to talk of yourself, but to listen while others talk" (137), and subordinates her future to his own perceived emotional and spiritual needs.[17]

St. John's qualifications as a master-narrator are more impressive: he is her rescuer from death, a deeply committed clergyman, and, as it turns out, her closest male relative. As a bedraggled stranger without money, Jane arrives at Marsh End as a figure cast out as well from the structures of social authorization, devoid of credibility. Once she becomes an object of suspicion, the more desperately she tries to convince Hannah of her honesty, the more sinister she appears: "You are not what you ought to be, or you wouldn't make such a noise," Hannah says, "I'm feared you have some ill plans agate, that bring you about folk's houses at this time o' night" (340). St. John is able to break Jane out of this vicious circle by overhearing her thoughts, spoken aloud when she thinks no one can hear—words that therefore constitute testimony to her state of mind unshaped by any consciousness of an audience to be influenced (340).

The role he thus adopts is not readily relinquished. Jane, once restored to neatness and respectability, is eager to reclaim authority as well, making it clear that she has her own reasons for maintaining an alias and offering a truncated version of her history. But while Diana and Mary are quick to accept this—"You are quite right, I am sure" (353)—St. John persists in viewing her skeptically as data for his own constructions. What ensues is a power struggle in which each tries to control the interpretation of the other as well as of themselves. For each, the ability to provide a compelling account of the hidden pattern of the other's past and present—its plot—will confer the power to plot the future as well.[18]

The struggle first crystallizes around Jane's portrait of Rosamond Oliver. Jane displays the portrait to St. John and offers to copy it as a way of unveiling his passion for Rosamond. By doing so, she hopes to bring about a marriage between the two, as part of a projected vision of their future she finds more meaningful than his own: "I—less exalted in my views than St. John—had been strongly disposed in my own heart to advocate their union. It seemed to me that, should he become the possessor of Mr. Oliver's large fortune, he might do as much good with it as if he went and laid his genius out to wither, and his strength to waste, under a tropical sun" (376–77).

Jane's skill in painting Rosamond's portrait accurately—capturing the personality of the original as well as its external features ("It smiles!" 376)—is thus meant to figure her skill in perceiving the true state of affairs between St. John and Rosamond, which she also boldly displays to St. John, as well as serving as a tool in her effort to bring about the end she desires.[19] St. John resists both constructions, refusing a copy of the portrait and telling Jane, "you partially misinterpret my emotions. You think them more profound and potent than they are" (379). Instead, he finds on the portrait cover a piece of unconscious evidence about Jane's identity, which will enable him to "assum[e] the narrator's part" (383) in relation to her past.

Nor does he limit himself to narrating her past. His interpretation of her ultimately offers a narrative trajectory that, he suggests, points inevitably to her future as his wife and assistant:

> God and nature intended you for a missionary's wife. . . . I have made you my study for ten months. I have proved you in that time by sundry tests: and what have I seen and elicited? In the village school I found you could perform well, punctually, uprightly, labour uncongenial to your habits and inclinations. . . . In the calm with which you learnt you had become suddenly rich, I read a mind clear of the vice of Demas. . . . In the resolute readiness with which you cut your wealth into four shares, keeping but one to yourself, and relinquishing the three others to the claim of abstract justice, I recognized a soul that

revelled in the flame and excitement of sacrifice. In the tractability with
which, at my wish, you forsook a study in which you were interested,
and adopted another . . . in the unflagging energy and unshaken temper with which you have met its difficulties—I acknowledge the complement of the qualities I seek. (407–8)

But St. John is wrong on almost every point. Just as he had claimed that
Jane's account of him overestimated the depth of his emotions, he here
underestimates Jane's. The narrator's own prior account of these same
events has offered a very different version of their meaning: Jane performs
well as a teacher in part because she teaches herself to feel affection and
respect for her pupils; she hears of her wealth not in calm but in a state of
distraction, being more interested in news of Mr. Rochester and the possibility of being related to people she has already come to love; she divides up
her wealth out of that same love—she wants to free her cousins from the
economic necessity that keeps them apart from her. Finally, she agrees to
work with St. John out of need for his approval. St. John thus continually
perceives abstract, "disinterested" virtues in events the narrator shows us
growing out of Jane's continuing hunger for affection and love—the hunger that so *ill*-suits her for a loveless marriage to St. John.

For both Jane and St. John, succumbing to another's plot for their life is
seductively attractive. It represents a form of giving way, relinquishing the
exhausting and often lonely labor of constructing one's own "plot." But
Jane's plot for St. John carries no authority outside of its own emotional
force, which he readily resists, and Jane herself is not strongly enough invest-
ed in it to fight for her constructions in the face of such resistance. His for
her, by contrast, is underwritten by all of his considerable religious authority and personal charisma. Claiming "to speak Heaven's message . . . direct
from God" (406), St. John puts himself in the position of the providential
plotter, and as such is able to integrate everything he knows about her into
his narrative—if not as direct evidence of the trajectory of her life toward
missionary work, then as temptations to be overcome, or failings to be
atoned for. He offers nothing less than the plot of her redemption, with
damnation the only alternative.

Jane's passionate defiance of both men's plots for her provides some of
the most powerful scenes of *Jane Eyre*. In both cases, though, at the crucial
moment of resistance, the narrator locates agency for the actual moment of
rejection outside of Jane herself. The determining impetus for leaving

Rochester is the image in the moon that tells her, "My daughter, flee tempt-ation!" (324), and in the flight itself, she says, "God must have led me on. As to my own will or conscience, impassioned grief had trampled one and stifled the other" (326). In St. John's case, of course, Rochester's mysterious call is what saves her. We can read these external forces as projections of Jane's own need (and clearly they are), but it is important that Jane *needs* to abdicate agency at the moments that most decisively move her "plot" forward.[20] It is not that we are given reason to doubt that Jane has the strength of character to resist the men's constructions herself: in both cases, the preceding struggle clearly shows her defying them in the face of consid-erable powers of persuasion and even the threat of violence (physical for Rochester, psychological for St. John). Jane also explicitly formulates all the arguments for her own right to resist on her own behalf, insisting in the face of Rochester's pressures that "*I* care for myself . . . I will respect myself" (321) and of St. John's that "God did not give me my life to throw away" (419). Instead of compensating for obvious weaknesses in her character, the intrusions of supernatural force allow the narrator to claim a deeper vulnerability than she in fact shows us, a vulnerability that is vital to our sympathy for her. Jane always in control would be as chilling as Crim-sworth; her ability always to assert her own narrative and material agency in the face of the male plots offered for her would be alienating, making her too much the deliberate plotter. Instead, she resists the narrative authority claimed by men not just on her own authority but on that of her mother, God, or Nature.

Jane's reunion with Rochester establishes the social value—and the au-thority—of her narrative powers even more firmly than her previous inter-actions with him. Jane's power to manipulate her audience through her narrative skill is put to use to revitalize Rochester rather than to keep him in check. She withholds narrative information, leaving the tale of her flight from Thornfield "half-told," to offer him "a sort of security that I shall appear at your breakfast-table to finish it" (443)[21] and hints at an alternative romance plot with St. John as a way of "fretting him out of his melancholy" (444).

As with Mr. B., Rochester's detailed acknowledgment of "the hand of God" (452) in his history ultimately aligns Jane Eyre's narrative with her husband's assertion of a providential plot of his own redemption. But because the same providential sequence of events has rendered Rochester permanently unable to read or write, he remains dependent on Jane's verbal constructions to experience the world, and is hence unable to reclaim the kind of authority Mr. B. does. For Rochester, Jane's very existence is as the narrator of his world.

*U*ltimately, *Jane Eyre* succeeds in creating a female character whom we can also accept as an authoritative narrator because it makes room for the kind of self-knowledge and purposive action that thus far had been the prerogative of both male characters and narrators. Perhaps the most important difference between Jane and the literary heroine-narrators who preceded her is her willingness to choose a course of action solely—and this is crucial—solely on the basis of its calculated effect on another person. That she is able to do so without becoming morally suspect as a manipulator in the process is a tribute to Brontë's skill in working self-consciously within and against the conventions of feminine narration. At the same time, *Jane Eyre* bears the marks of Brontë's negotiation with the convention: most clearly in Jane's struggle against the negative image of her as a plotting woman and the projection of those qualities onto Bertha Mason, and in her shifting of the agency for moving her plot forward at crucial moments onto an external, supernatural force.

Four

"MY BROKEN TALE"

Gender and Narration in *Aurora Leigh*

*W*ith *Aurora Leigh,* Elizabeth Barrett Browning set out to write what she called a "novel-poem" about the growth of a woman artist. As several critics have pointed out, Barrett Browning used her crossbreeding of novel and verse to break out of the gendered restrictions imposed on her by a male poetic tradition.[1] The novel, with its long tradition of female authors and protagonists, provided a less anxious precedent for a poetic narrative centered on a woman than the unrelentingly masculine tradition of epic poetry. But viewing the novel form as a largely unproblematic release from more strictly gendered poetic genres obscures the more problematic aspects of novelistic convention and its impact on *Aurora Leigh.* In particular, in producing a story narrated by its artist-heroine, Barrett Browning had to work within and against the conventions of feminine narration.

If Barrett Browning broke up the conventions of epic poetry with her novel in verse, she also transgressed the conventions of the novel, and by more than her employment of poetic meter and flights of poetic language. Indeed, the sense among both Barrett Browning's contemporaries and modern critics that *Aurora Leigh* is "unwieldy" and "shapeless" as a novel[2] suggests that Barrett Browning was taking on novelistic conventions concerning plot structure and control of narrative that she was unable to fulfill according to a novel-reader's expectations. Most disruptive of such expectations are her first-person narrator Aurora's confusing switches between retrospective and present-tense narration. C. Castan, for example, in the most extensive discussion to date of the work's narration, concludes that the "complaints" of some nineteenth-century critics about the novel's narration are "understandable," since "Mrs. Browning did not have the narrative skill to solve the problem that she set herself in writing *Aurora Leigh.*"[3] But I will argue that *Aurora Leigh*'s violations of novelistic genre, too, are a response to restrictions that generic conventions imposed on the expression of female artistic self-determination. The narrative confusions result from the coexistence of two seemingly incompatible plots: a female

Künstlerroman and a feminine love story, for both of which Aurora serves as heroine-narrator. In the former, she confidently traces her intellectual and moral development as an artist in a retrospective mode; in the latter, she reveals to the reader, through the twists and turns of her more immanent and less self-aware narration, the self-delusions and misunderstandings that the plot will clear away to make possible her reunion with Romney.

Each narrative mode is suited to its particular plot. A first-person *Künstlerroman,* for example, ideally exemplifies the very artistic mastery whose acquisition it recounts.[4] A conventional love story of the period, by contrast, typically offers us either a "perfect" heroine whose happiness is withheld through accidents or the machinations of others, or an "imperfect" heroine who overcomes her faults (usually pride and self-will) through a series of mortifications, and thereby becomes worthy to marry the hero. Both patterns (and *Aurora Leigh* participates in both) derive much of their pleasure from our participation in the heroine's naively unsuspecting state of mind at any given point in the story. They are hence well-suited to narrative forms that separate teleological narrative ordering from the protagonist's consciousness, whether omniscient third-person narration or forms of feminine narration such as letters or diaries. Like the feminine narrator, the conventional love-heroine, whether she narrates or not, is closed out of conscious participation in the hermeneutic and proairetic codes that structure the novel, while remaining subject to them.[5] It is in this sense that Aurora, particularly in the later books, can be termed *unreliable* as a narrator.

The conflict between Aurora's dual literary roles itself represents a deeper tension within the text: that between the impulse to rebel against the restrictions of the traditional role of Victorian womanhood—an impulse that in the early books places a defiant Aurora squarely in the position of the traditionally male artist-hero—and the desire to co-opt the ideological power of that role, to form her "perfect artist" on the foundation of a culturally recognizable "perfect woman." As many feminist critics have argued, Barrett Browning's novel-poem enacts a triumphant reconciliation of woman and artist, which necessarily rejects many aspects of the conventional Victorian dichotomy between femininity and artistic power.[6] But its blissful denouement does not resolve all of the tensions between love-heroine and artist-heroine that it lays to rest. I would suggest that Barrett Browning's juggling of narrative modes does not so much reconcile these conflicting roles and impulses as allow them an uneasy coexistence.

Aurora Leigh presents itself in the first few lines as a retrospective first-person narrative, written by the narrator as part of an effort to make sense or order out of her own life:

> I who have written much in prose and verse
> For others' uses, will now write for mine,—
> Will write my story for my better self,
> As when you paint your portrait for a friend,
> Who keeps it in a drawer and looks at it
> Long after he has ceased to love you, just
> To hold together what he was and is.[7]

In its declaration of a plan to write a "story" of one's life, this opening is analogous to that of *David Copperfield*, the other prominent first-person *Künstlerroman* of the Victorian period. Both promise not just an account of the events of a life, but a work of art of a recognizable form: David will produce a story that demands a "hero," while Aurora will produce something analogous to a "portrait." Both, too, posit a potential "other" central to this production, who may or may not be identical with the self who narrates: David suggests that "the hero of [his] own life" may prove to be someone other than himself, while Aurora ambiguously compares or associates her "better self" with a "friend" who has "ceased to love" her. Finally, the two are parallel in the ambiguity they suggest about whether the self-understanding that will provide coherence to the story—the "hero of my own life" whom David Copperfield expects his tale to identify; the "self" that Aurora writes to "hold together"—is the foundation for the narrative or only a hoped-for result of its composition ("these pages must show").[8]

But the ambiguities of *Aurora Leigh*'s opening are deeper and more troubling than those of *David Copperfield*'s, for they threaten more profoundly our sense of what the "story" Aurora means to write will be about. Aurora's immediate self-identification as a successful writer—the first *I* of the novel-poem is one who has "written much in prose and verse"—asks that we be conscious of the work's status as a highly crafted *literary* autobiography; in other words, that we read with a certain faith in the narrator-poet's literary control. Doing so, we are presented with a complex metaphor for a self-consciously created and yet internally divided self. While narrative self-portraiture promises to reconcile past with present—to "hold together" what the poet "was and is," and thereby create a unified self—the metaphor as a whole still leaves open the problem of how to reconcile the deeper self-alienation implied in the narrator's comparison of her "better self" to a "friend" who has "ceased to love" her.

At the same time, the oddness of the comparison, and particularly the fact that the "friend" is male, invites a counterreading: that behind the advertised story of artistic self-creation lies a tale of thwarted or denied romantic love. And this in turn undermines our faith in the poet-narrator's artistic control, her understanding of the shape or meaning of her story. It asks us to read her, not as a poet shaping her life into a work of art, but as a woman who does not know her own mind. The point is not that we must or do decide to read the work one way or the other. It is rather that the ambiguities inherent in the work's opening already reflect the tensions of dual narrative possibilities.

And in fact the narration of *Aurora Leigh* does not remain, like that of *David Copperfield,* consistently retrospective. Aurora writes herself into the present early in book 5. From there the narrative proceeds at times with a diary-like immediacy, as in her comment,

> It always makes me sad to go abroad,
> And now I'm sadder that I went to-night,
> Among the lights and talkers at Lord Howe's.
>
> (5.580)

and at times from a perspective somewhere in the future, the exact location of which is often difficult to determine.[9] The vantage point from which Aurora delivers the account of her early life and development as an artist, then, is not, as the conventions of pseudo-autobiographical novels like *David Copperfield* would lead us to expect, somewhere at or beyond the satisfactory conclusion of her adventures.

At least one contemporary reviewer was considerably annoyed by these narratological mixed signals:

> It is difficult to conjecture at what epoch of the story the book purports to have been written. It does not seem to have been written in the form of a journal, while the events were taking place; nor yet after the story was completed. It opens, indeed, as if this latter were the case . . . and the reader supposes that she had it all in her mind at that moment. When she says, therefore, in regard to Romney Leigh, "I attest / The conscious skies and all their daily suns, / I think I loved him not . . . nor then, nor since . . . / Nor ever," the reader believes it.
>
> In the third book we find her sitting, a maiden lady and an authoress, reading letters and commenting upon them . . . and the reader

thinks that that is where the story must have left her; and though it looks very much as if she were in love with her cousin, yet he must be mistaken about it. Notwithstanding all this, she says in the last book: "I love you, loved you . . . loved you first and last, / And love you on forever. Now I know / I loved you always, Romney." This contradiction confuses the reader, and he feels almost as if he were trifled with.[10]

The problem for this reviewer is not just that Aurora is unreliable as a narrator: the narrators of epistolary or journal-style novels, for example, often jump to conclusions about the state of their own feelings that later events call into question, and even the most authoritative retrospective narrators sometimes engage in what looks like emotional self-deception, as in David Copperfield's assertions of his abiding love and tenderness for Dora. But the one thing retrospective narrators can always be expected to know is the way events or feelings are tending—however little they may want to tell us about them. They are expected to have the interpretive advantage of hindsight, and to use that knowledge to guide the reader's responses and expectations. When Copperfield says that he sometimes wishes Emily had drowned when they were both children, for example, we may not know exactly why, but we know enough to be on our guard about Emily. By the same token, this reviewer complains, when the narrator of *Aurora Leigh* assures us that she did not and never would love Romney, the reader ought to be able to feel reasonably assured that whatever this book may prove to be about, it will not be the love story of Aurora and Romney Leigh. But of course, this is precisely what the novel, by the end, turns out to be.

It is easy to dismiss such a response as naive: there are a number of hints in the first few books of the poem that Aurora's feelings for Romney run deeper than she claims. But the reviewer has hit upon a real difficulty: at the point in the narrative where it occurs, Aurora's implicit claim of retrospective reliability asks that we take her renunciation of Romney at face value—a task that is made easier by her comparatively unerotic presentation of him. But if we do so, like the reviewer, we find our assumptions and narrative expectations rudely disrupted when the narrative perspective changes and the romantic plot assumes greater prominence later on. On the other hand, if we have been made suspicious by the hints of romantic self-deception in this section, or (more likely) if we already know how the novel will end, the disturbing dissonance between the claim of narrative authority and our sense of the actual direction of the narrative remains. As in the opening lines, we seem left with a choice between denying the romantic plot (only to find that we have been deceived) and denying the artistic/narrative mastery that validates the *Künstlerroman*.

The reviewer initially suggests authorial "carelessness" as the reason for his confusion—again, attributing the problem to Barrett Browning's imperfect command of novelistic conventions—but his complaint at the end of the paragraph that "the reader" feels "almost . . . trifled with" hints at his suspicion of an intent to deceive, a hint abandoned in the absence of any sense of what purpose such a deception might serve.[11] But I would argue that there is a purpose to the deception—or to what is, at least, a temporary confusion—Aurora's narration creates, and it has to do, again, with the two kinds of stories that *Aurora Leigh* is telling: it is no coincidence that the central confusion created by *Aurora Leigh*'s narrative oddities concerns that essential element in any novel about a young woman—her romantic entanglements and matrimonial fate.

In a male *Künstlerroman* like *David Copperfield,* love and artistic achievement can be made to coincide relatively easily: the male artist's lady-love can always be subordinated to or integrated into his artistic life as assistant or as inspirational muse—as Dora supplying David with pens, or as Agnes, pointing him upwards to ever-greater moral heights in life and art. The social and literary conventions by which the beloved woman finds her ultimate purpose in the man she loves—and therefore in his concerns—make for an easy integration of romantic love and male self-fulfillment. But when the sexes of artist and beloved are reversed, the conventions of the marriage-plot work against the artist's needs. For the woman to lose herself in love, to subordinate her interests and aspirations to those of her lover, necessarily means foregoing the self-exploration and intellectual independence that are needed to develop as an artist. For the author simply to reverse genders, to create a submissive and self-sacrificing male lover prepared to devote himself to his wife's career, generates problems of its own, running as it does against literary codes of acceptable and attractive masculinity.[12]

This conflict between romance and vocation, indeed, is the subject of Aurora's and Romney's great argument in book 2. Romney asks his cousin to abandon poetry to help him in his social projects with her love and "fellowship / Through bitter duties" (2.354–55), explaining that, as a woman, she is "weak for art" but "strong / For life and duty" (2.372–75). Aurora, in her defiant reply, contrasts herself with the kind of woman likely to respond to such a plea to "Love and work with me":

> Women of a softer mood,
> Surprised by men when scarcely awake to life,
> Will sometimes hear only the first word, love,
> And catch up with it any sort of work,
> Indifferent, so that dear love go with it.
>
> (2.443–47)

Such women may make "heaven's saints" (2.450)—not to mention good heroines for male novels—but their way is at odds with Aurora's own developmental agenda as a would-be artist: as she insists to Romney,

> *me* your work
> Is not the best for,—nor your love the best,
> Nor able to commend the kind of work
> For love's sake merely. Ah, you force me, sir,
> To be over-bold in speaking of myself:
> I too have my vocation,—work to do,
> The heavens and earth have set me since I changed
> My father's face for theirs, and, though your world
> Were twice as wretched as you represent
> Most serious work, most necessary work.
>
> (2.450–59)

We can see then, why it was important for Aurora to reject Romney at the time of his proposal—he demands her vocation with her love, and she is only—perhaps—prepared to give him the latter. But why should it be important to convince the reader, with all the authority of a retrospective narrator, that she "loved him not,—nor then, nor since, / Nor ever"? (2.713–14).

Narrators, of course, do more than tell the reader where things are heading; they also have to suggest what they will mean, and the two functions are closely intertwined. The stopping point of a novel becomes its center of value as well, the telos of a character's adventures—a convergence neatly signaled by the dual meaning of the term *end.* The point of view at which a hero or heroine arrives will tend, by its mere position, to represent the truth, in relation to which earlier deviations can be seen as error. Part of what a retrospective first-person narrator does, then, in establishing a relationship between events narrated and the *end* of the novel, is to signal a state of error—as David Copperfield does, for example, through his parodic account of his infatuation with Dora.

This pattern of making the end point a center of value from which all previous positions are seen as error is readily apparent at the end of *Aurora Leigh*. After many misunderstandings, both trivial and profound, Aurora and Romney are united, and the meaning of their lives is seen retroactively to lie in the struggle to bring art, love, and social improvement into relation with each other—a struggle that achieves symbolic success in their marriage. This truth established, both lovers rush to attribute all previous deviations from it to grievous error. Even before the clearing away of imagined obstacles on both sides has made it possible for Aurora and Romney to declare their love, Aurora suggests that, while she was "right upon the whole" (8.536) about the social value of art, she may have been wrong to reject him quite so vehemently (8.496–99).

By the time their love has been declared, Aurora's recantation of her birthday speech is virtually complete. She was "wrong in most," she confesses: wrong to see his love for her as selfish or limited, to question his "power to judge / For me, Aurora" (9.630–31), and to insist on using her own gifts "according to my pleasure and my choice" (9.633). In the course of this repudiation, Aurora ultimately turns her back on all the most forcefully stated claims of that original speech: she wishes now that she had been "a woman like the rest / A simple woman who believes in love" (9.660–61) and castigates herself for having taken offense that Romney

> sought a wife
> To use . . . to use! O Romney, O my love,
> I am changed since then, changed wholly,—for indeed
> If now you'd stoop so low to take my love
> And use it roughly, without stint or spare,
> As men use common things with more behind
> (And in this, ever would be more behind)
> To any mean and ordinary end,—
> The joy would set me like a star, in heaven,
> So high up, I would shine because of height
> And not of virtue.
>
> (9.671–81)

Such a full repudiation of the position taken in her youth may be necessary given the symbolic weight Aurora and Romney carry in the poem. As mere individuals, they might reasonably be seen as having only now changed and matured to the point where it was possible for them to love each other, but as representatives of the artist and the social idealist, their love needs to be seen as inevitable, foreordained. Aurora must have "always loved" Romney, because art must always need the connection to human strivings that he represents. That this should apparently entail embracing a position of feminine subservience to her husband's aims can be better understood in the light of Deirdre David's work on Barrett Browning's beliefs about the social role of the woman artist, beliefs David tellingly argues are more conservative than feminist critics have been willing to acknowledge.[13]

The thoroughness of Aurora's repudiation here of her earlier choice to reject Romney in favor of her artistic vocation should also begin to make clear how *Aurora Leigh*'s peculiar narrative form came about. It is difficult to imagine how the Aurora of the conclusion could have narrated the scene in the garden with anything like the emphasis and conviction it deserved. It would have to emerge as the foolish and arrogant mistake she now believes it to be—to be represented, at best, with the gentle, distancing irony David Copperfield employs toward his own early errors. But in fact, Aurora's early conviction that art matters more than Romney is crucial to her development—not simply as an erroneous and misguided position the discovery of which will later make her repose more gladly in the truth; it is also the precondition of her development as an artist, and hence what makes possible the later position from which she can repudiate it. However mistaken Aurora may be about the state of her own unconscious feelings for Romney, she seems essentially right in her assessment of her own vocational needs: the poem itself is proof of that. She is right, too, in seeing marriage to Romney as likely to compromise seriously her artistic aspirations: while Aurora later casts herself as having unfairly distorted Romney's good intentions (as indeed she later often does), his own words here condemn him as arrogantly dismissive of Aurora's artistic efforts or prospects, and contemptuous of any suggestions that she may have plans of her own for easing the world's miseries. He does not even glance at the book of her poetry he finds, convinced that, even if it is better than the average woman's work, it can still have little to offer:

> The chances are that, being a woman, young
> And pure, with such a pair of large, calm eyes,
> You write as well . . . and ill . . . upon the whole,
> As other women. If as well, what then?
> If even a little better, . . . still, what then?
>
> (2.144–48)

Romney here represents the whole weight of male social authority, discouraging women from writing by assuring them that anything they do will inevitably be second-rate. It is a position he takes up quite self-consciously, as he ventriloquizes for Aurora the kind of critical response she can expect for her work:

> "Oh excellent,
> What grace, what facile turns, what fluent sweeps,
> What delicate discernment . . . almost thought!
> The book does honour to the sex, we hold.
> Among our female authors we make room
> For this fair writer, and congratulate
> The country that produces in these times
> Such women, competent to . . . spell."
>
> (2.236–43)

It is hence as symbolically necessary for Aurora to reject Romney the male critic at the outset, and prove herself independently as an artist, as it is at the end of the novel for her to realize she has "always" loved Romney the social idealist. Furthermore, to prevent the scene from being undercut by the undeniable foolishness of Aurora's position—she has been caught in the act of crowning herself with ivy and imagining herself as a great poet before she has fairly begun to create, and she defends her fledgling genius to Romney with all the high seriousness of someone who fully intends to become a great artist—it is important that the scene be narrated with all the authority of a now-accomplished artist, a later self who sees this moment, foolishness and all, as a crucially *right* choice in her own development.

Thus while the view from the conclusion would see Aurora's error as lying in her rejection of Romney—reunion with him being the telos of the novel as a whole—when the scene is narrated from a perspective that recognizes as an end the fulfillment of artistic talent, the configuration of error and truth is crucially different. The error now lies primarily in Aurora's foolish optimism about her own art. Writing "false poems" that she believes to be "true," (1.1023) and accomplishing "mere lifeless imitations of live verse" (1.974), she sees the struggle of the artist as an easier one than her later self knows it to be, and crowns herself too soon. But even this foolishness is in some sense necessary for her later success: the bad verse is a useful apprenticeship, and without her artistic overconfidence she might never have braved the critical odds against the woman artist. Aurora's self-caricature in her account of her early artistic efforts is, significantly, as close to that of

David Copperfield as anything in *Aurora Leigh*—it is the laughter of a narrator who sees in his or her earlier foolishness one's own best qualities: David's loving trustfulness, Aurora's artistic seriousness and aspiring soul.

What begins to emerge from *Aurora Leigh*, then, are two different kinds of story, which have in turn two different kinds of narration. The first, which corresponds roughly with the first four books of the poem, is the *Künstlerroman*. It is told as a fully conceived, retrospective narrative: as the reviewer says, "she had it all in her mind at that moment." The form and subject here complement each other, the reader's sense of the narrator's conceptual control of her story, her authority over it, contributing as much to a belief in the tale's telos—successful authorship—as the events of the story itself. If we are aware of a potential counternarrative in her relations with Romney, it remains a dormant or subordinate one, precisely because of the narrator's conviction that it is tangential to the most important trajectory of her life: her development as an artist.

In book 5, the novel shifts both its subject matter and its mode of narration. At the opening of this book, Aurora makes her most forceful and coherent statement of what art in her age can and should be. She chides fellow poets for preferring a romanticized distant past to the heroism and beauty of the everyday present, speaking as someone confident both of her abilities and of her right to judge her fellow artists. Unsurprisingly, this section of the poem is frequently cited as Barrett Browning's own poetic manifesto. Thus, while Aurora expresses frustration with the shortcomings of her own artistic efforts, complaining that "what I do falls short of what I see" (5.345), it is clear that this is the frustration of the accomplished artist who cannot be satisfied with anything less than unattainable perfection. Indeed, even these frustrations, as they force Aurora to "set myself to art" (5.350), eventually issue forth in a work that Aurora implies is the long-awaited masterpiece: "Behold, at last, a book" (5.352).

But if Aurora's position as an artist is now as self-assured as it can be without casting doubt on her perfectionism, her emotional state is much more unclear. And as Aurora makes explicit in her discussion of her fellow poets Graham, Belmore, and Gage, the reasons for this have to do with the conflicts between her gender and her role as artist. While Aurora insists that she "never envied" these male poets for their "native gifts" or "popular applause" (5.505–17), she confesses to envying them for the adoring women who provide emotional support for their work and fill out the void in their personal lives: Belmore has a girl who, hearing him praised, "Smiles unaware as if a guardian saint / Smiled in her"; Gage's mother murmurs wonderingly,

"Well done," at each "prodigal review" of his new work, as unthinkingly proud of his poetry now as she was of his "childish spelling-book" years before, while Graham has "a wife who loves [him] so, / She half forgets, at moments, to be proud / Of being Graham's wife" (5.524–37).

Aurora herself suggests that the emotional lack she feels is that of orphanhood, but it is hard to see how either Aurora's silencing mother—whose only remembered words are "Hush—here's too much noise" (1.17)—or her melancholic, intellectual father could provide the kind of self-effacing, unconditional adoration these male poets receive from mother, lover, or wife.[14] The passage points rather to Aurora's frustration at the gap her gender creates between artistic and emotional self-fulfillment—between the happy ending of a *Künstlerroman* and that of a love story.[15] Indeed, in case we miss the connection, Aurora immediately shifts to a forcedly casual mention of the fact that she has "not seen Romney Leigh / Full eighteen months . . . add six, you get two years" (5.572–73). The passage thus makes an appropriate transition from one tale to the other—from the quest for artistic achievement and recognition to that for emotional fulfillment. The quest will lead her (unwittingly) first to Marian Erle, who with her "dog-like" (4.281) devotion seems a potential stand-in for the adoring women Aurora feels the lack of, and finally to Romney Leigh.

The discussion at the opening of book 5 not only marks the transition in subject matter from *Künstlerroman* to love story, it also, significantly, marks the switch to a different mode of narration. The peculiar account of time in the passage quoted above—with the poet apparently noting with ellipses a lapse of six months during which the manuscript had been abandoned literally midline—suggests a more immediate relation between the narrator and her tale. Immediately afterward, Aurora refers to "tonight['s]" events, and from here until the end of the novel, her narration approximates most closely to that of a journal, written, as she says at the end, "day by day" (9.725), sometimes in the immediacy of strong emotion—as when, after discovering Marian in Paris, she has to break off writing because her "hand's a-tremble" (6.416)—and sometimes with a degree of calm retrospection. Just as the retrospective narrative of the preceding portion of the novel-poem exemplifies the artistic control the acquisition of which it recounts, so here Aurora's more fragmented narrative reflects a certain lack of control and an absence of conscious purpose appropriate to her problematic relationship to the love plot.

Of course, the division between narrative modes is not absolute. As I have mentioned, there are buried strains in the early account of Aurora's dealings with Romney. The tensions between romantic involvement and artistic control show themselves in other ways with the introduction of Marian Erle and Lady Waldemar in books 3 and 4. From the beginning of book 3, in which the narrator lapses briefly into present tense to hint at her unhappiness—claiming that she has grown "cross" and "pettish" (3.35–36) for reasons she does not elaborate—Aurora's artistic self-confidence and determination begin to run parallel with an emotional dissatisfaction and even a certain self-distrust, as when she chides herself for failing to warn Romney and Marian about Lady Waldemar. This loss of control takes its most interesting artistic toll in the form of some curiously misused metaphors in book 4. In the first, Aurora attempts to account for her feeling of awkwardness with Romney by comparing the two of them to two clocks:

> Perhaps we had lived too closely, to diverge
> So absolutely: leave two clocks, they say,
> Wound up to different hours, upon one shelf,
> And slowly, through the interior wheels of each,
> The blind mechanic motion sets itself
> A-throb to feel out for the mutual time.
>
> (4.420–25)

But, she goes on, "It was not so with us, indeed: while he / Struck midnight, I kept striking six at dawn" (4.426–27). The point of the metaphor seems to be to demonstrate its inapplicability to herself and Romney, as if its very inappropriateness would account for her discomfort.

Later, Aurora attempts to comfort Romney after Marian's disappearance by assuring him that Marian,

> "however lured from place,
> Deceived in way, keeps pure in aim and heart
> As snow that's drifted from the garden bank
> To the open road."
>
> (4.1068–71)

Romney is quick to point out the flaw in her comparison:

> "The figure's happy. Well—a dozen carts
> And trampers will secure you presently
> A fine white snow-drift. Leave it there, your snow:
> Twill pass for soot ere sunset."
>
> (4.1072–75)

In both instances, Aurora introduces a comparison that seems curiously at odds with her intention, as each points to an end—in the first, reunion with Romney, in the second, defilement for Marian—that is the direct opposite of the situation it is intended to illuminate. Interestingly, the "mistake" in each metaphor lies not in Aurora's initial comparison but in the ending she assigns to its implicit "plot": the clocks that should align themselves remain discrepant; the snow remains pure in a place where in fact it would be defiled. What is most significant about these mistaken metaphors is not simply the unconscious desires they presumably reveal (desires that the novel goes on to fulfill), but the fact that such desires should reveal themselves precisely in a lapse of artistic control—of the poet's power to make metaphors. The metaphors hence provide brief hints of a narrator not fully conscious of her own ends.

It is no coincidence that some of the most distinctive disturbances of Aurora's retrospective authority should be associated with Marian Erle and Lady Waldemar. Like Helen Burns and Bertha Mason in *Jane Eyre*, the two figures represent Barrett Browning's engagement not only with the angel/whore dichotomy of Victorian culture, but with the artless/artful split that is its narratological equivalent. Initially the two figures appear to work to consolidate Aurora's status as master-narrator on a masculine model: Aurora appropriates and retells the artless Marian's story, highlighting its moral significance, broader social implications, and redemptive trajectory of plot in ways Marian is presumed to be unable to formulate for herself. Meanwhile, she frames the artful Lady Waldemar's speeches in terms that invite suspicious reading, calling attention to their duplicity and hidden "plots." But unlike Helen and Bertha, Marian and Lady Waldemar both come to resist (with different degrees of success) their status as the feminine props of Aurora's narrative mastery, as both eventually offer narratives that explicitly contradict Aurora's readings of their characters, the meaning of their actions, and the appropriate endings of their plots. These resistant narratives not only disrupt Aurora's sense of narrative control (it is after one such episode, Marion's account of her rape, that Aurora confesses her "hand's a-tremble" as she writes), they also materially affect the end of Aurora's story: Marian's new self-understanding releases Romney from the obligation to marry her, while Lady Waldemar's embittered reflections help to reveal to Aurora the denied love between herself and Romney.

Aurora's eroded control over the ends of her narrative becomes more pronounced once the retrospective portion of the narrative stops. The relationship of events to the novel's ending—in other words, Aurora's continuing state of error—can no longer be signaled authoritatively by Aurora herself, as she now writes from a position of immersion in events rather than of confident hindsight. Instead, Aurora as narrator is continually revealed as unreliable, in error, both through her conspicuous repressions and denials regarding her feelings for Romney, and through the reversals in her dealings with Marian, in which she must confess to her own hasty misjudgments.

The best example of the former is Aurora's prolonged attempt to come to terms with Romney's (supposed) new engagement to Lady Waldemar, news of which she has picked up at Lord Howe's evening party. This section is apparently written immediately after her return—the party is referred to as having occurred "tonight"—and it shows Aurora in the very process of assessing and resolving her feelings by writing about them. Her reflections continually change direction, as she recognizes the significance of what she has already written and then pauses to redirect her thoughts. She opens, for example, with an effort to attribute her unhappiness after the event to a general discomfort with such occasions—"It always makes me sad to go abroad" (5.579)—but by the end of her poetic reproduction of the evening's conversation it has become clear to her that the real source of discomfort is Lady Waldemar:

> The charming woman there—
> This reckoning up and writing down her talk
> Affects me singularly.
>
> (5.1041–43)

Aurora goes on to attribute this to what she sees as Lady Waldemar's genius for indirect social torture, but eventually pauses again to reflect:

> And after all now . . . why should I be pained
> That Romney Leigh, my cousin, should espouse
> This Lady Waldemar?
>
> (5.1054–56)

From here she launches into an elaborate series of reflections on marriage, men, and Romney in particular, in an attempt to confront this "pain" and resign herself to the marriage. In the course of these, she examines and rejects every possible ground for objecting to Romney's marriage except the one that naturally presents itself to a reader—personal jealousy. That her attempt at resignation has ultimately failed is made clear by the broken, halting tone of her conclusion—

> And then at worst,—if Romney loves her not,—
> At worst—if he's incapable of love,
> Which may be—then indeed, for such a man
> Incapable of love, she's good enough;
> For she, at worst too, is a woman still
> And loves him . . . as the sort of woman can.
>
>   (5.1120–25)

—and by her sense of physical irritation and discomfort at the close: "My loose long hair began to burn and creep, / Alive to the very ends, about my knees" (5.1126–27).

The repression and confusion that this passage reflects, the alternating suggestion and denial of romantic interest in the man being discussed, make the narration here closest to that of the heroines of epistolary novels. As innocent girls, such narrators are expected to be unable to hide or repress their tender feelings; as well-bred young women, however, they are not supposed to acknowledge, or even be fully conscious of, romantic feelings that are not (yet) reciprocated or approved. To the extent that, like Clarissa, they are being presented as morally serious and intelligent, such heroines often go through the kind of elaborate self-questioning and efforts at resignation that we see here, but as in Aurora's case, these reflections are often at least as significant for what is not recognized or acknowledged as for what is—for what they witness to, rather than what they consciously intend to convey. Aurora has become a feminine narrator.

Such a narrator, as we have seen, necessarily has a fundamentally different relationship, to her story and to a reader, from the authoritative retrospective narrator to which we were initially introduced. In essence, we are asked to read against her more than with her. Instead of trusting the narrator to signal the shape her own life is to take, we focus on the gap between narrator and implied author, and trust the author to make the narrator betray herself, to signal the novel's telos between the lines of her own ignorance. And with the loss of the power of narrative ordering, Aurora also comes to seem less the plotter of her own fate and more its passive object; it is no coincidence that the end of the novel sees such a concentration of accidental misunderstandings, missed meetings, and other twists of fate. Inevitably, the novel's satisfactory resolution comes to seem more the doing of the author acting as deus ex machina than of the narrator.

Herein lies one of the most recalcitrant discomforts of *Aurora Leigh*. Even after its sources and purposes have been traced, the contradiction between Aurora's initial "I loved him not, nor then, nor since, nor ever" and her later "I loved you always" remains as unsettling to modern feminist readers as it was to that early reviewer, for it points to a deeper contradiction between Aurora's self-confident, bitingly insightful argument for her right to vocational self-determination and her abject retroactive repudiation of that right after her reunion with Romney.[16] Barrett Browning puts this repudiation in a context that ensures that it is materially irrelevant to Aurora's fate, since it is matched (after she has made it) by Romney's own implicit disavowal of the right he earlier claimed to "use" Aurora for his own ends. Indeed, it is now he, moved by the power of her poetry, who will provide the kind of full-time emotional support for her work he once asked her to provide for his: "[W]ork for two," he tells her, "As I . . . for two, shall love!" (9.911–12). I do not wish to underestimate the power and importance of this final vision of a nonhierarchical union between a man and a woman. But this balance is not Aurora's compromise. While Barrett Browning's plot balances, against Aurora's unconditional self-abasement to Romney, Romney's own change of heart, her artist-narrator cannot reaffirm, in the face of romantic fulfillment, her right to have held out for that balance— calling instead for women to "believe in love" as a power to overcome the romantic/vocational contradictions she has experienced. The shift from the story of Aurora's artistic achievement to that of her romantic fulfillment is accompanied by a shift to a feminized narrative mode that distances Aurora from the shaping of her own fate. Yet, significantly, the same narrative shift is what allows her earlier affirmation to remain within the novel-poem in all its original force, in the form of Aurora's initial retrospective narrative.

Nancy Miller suggests that "implausibilities" of plot in many women's novels represent efforts to express an "ambitious wish," a "fantasy of power" whose expression is impossible within the patriarchal conventions of the novel, because those conventions permit to female heroines only plots based on erotic wish-fulfillment. "The inscription of this power," she writes, "is not always easy to decipher," because it is necessarily covert. "When these modalities of difference are perceived, they are generally called implausibilities. They are not perceived, or are misperceived, because the scripting of this fantasy does not bring the aesthetic 'forepleasure' Freud says fantasy scenarios inevitably bring: pleasure bound to recognition and identification, the 'agreement' Genette assigns to plausible narrative."[17] Miller's argument about the conventions that govern "plausible" plots could be extended to cover those that govern "consistent" narration, for, as we have seen, the narrative improprieties of *Aurora Leigh* served to fold into the work its plot of female ambition. Barrett Browning would not, given the conventions she had taken on in writing a *novel*-poem, throw away altogether the idea of marriage as the required telos of a young woman's story—nor even fully subordinate it to a "higher" aim of artistic achievement. Nor, apparently, could she allow her heroine-narrator the same kind of self-conscious control over the shaping of her romantic experience into narrative as she did over her development as an artist. But the mixed narration of *Aurora Leigh* did allow her to create a kind of double teleology for the novel, in which the struggle toward artistic independence and success, the plot of poetic "ambition," could be kept relatively isolated from the undermining influence of the traditional love-story, with its emphasis on female passivity and lack of emotional or sexual self-knowledge, its insistence on loving self-abnegation as the proper "end" of female existence.

Aurora Leigh seems, on the whole, less uniformly successful than *Jane Eyre* in its challenge to the convention of feminine narration. But it is also more ambitious: Barrett Browning seeks—and apparently achieves—an explicitly public and preacherly authority for her artist-heroine, and at the same time engages more self-consciously and complexly with the counter-figures of the plotting woman and the artless victim, granting them, at least provisionally, the power to speak for themselves.

Five

FEMININITY AND OMNISCIENCE

Female Narrators in *Bleak House* and *Armadale*

If the feminine narrator has a polar opposite, it would surely be the classic Victorian "omniscient" narrator, who understands the narrative and its world in a way ontologically unavailable to any of its characters, male or female.[1] But in two novels written in the period after the publication of *Jane Eyre* and *Aurora Leigh*, omniscient narrators share the stage with women narrating in the first person: Dickens's *Bleak House*, with the retrospective narrative of Esther Summerson, and Wilkie Collins's *Armadale*, with the correspondence and then the diary of Lydia Gwilt. The omniscient voice in both novels does not—as, say, in *Redgauntlet*—explicitly frame the autodiegetic sections or explain why they have been included; transitions from one narrative mode to the other are silent, a feature that gives the female voice a certain narrative autonomy.[2]

This particular combination of narrative voices is an intriguing one: the conventions of omniscience necessarily undercut the illusion of documentary verisimilitude in the memoir or diary sections, while the omniscient narrator's otherwise superhuman range of knowledge about characters and events raises the question of why he needs to rely so heavily on the supplement of a female narrative witness in the first place. In both cases, though in very different ways, it is precisely the totalizing qualities associated with the omniscient voice that motivate the use of feminine narration: in *Bleak House*, Esther's apparently artless vision offers an alternative to the oppressively systematic exposition of social decay and despair that would otherwise leave no space for resistance to or escape from the evils it addresses. In *Armadale*, by contrast, the oppressive fatalism that haunts the novel is finally exorcised by being permitted to destroy the artful, plotting woman who has hitherto contributed to it. In these novels, in other words, the employment of feminine narration is not exclusively, or even primarily, driven by ideas or concerns about women—although these certainly play an important role in the characterization of the narrators, with *Bleak House*, particularly in conjunction with Miss Wade of *Little Dorrit*, acting as a kind of corrective response to *Jane Eyre.* Rather, the convention becomes a way of managing a classically Victorian anxiety about the power and autonomy of individuals in relation to larger, apparently deterministic structures or processes. In *Bleak House,* this management occurs in relatively static terms—Esther may change somewhat over the course of her tale, but the essentials of her narrative status and function in relation to the omniscient voice do not. In *Armadale,* the interaction is more dynamic, as Collins characteristically plays with more drastic violations of gender roles—in narrative as well as social terms—before reestablishing a version of conventional "normality."

From Jane Eyre to Esther Summerson

Dickens's first venture into first-person narration, in *David Copperfield,* came only two years after the publication of *Jane Eyre,* and several critics have posited a direct influence between the two, particularly in the representation of the hero/heroine's childhood.[3] *David Copperfield* is of course also Dickens's most autobiographical novel, so that we could see the novel as emerging from a crossbreeding of *Jane Eyre* with his own remembered past. The conjunction is not coincidental. *Jane Eyre* seems to have made it possible for Dickens to write about the painful experiences of his own childhood by offering a model for representing the experience of an abused child that did not split the representation of that child apart from the resentment generated by his or her treatment. Dickens's earlier children (for example, Oliver Twist, Florence Dombey, Little Nell) had won readerly sympathy by virtuously and pathetically enduring abuse without complaint, while recognition and judgment of their mistreatment was limited to an external narrative voice or to adult savior-figures within the text. Jane, by contrast, gains our empathy by struggling not only with an externally painful situation but with her own violent and confusing feelings about it. Her anger at her abusers conflicts with her longing for love and approval from a parental figure, and with the difficulty, particularly for a child, of holding onto moral judgments at odds with every authority she knows. By making Jane's lonely and painful efforts at self-assertion and self-control an integral part of her childhood pathos, Brontë made it possible to bridge the gap between the victimized child and an authoritative adult voice capable of commanding the reader's moral assent, and in doing so, she also produced a much more convincing portrait of childhood than Dickens had yet managed. This is the strategy Dickens adopts in *David Copperfield* to make

David's childhood as a mistreated and then neglected orphan lead convincingly to his adult identity as a confident and successful writer capable of narrating that past.

Given the autobiographical elements of *David Copperfield,* the switch from a female to a male autodiegetic narrator is hardly remarkable. But Dickens's next venture into the form, in *Bleak House,* returned to the female autodiegetic narrator as well as to the story of the abused and rejected orphan in quest of "a little love." If *David Copperfield* merely suggests Brontë's influence, *Bleak House* looks more like a deliberate revision.[4] I want to suggest that the two novels, taken together, represent a taming of the *un*feminine narrative possibilities raised by *Jane Eyre.* That is, while Jane's confidence, competence, and control are converted to a more conventional male form in *David Copperfield*—indeed, pushed further, in that David is also represented as a successful novelist, and thus publicly authorized as a storyteller—the female version given us in *Bleak House* returns much more closely to the conventions of feminine narration.

No Victorian novel has provoked more discussion and debate of its narrative structure than *Bleak House,* with its alternation between omniscient and first-person narration. At the center of the controversy is its part-time narrator Esther Summerson, who continues to generate a range of responses —from idealization to discomfort to debunking outrage—reminiscent of *Pamela.* Esther, like Jane, is a retrospective narrator, but one with a more troubled relationship to narrative authority.[5] From the novel's publication onward, readers have been puzzled to decide just how much Esther knows about the story she tells and the effects she creates, and how much and what kind of reliability her creator meant to assign to her. But the most troubling features of Esther's narration are also those most closely associated with the conventions of feminine narration, and much of the response to her is in keeping with the dichotomy between artfulness and artlessness that has dogged feminine narrators from Pamela on—the feature whereby it is always possible to assign agency for the rhetorical canniness of narrative "artlessness" to a now-artful narrator rather than solely to her creator. In this case, though, the problem is exacerbated by the inherent tension between what is in some respects a classically feminine narrative stance and the authority implicit in Esther's role as an unframed retrospective narrator.[6]

Esther opens her narrative with exactly the kind of conventionally deferential and apologetic gesture Brontë had so pointedly omitted in *Jane Eyre:* "I have a great deal of difficulty in beginning to write my portion of these pages, for I know I am not clever."[7] The tone of reluctance and reference to "my portion" indicate that the narrative is an assigned task, and later in the same chapter she speaks of herself as "obliged to write all this" (26). The implication is that the impetus for the act of narration comes from outside herself, that the task is undertaken out of obedience to a higher authority presumed to know what place her "portion" has within the larger whole.[8] In short, Esther constitutes herself as a narrative witness, producing requested testimony without a full understanding of the ends it is to be used for. Her opening thus disclaims both narrative agency and narrative authority: if she believes she is "not clever," she can hardly be presumed to be claiming full understanding of the shape and meaning of the story she tells. Esther's subsequent narrative is full of gestures that reinforce this opening position by disclaiming or effacing her potential for either self-consciousness about the shape and trajectory of her narrative or authoritative moral judgment about its content—her potential, in other words, as a plotter or a preacher.

While the reader quickly realizes that Esther is the moral as well as the narrative center of her tale, she herself appears to be blind, or at least resistant, to this fact, and expresses surprise and even distress that she continues to dominate her own narrative: "I don't know how it is, I seem to be always writing about myself. I mean all the time to write about other people, and I try to think about myself as little as possible, and I am sure, when I find myself coming into the story again, I am really vexed and say, 'Dear, dear, you tiresome little creature, I wish you wouldn't!' but it is all of no use" (112).

Esther's account of her irritatingly persistent appearance in her narrative is oddly reminiscent of "King Charles the First" infesting Mr. Dick's Memorial in *David Copperfield*. But while Mr. Dick's lack of narrative control signifies his madness, and thus presents a problem that he must struggle to overcome, Esther seems merely to accept that the shape and meaning of her narrative will necessarily come about involuntarily. If her narrative continues to belie her conscious aim "to think about myself as little as possible," she suggests, "it must be because I really have something to do with [it], and can't be kept out" (112). Interestingly, Esther's puzzlement at her narrative centrality results partly from her denial of her own agency as a character within the story: she refuses to acknowledge that her centrality is a product of the way she makes things happen for other people.

Consonant with this denial of control is an effacement of the retrospectivity of the narrative, an effect reinforced by its alternation with the present-tense omniscient voice. While *Jane Eyre* self-consciously reproduces the intimacy and immediacy of epistolary fiction, Dickens goes a step further by reproducing its characteristic moments of confusion, ignorance, and self-contradiction. Hence the narrator of the opening chapter tells us that her godmother was "a good, good woman" (15) and that she herself culpably "never loved [her] as I ought to have loved her" (16), without making a distinction between what she felt or believed as a child and her current perspective. In later chapters, though, we learn that Jarndyce has described the godmother as "cruel" and "distorted" (237), that she had used deceit to deny Esther her real mother, and that Esther herself now believes that she is "as innocent of my birth as a queen [is] of hers" and that she "should not be punished for birth" (516). The narrative perspective of Esther's opening chapter, then, is aligned with that of the narrated self of Esther's childhood rather than with the self she becomes before she begins that narration. Recursiveness—the capacity to edit or revise what she writes—is similarly effaced. Such comments as "six quiet years (I find I am saying it for the second time)" (26), or "that particular . . . which I have no intention of mentioning any more, just now, if I can help it" (519) suggest that Esther's words, once written, cannot be altered.

Nowhere is the effacement of both retrospectivity and recursiveness more apparent than in the treatment of Woodcourt, whose every appearance is marked by abrupt self-corrections: "I think—I mean, he told us" (238); denials: "Ada laughed and said—But, I don't think it matters what my darling said" (202); or other signals of hesitation or embarrassment. Since his appearances provide the outlines of the romance plot a reader conventionally expects in the narrative of a young and attractive heroine, they take on a prominence out of proportion to their frequency. These self-correcting gestures suggest that Esther cannot simply cover up her hesitations and second thoughts by editing out the slips she makes, while the embarrassment and uncertainty they signal about the possibility of Woodcourt's love are obviously more appropriate to the narrated self than to the narrator, who has been happily married to him for seven years. They again associate her writing with personal letters, which offer more emotional immediacy as well as less opportunity for inconspicuous revision, but they come even closer to the effect of oral conversation. We can almost see Esther blushing, tittering, shaking her head, trying to change the subject. To take these moments at face value, in other words, would be to efface our consciousness of Esther *as narrator* altogether.

Even more obtrusive is the portrayal of Esther as *morally* artless. As with Pamela and her descendants, making Esther the sole narrator of her story creates the problem of having her convey her own transcendent virtue and goodness without implying any vain consciousness thereof. This is achieved, or at least attempted, by means of her constant assertions of humility and her detailed recording of the praise and devotion of others, accompanied by simultaneous disclaimers like "(The idea of my wisdom!)" (97) or "It was only their love for me" (426). Esther also pointedly disclaims any effort to elevate her own opinions, particularly on general matters like the education of boys, to authoritative status: "I write down these opinions, not because I believe that this or any other thing is so, because I thought so; but only because I did think so, and I want to be quite candid about all I thought and did" (227). With gestures like these, Esther projects the image of a quintessentially artless feminine narrator. Under an impetus distinct from any "design and intention" of her own, they imply, she offers unshaped, unedited written testimony of her experience—testimony whose true significance for the novel as a whole, particularly as regards her own feelings, character and influence, is to be understood by the reader as often at odds with her own explicit pronouncements.

For contemporary readers who were content to take her at face value, Esther's role as feminine narrator enhanced both the impression of her virtue and the narrative pleasures of reading *Bleak House*. So *Bentley's Monthly Review* described her:

> anything more simple and modest than [her] account, cannot be imagined. There is not a grain of self-praise in her autobiography, nor is there on the other hand that mock-depreciation of herself which a person of real vanity, but pretended humility, would assume. All is perfectly natural and easy. . . . She does not once give us her intellectual or moral portrait, yet we recognize the clever head, and the noble, generous, single-purposed, sympathizing heart, which is all that woman's should be, and all that man's so seldom is. Consummate art this in the author! He does not draw his heroine's picture: he does not even make *her* do it: he leaves the reader to do it himself, and yet the latter (be he ever so dull-witted) can draw it only one way, under his unseen guidance.[9]

This reviewer closely associates Esther's virtue with her perceived lack of deliberate narrative shaping, and both specifically with her femininity ("all that a woman's should be"). The review also suggests the special pleasures associated with the do-it-yourself quality of feminine narration, which leaves it up to the reader to "draw his heroine's picture" (though under Dickens's direction) instead of being subject to the narrator's explicitly exercised authority. Like Pamela, what this version of Esther gains in perceived moral authority she loses in perceived narrative control.

But many readers were more suspicious, and in fact the majority of contemporary reviews included some criticism of what John Forster would later term Esther's "too conscious unconsciousness" as narrator, even when they liked her as a character. Hence the *Westminster Review* complained that "Esther Summerson fatigues us by the pains she takes to show how wonderfully good she is, and how unconscious of her goodness,"[10] while *Blackwood's* observed that "there is no affectation so disagreeable as the affectation of ingenuous simplicity."[11] What is striking about these responses is how often they object not just to the way Dickens managed Esther as narrator, but to the fact that she narrates at all: "Such a girl would not write her own memoirs," wrote the *Spectator*,[12] and Forster termed the experiment not only "not successful" but "not worth success."[13] These comments form the beginning of a long critical tradition that sees Esther as an aesthetic mistake, in that the feminine ideals she represents as character are simply at odds with her authoritative role as a retrospective narrator.

Interestingly, the effacement of retrospectivity in Esther's narrative has proved far easier for readers to accept than the artlessness of her moral self-portraiture. Despite the fact that Esther occasionally signals her retrospectivity explicitly,[14] W. J. Harvey suggests that the device whereby "Esther *seem[s]* to be living in the dramatic present, ignorant of the plot's ramifications . . . is a convention most readers readily accept."[15] Even contemporary reviewers who were otherwise sharply critical of Esther often accepted without question the temporal immanence of her narration, equating her with the female epistolary narrators of eighteenth-century fiction, and in one case referring to her narrative as a "diary."[16] And as Michael Kearns notes, even more recent critics like Alex Zwerdling and Judith Wilt who claim to be focusing on "Esther as narrator" frequently fail to make temporal distinctions between the narrating and the narrated self.[17] The readiness with which even suspicious or hostile readers have perceived Esther as lacking control over the temporal dimensions of her narrative, despite her occasional overt signals of retrospectivity, suggests the grip that the conventional association of femininity with lack of narrative control continues to exert, on both sides of the artful/artless divide.

More recently, there has been a critical "rehabilitation" of Esther as narrator, with the signs of her "too conscious unconsciousness" read as indicators of psychological depth:[18] Esther's "coy" self-deprecation and evasions are seen as the scars left on her self-esteem by her unloving and abusive godmother, the product of her insecure need to reassure herself that she is loved and valued. Esther is hence absolved of the charge of self-conscious artfulness, becoming instead, like Jo, another damaged and pathetic product of the system Dickens excoriates. In effect, this reading rescues Esther's reputation for artlessness by attributing the agency for her seemingly artful gestures to her unconscious. In doing so, it also locates the "real" meaning of her narrative—which now includes the perception of her psychologically damaged state—even further from her own consciousness.

Suzanne Graver offers an intriguing variation on this view by arguing that in Esther, Dickens reproduces the "double-voicedness" feminist critics now see as characteristic of women writing under patriarchal constraints— "a dominant [voice] that is cheerfully accepting and selflessly accommodating; and a muted one, itself double-edged, that is inquiring, critical, and discontented but also hesitant, self-disparaging, and defensive."[19] But while Graver persuasively demonstrates that Esther exhibits these features, and establishes their relationship to contemporary ambivalence about women's intelligence and judgment,[20] I am not convinced that they represent Dickens's "brilliant" self-conscious mimesis of women's writing, so much as the fact that he found himself in a situation closely parallel to that experienced by many nineteenth-century women—needing to assert his own vision and judgment through a mask that conformed to social expectations (including his own) of virtuous womanhood.

My aim, though, is not ultimately to decide whether Esther is artful, artless, or artlessly revealing the artfulness of her wounded unconscious. It is rather to point out how the interpretive problems she poses—and the resentment she generates—relate to the tradition of feminine narration. I have suggested that Esther be read as a conservative revision of *Jane Eyre*. Esther "refeminizes" Jane Eyre as narrator not only through the overtly feminine features of her narration, but through her relationship to the omniscient voice with which she alternates. *Bleak House* is not "about" Esther in the sense that *Jane Eyre* is "about" Jane. Her narration and her character, however problematic the relationship between them, are both part of a larger whole.

Though *Bleak House* is divided roughly equally between its two narrators, they are far from equal in status. Esther's narrative is not only technically "subordinate" to that of the omniscient narrator, hers is also far more limited in scope and vision. This limitation has long been accepted as part of its function. My students routinely describe Esther's chapters as a "relief" from the omniscient narration. Like the women correspondents in *Humphrey Clinker*, Esther provides a welcome break from the other narrator's insistence that we acquiesce in his darkly satiric vision, as well as from his penchant for sometimes exhausting rhetorical excess. Esther, by contrast, keeps assuring us that she is not one to judge, that she is "confused" (70) by the people and situations she describes for us. And however we eventually choose to paint her portrait, there is no question that Dickens "leaves the reader to do it himself." For Harvey, "plodding" Esther is a "brake" on "the runaway tendency of Dickens's imagination," offsetting the "centrifugal" forces of his creativity exemplified in the omniscient portions.[21] For J. Hillis Miller she offers a limited solution to the novel's moral despair, by representing "an ideal which is impossible for the [omniscient] narrator because he is not so innocent as she is."[22] John Frazee, focusing on the emotional dynamic of the novel, stresses the need to quarantine Esther from the totalizing outrage and despair of the omniscient narrator so that they do not overwhelm the reader's experience: "by bifurcating the narrative . . . Dickens avoids what would be a fatal centrality of focus."[23] Esther, in other words, is thematically significant for what she cannot see or understand at least as much as for what she can.

While Dickens's narrative method in *Bleak House* is technically unprecedented, conceptually it is in fact highly conventional. Esther's relationship to the omniscient voice closely mirrors that of feminine narrator to master-narrator. Even though we never see the omniscient narrator explicitly introducing or otherwise framing her narrative, his is understood to be the more comprehensive view. Esther as retrospective narrator seems as if she ought to have the potential to know more and do more than the likes of Pamela. But whether we see her as artless feminine ideal, as a figure innocently "blind" to the overwhelming truth of Dickens's own vision, or as someone whose self-conscious self-aggrandizement is to be read only as a symptom of her unconsciously damaged psyche, Esther, like her predecessors, continues to be as significant for what she does not know—about others, about her narrative, or about herself—as for what she knows.

Miss Wade and Tattycoram, or, How Not to Have a Narrative

Dickens's next—and last—venture into female narrative voice was much more modest. Miss Wade's narrative in *Little Dorrit* is brief (one chapter) and explicitly framed as a subordinate, embedded narrative. It is far more univocal than Esther's—in itself, in the external signals we are given about how to interpret it, and in its function within the larger narrative. Miss Wade is in many ways the direct inverse of Esther—self-aggrandizing where she is self-effacing, suspicious where she is trusting, assertive where she is retiring. Whereas Esther writes reluctantly in response to an unspecified external authority, Miss Wade writes her narrative under her own impetus and thrusts it without apology upon Arthur Clenham. Whereas Esther opens her narrative with a denial of her own authority—"I know I am not clever" (15)—Miss Wade begins with an assertion of hers, "I have the misfortune of not being a fool."[24] Miss Wade's narrative reads as a kind of postscript to both *Bleak House* and *Jane Eyre.* If Esther Summerson represents Jane Eyre drained of passionate self-assertion, Miss Wade is a distillation of her most defiantly resistant moments, heightened to the point of parody. But more importantly, through her interactions with the maid Tattycoram, Miss Wade acts to disqualify female interpretive self-assertion altogether.

The chapter title Dickens provides for Miss Wade's narrative, "The History of a Self-Tormentor," immediately sets both author and reader in opposition to her perspective, and this is reinforced by his later addition of a running title at the top of that chapter's pages, "Distorted Vision." While Miss Wade clearly sees herself as the victim of the deliberate torments of others, we are to read her as a "Self-Tormentor," victimized by nothing more than her own distorted process of interpretation. It soon becomes clear, though, that a large part of the problem is the effort to interpret at all. Miss Wade's problem is less that she reads people incorrectly than that she *over*reads them, assigning to their words and actions deeper and more complex motives than they in fact possess. Thus the little schoolgirl friend who "distribute[s] pretty looks and smiles to every one," is in Miss Wade's eyes doing so "purposely to wound and gall me!" though we are clearly meant to see the girl's actions as a natural outgrowth of her "affectionate temper" (663). Miss Wade later insists on leaving the school to escape the sight of the "plotting faces" of all the girls who, in their own words, "try hard to make it better" for her (664). And so on throughout her life. Confronted with what Dickens means us to see as straightforward goodnaturedness on the part of schoolmates, employers, fiancée, and so forth (Miss Wade seems to meet with an unending stream of people whose consistent kindness, tolerance, and egalitarian principles are little short of miraculous), she persists in unraveling (and thwarting) what she sees as complex plots to humiliate her, thereby destroying all her own opportunities for happiness. Needless to say, she is also easily seduced by Henry Gowan, the first man who can read her sufficiently well to feed her private obsessions for his own ends.

Miss Wade's narrative is largely consistent with the patterns of feminine narration: that is, her efforts at "plotting"—at perceiving patterns in what happens to her, as well as at mounting plots or counterplots of her own—

are represented as both deviant in themselves (with suggestions of sexual deviance in her passion for the schoolgirl, her unrepentant account of her affair with Henry Gowan, and the masturbatory implications of the term *self-tormentor*) and inadequate, easily superseded by the first devious male who comes her way. Her narrative is too univalent to be very engaging in itself: the pleasure it provides for a reader is largely the quasi-sadistic one of picking it apart—as is implied in Dickens's original notes for the chapter: "From her own point of view. Dissect it."[25]

But of course Miss Wade's narrative—indeed, Miss Wade's character—is in the novel less for its own particular pleasures than for the perspective it provides on Tattycoram, with whom she is closely associated.[26] Tattycoram's situation, though, is less straightforward in its interpretation than Miss Wade's. Tattycoram's resentment, if it is not obviously well-justified, at least comes a good deal closer to winning our sympathy. Whereas Miss Wade is surrounded by people who treat her as equals, even beyond her rights—the woman who cares for her in her childhood calls her a granddaughter; her first employer treats her with such "great delicacy" that she is actually hurt when Wade calls her "Mistress" (666), and her final employers are happy to see her engaged to their beloved nephew—Tattycoram is taken in only to serve as a maid to an excessively indulged and pampered daughter. And while Miss Wade's supposed tormentors treat her resentment with great seriousness, going to saintly lengths to try to unearth, understand, and resolve her grievances, Mr. Meagles responds to Tattycoram's rages merely by amiably commanding her to repress them, to "count five-and-twenty" (322). To others, he is quick to account for her resentment by reference to her sexually shameful heritage: "It was of no use trying to reason then, with that vehement panting creature (Heaven knows what her mother's story must have been)" (323).

This is not to say that we should accept Miss Wade's "perverted" account of the Meagleses' true motives in taking in Tattycoram (328): those motives seem as unreflectively good-natured as we could wish. But elsewhere in Dickens's representation of the Meagleses, good nature is not always enough. At one point, Clenham reflects on "whether there might be in the breast of this honest, affectionate, and cordial Mr. Meagles, any microscopic portion of the mustard-seed that had sprung up into the great tree of the Circumlocution Office." The reflection is sparked by Meagles's unjustified "sense of a general superiority to Daniel Doyce" (194), and is confirmed later in the account of Meagles's slavish admiration of the "high company" of the Barnacles (409).

It seems not inconceivable, then, that a man who assigns far too much dignity to Lord Decimus for being a lord and a Barnacle might grant too little dignity to Tattycoram for being a bastard and a dependent, thus giving grounds for her feeling that they treat her "like a dog or a cat" (323). Tattycoram's most compelling moments come, not when she is imagining perverted motives in the Meagleses, but when she is simply crying out against the huge gap between her treatment and that of Pet: "she was younger than her young mistress, and would she remain to see *her* always held up as the only creature who was young and interesting, and to be cherished and loved? . . . What did we think she, Tattycoram, might have been if she had been caressed and cared for in her childhood, like her young mistress? As good as her? Ah! Perhaps fifty times as good (322–23). Dickens is quick to close down the possibility of taking Tattycoram's complaints on their own terms: here, by having her move on to what are obviously fantasies of deliberate persecution, and later by holding up Miss Wade as a cautionary tale. If Tattycoram engages in the same kind of interpretive activities Miss Wade does, Dickens implies, she will become like Miss Wade —"miserable, suspicious, and tormenting" (811). The point is, though, that what Dickens opposes to Miss Wade's *mis*interpretation of others is really no interpretation at all. Arthur Clenham may draw conclusions about the shortcomings of the Meagleses' social assumptions, and readers may sense that Tattycoram's rages at least hint at her author's real ambivalence about the justice of class divisions, but Tattycoram herself must learn to replace independent interpretation, and the impulse to active defiance it provokes, with the empty iteration of counting: "I won't stop at five-and-twenty, sir. I'll count five-and-twenty hundred, five-and-twenty thousand!" (812).

Miss Wade's narrative is thus doubly feminized—first by the unreliability of the narrative itself, which invites us to interpret it at cross-purposes to her own intentions, and second, in that its explanatory value within the larger whole is completely distinct from her own sense of its value: she offers it as an explanation of why she hates Henry Gowan, when in fact it proves more significant to explain her interactions with Tattycoram. Every hint of narrative authority is thus stripped from her tale. But while Dickens (and many of his readers) clearly found a certain vengeful delight in the "dissection" of Miss Wade's overassertive, quasi-feminist consciousness, making it a kind of "set piece" within the novel, its larger thematic role as a gloss on and warning about Tattycoram's resentment, has at least as much to do with class as with gender. In fact, we might see the piece as a kind of deflection of class *onto* gender, as Tattycoram's class resentment is equated with and translated into the deviant sexual and interpretive ambitions of an artful woman.

Miss Wade and Esther Summerson could not be more different in the kind and degree of narrative authority they claim, or in what is granted to them by the larger text. What they share in common, though, with each other and with the conventional feminine narrator more broadly, is the inverse proportion between the two.

Plotting Women, Plotted Men: Fate and Narration in *Armadale*

Wilkie Collins's *Armadale* offers the conjunction of a nefariously plotting female villain, Lydia Gwilt—whose plots are revealed to us largely through her own letters and diary—with what one critic has called "one of the most overplotted novels in English literature"[27] (there is actually a chapter titled "The Plot Thickens"), all in a text whose thematic obsession is with questions of heredity, predestination, and free will—in other words, with the question of who, or what, plots human lives.

The structure of the narration is unusual. *The Woman in White,* Collins's first best-seller, had been framed as a collection of first-person accounts gathered and collated by the hero, a format he would return to for *The Moonstone,* and one that Bram Stoker later picked up and elaborated for *Dracula. Armadale,* by contrast, is dominated by an omniscient narrator who carries through to the end of the novel, but in the second book the omniscient narration begins to be punctuated by occasional short chapters composed entirely of correspondence, mainly between Lydia Gwilt and her older accomplice Mother Oldershaw. In the latter half of book 3, we begin to get long chapters of Gwilt's diary, which also takes up the whole of book 4, until it is "Broken off" and the omniscient narrator resumes for book 5 and the epilogue. In total, the diary accounts for more than half the narrative from the time it appears until the end of the novel. Unlike Collins's documentary novels, there is no effort to explain how this mix of narrative modes came about, or why a narrator who readily enters the consciousness of all the major characters (including Lydia Gwilt) should need to rely on the contrivance of a diary to show us what Gwilt is thinking. Some reviewers complained about this feature of the novel,[28] and T. S. Eliot later agreed, writing that "[i]f Miss Gwilt did not have to bear such a large part of the burden of revealing her own villainy, the construction would be almost perfect."[29]

Despite its narrative oddity, though, *Armadale* largely follows the pattern of *The Woman in White* in its use of a female narrator: a woman initially granted unusual power or authority is eventually put in her place as a narrator and a character, while initially weakened males regain narrative and social authority and "resolution."[30] What makes *Armadale* distinctive is the ideological burden carried by this gender struggle. Here, as in *Redgauntlet*, the use of epistolary and diary narration, with its record of the struggle to master a narrative whose events threaten to master the writer,[31] is linked with the novel's exploration of the tension between individual agency and the broader forces of history, heredity, or fate. But while Scott initially invokes gendered relationships to narrative and material agency only to dissolve the difference between them in the end, *Armadale* ultimately manages the tension between freedom and determinism by gendering it, and does so in part through the shifting power dynamics of its narrative voices.

For most of *Armadale*, it is men who are threatened with a subjection to what might be termed the "already-written" or "already-plotted." The story turns on a prehistory, given in the prologue, in which two men, both named Allan Armadale, destroy each other's lives, with one eventually murdering the other for stealing the woman he loves. The murderer dies a few years later, haunted by guilt, but not before marrying, then fathering a son, also christened Allan Armadale (against his will), and not before discovering that his namesake's widow has borne a posthumous son with the same name. Terrified that their sons will somehow reproduce their own fatal interaction, the murderer on his deathbed writes a confession of the whole story for his infant son, to be given to him when he comes of age. The letter ends with the following peroration:

> My son! the only hope I have left for you, hangs on a Great Doubt— the doubt whether we are, or are not, the masters of our own destinies. It may be, that mortal freewill can conquer mortal fate; and that going, as we all do, inevitably to death, we go inevitably to nothing that is before death. If this be so, indeed, respect—though you respect nothing else—the warning which I give you from my grave. Never, to your dying day, let any living soul approach you who is associated, directly or indirectly, with the crime which your father has committed. Avoid the widow of the man I killed—if the widow still lives. Avoid the maid whose wicked hand smoothed the way to the marriage —if the maid is still in her service. And more than all, avoid the man who bears the same name as your own. Offend your best benefactor, if that benefactor's influence has connected you one with the other. Desert the woman who loves you, if that woman is a link between you

and him. Hide yourself from him under an assumed name. Put the mountains and the seas between you; be ungrateful, be unforgiving; be all that is repellent to your own gentler nature, rather than live under the same roof, and breathe the same air with that man. Never let the two Allan Armadales meet in this world: never, never, never! There lies the way, by which you may escape—if any way there be.[32]

The remainder of the novel focuses on this younger generation of Allan Armadales. By the time the murderer's unsuspecting son gets this letter, it is already too late to obey it: traveling under the pseudonym Ozias Midwinter to escape from his hateful stepfather, and knowing nothing about his past, he has already formed an undying friendship with the other Allan Armadale, who saved his life. The bulk of the novel concerns Midwinter's struggle between faith in his father's prophetic injunction and his own passionate devotion to Allan, who is ignorant of his family history, and whose naive, scatterbrained impulsiveness leaves him sorely in need of Midwinter's guidance and protection—particularly after an unlikely string of deaths leaves Allan heir to a large estate. In other words, Midwinter's fear is that the trajectory of his relationship to Allan has been predetermined by a plot laid down before his birth, by his father, by heredity, by destiny. His hope, encouraged (and indeed enjoined) by a sympathetic clergyman, Mr. Brock, in whom he has confided everything, is that all this is idle superstition, that his own good intentions make it impossible for him to pose any danger to his friend. But from the reader's perspective, the deck is stacked against him simply by the nature of the narrative that he is in. His effort to believe, at Brock's insistence, that a series of increasingly uncanny repetitions are just "coincidence" is at odds with everything we expect from narrative—from the sensation novel in particular, in which, as D. A. Miller notes of *The Woman in White*, the most hysterical and improbable suspicions of unlikely correspondence are precisely those most likely to prove correct.[33] Hence, just as Midwinter suspects, the woman in the red paisley shawl whose mysterious visit to Allan's mother in Somersetshire induced her fatal heart attack *is* the "wicked" maid, and is also the same as the similarly clad woman whose attempted suicide off a boat in London initiated the chain of deaths that left the Thorpe-Ambrose estate to Allan.

Midwinter's fatalism receives an added boost from a dream Allan has one night when a midnight adventure leaves them stranded on the deck of an abandoned ship—which turns out to be, of course, the very same ship the murder took place on all those years before. The dream opens with a scene that Midwinter (though not Allan) recognizes as that of the murder, and moves on through a series of vaguely threatening vignettes peopled by the shadowy figures of a man and a woman. Though a local doctor puts in a virtuoso performance tracing each of the dream's elements to events of the preceding twenty-four hours, Midwinter remains gloomily convinced that the male shadow must be himself, the female shadow must be the evil maid, and the whole must be prophetic of disaster to his friend if he persists in their friendship. The chapter immediately following is our first dose of Gwilt's correspondence with her accomplice Mother Oldershaw, and it immediately informs us that Gwilt is not only the evil maid, the mysterious visitor, and the attempted suicide, but that she is also actively plotting to get money from Allan Armadale—and revenge on his family for the suffering she attributes to them—preferably by marrying him.

If *Armadale* seems "overplotted"—claustrophobically overdetermined in its development—it is because we now have three different versions of the already-plotted, the already-written, all working in conjunction: the father's letter, with its detailed and portentous injunctions, Allan's dream, with its fixed sequence of vignettes, and Lydia Gwilt's schemes. From here, events seem to march inexorably on through the fulfillment of warning after warning, dream-vision after dream-vision, and condition after condition for Gwilt's nefarious plans. And lest we forget, the omniscient narrator continually reinforces the effect of these prophetic structures—pointing out, for example, that Midwinter's decision to resist his fatalism by introducing Allan to his mother's sitting room "actually favoured the fulfilment of the Second Vision of the Dream" (285).

For the men of the novel, the deck at this point seems heavily stacked against any notion of free will or autonomy. Lydia Gwilt, however, is proving astonishingly successful at continuously and creatively reshaping her identity and the course of her own and others' lives. At this point, then, it is the woman who is identified with the mastery of plots, and the men who are its objects. Allan Armadale, whom the narrator often refers to as "artless," is ignorant of his past and incapable of planning coherently for the future. Devoid of foresight, judgment, or consistency, and easily swayed by others, his character cries out for someone else to take over the planning and control of his life. Midwinter has more potential, but is crippled by his neurotic fatalism, which is continually being reinforced by the action of the plot. Whereas Gwilt's plans to write her own future are in a sense endorsed by their consonance with the novel's other prophetic structures (the dream and the letter), Midwinter's efforts to gain mastery over his consciousness and his life are undercut not only by those prophetic structures but by the concrete circumstances we are made aware of by Gwilt's letters, of which he knows nothing.[34]

Introducing Lydia Gwilt as a voice independent of the omniscient narrator, then, seems to parallel her status as a co-plotter of the novel's action.[35] In this respect, Gwilt's role as epistolary narrator closely parallels Lovelace's in *Clarissa*. As I have argued, for an archplotter like Lovelace, letter writing serves to show off his strategic skills to best advantage by demonstrating that events are shaped by his plotting imagination before they even take place. They thus seek to display a seamless continuum between the plots he has for the future and the plot of his unfolding narrative. In fact, I would argue that *Armadale* deliberately echoes *Clarissa:* the machinery of Gwilt's plotting— her procuress/accomplice Mother Oldershaw, who recalls Richardson's Mother Sinclair, and her ready construction of fake households and identities and resourceful turning-to-account of adverse circumstances —closely parallels Lovelace's. So does the tone of her letters: the playful and not-so-playful abusiveness and power-moves between the allies—"Oh, Mrs. Oldershaw, how intensely I enjoy the luxury of irritating you!" (402)—the punitive rage directed at those, like Miss Milroy, who thwart any aspect of a plot; the scorn and incredulity expressed toward anyone who professes sincere emotions or virtue, and so on. The epistolary chapters also recall *Clarissa* in the juxtaposition of the plotters' correspondence with letters from their virtuous opponents and victims (in this case largely Midwinter and Brock) that reveal the plotters' success all the more vividly through their victims' unconsciousness of it. By associating Gwilt so directly with Lovelace, Collins emphasizes the novel's reversal of conventionally gendered relationships to plots and plotting.

This reversal poses a problem for the rest of the novel to solve. Power relations begin to shift as soon as Gwilt and Midwinter are brought into contact, largely through the effects of sexual desire. Though still planning to seduce Allan, Gwilt also turns her charms on Midwinter—as she does on other strategically placed males—to keep him amenable to her control. But to her surprise, and much against her will, she finds herself returning his desire, a development that eventually leads to her undoing when love overpowers self-interest. At the same time, in a process that is not adequately explained or motivated within the text, Midwinter undergoes a gradual empowerment as a writer and a man that closely parallels Gwilt's gradual incapacitation as a plotter.

One step in this process comes with the letter Midwinter sends Gwilt after the fulfillment of another vignette from the dream, explaining that he has to run away from her and Allan. Borrowing his father's words, he writes, "A merciless necessity claims my future life. . . . I must hide myself from him, under an assumed name. I must put the mountains and the seas between us. I have been warned as no man has ever been warned before" (401). Though it explains nothing about the reasons behind this resolution (and hence about Midwinter's still-secret association with the Armadale family history), this letter has the effect of psychologically undermining Gwilt's capacity to plot. For example, she confesses: "I tried hard all night to think of a way of making our interview of the next evening safe from discovery, and tried in vain. Even as early as this, I began to feel as if Midwinter's letter had, in some unaccountable way, stupefied me" (403); and, later: "Ever since I got that strange letter of Midwinter's last Sunday, my usual readiness in emergencies has deserted me. When I am not thinking of him or of his story, my mind feels quite stupefied. I who have always known what to do on other occasions, don't know what to do now" (421).

"Unaccountable" seems the right word here. Given that Gwilt knows (as Midwinter clearly does not) that her intentions toward Armadale are harmful, she might well be somewhat unnerved by Midwinter's mysterious conviction that his association with her will have "fatal consequences" for his friend. But up until now, Gwilt has been resourceful, confident, and not easily discouraged by omens; when an idle game with cherry stones on her plate suggests that Midwinter will not return to her, she writes, "I contradicted Destiny quite fiercely. I said, 'He will,'" (402)—as indeed he does. Her hostility toward Armadale, too, should make Midwinter's fears for his friend less than worrisome to her. The letter's negative effect on Gwilt's powers as a plotter, in other words, seems to far exceed any plausible explanation the text offers. Rather than revealing anything significant about her as a character, the episode points to Collins's need both to begin undermining Gwilt's powers and to link her decline to Midwinter's more positive process of resolving his own vexed relationship to fate and destiny. That is to say, it is a point at which the ideological needs of Collins's use of gendered relations to plotting and narrative exceed his ability to provide adequate textual motivations for them.

Gwilt's response to Midwinter's letter marks the transition in her narration from letters—her Lovelacean mode—to the diary. While the letters demonstrated, and at times enacted, her domination of people and circumstance, the diary testifies primarily to self-division, confusion, and ebbing confidence. After learning Midwinter's full history and the prophecies that go with it, she begins to become infected with his fatalism—the more so since she knows, as he does not, that she is the woman mentioned in the father's warning. "I begin to fancy that *I* believe in the dream, too!" She then bursts out, "I won't write any more. I hate writing. It doesn't relieve me—it makes me worse. I'm farther from being able to think of all that I *must* think of, than I was when I sat down" (414). It is as if the encounter with the already-written, through Midwinter, drains her ability both to plot and to write.

From here, it becomes more and more obvious that she is uncontrollably in love with Midwinter, while her plots—the latest involves marrying Midwinter under his real name, murdering Allan, and then claiming a substantial jointure as his widow—come to seem less something she plans and seeks to execute herself than something that emerges, inexorably and involuntarily, from the process of keeping the diary: "The whole thing has been in my diary, for days past, without my knowing it! Every idle fancy that escaped me, has been tending secretly that one way!" (434); and, later: "there is no resisting it! One after another the circumstances crowd on me. They come thicker and thicker, and they all force me one way" (440). Gwilt, then, has begun to constitute her own plots—and even the continuing work of her plotting imagination—as an oppressive force to which she submits, rather than as a source of autonomy and power.

Gwilt's gradual loss of control is paralleled by Midwinter's growing empowerment. One crucial factor in his transformation is a letter he receives, written by Brock from his deathbed. Brock has been a kind of alternative father-figure to Midwinter all along, and this deathbed letter can be seen as a substitute for the earlier deathbed letter from Midwinter's real father. In it, Brock finally abandons his earlier attempt to dismiss the prophecies that terrify Midwinter; instead, he reinterprets them with a clergyman's authority as a spokesman for divine providence. As a Christian, he argues, Midwinter should find it unthinkable that God would allow his best qualities—"all that is loving, all that is grateful, all that is patient"—to be the instrument of destruction to his loved friend. Faith, he says, "will show you another purpose in the events which brought you and Allan together than the purpose which your guilty father foresaw. Strange things, I do not deny it, have happened to you already. Stranger things still may happen before long . . . the great sacrifice of the Atonement . . . has its mortal reflections, even in this world. If danger ever threatens Allan, you, whose father took his father's life—you, and no other, may be the man whom the providence of God has appointed to save him" (503).

Brock's letter effectively converts the novel's prophetic structures from a fatalistic plot of hereditary destructiveness to a providential plot of redemption and salvation. Unsurprisingly, Midwinter finds this interpretation compelling, since it converts him from the helpless puppet of a malevolent fate to the more or less self-conscious agent of providence.

For Gwilt, the letter crystallizes into near-certainty her anxieties about her declining power to shape the future: "If the favoring circumstances which have driven me thus far, drive me to the end; and if that old man's last earthly conviction is prophetic of the truth, Armadale will escape me, do what I may" (504). Combined with her passion for Midwinter, these reflections drive her to abandon plotting altogether (only temporarily, as it turns out) and to resolve henceforth to devote herself to her marriage to Midwinter: "I will not have a thought in my heart which is not *your* thought as well as mine!" (504). Having essentially forbidden herself independent thought, Gwilt also vows to "close and lock" the diary (504).

When the diary reopens two months after the marriage, it details a new shift in their relationship. Midwinter has become a writer—a public, authoritative figure as foreign correspondent for a London journal. The only impact this has in the novel is that for some reason it erodes his passion for Gwilt, and hence her power over him: "Day after day, the hours that he gives to his hateful writing grown longer and longer; day after day, he becomes more and more silent, in the hours that he gives to Me" (532–33). No explanation is given for the decline of Midwinter's passion: although Gwilt eventually speculates that his alienation must result from some ineffable taint from her immoral past, there is no indication that he has any doubts, or any grounds for them, about either her moral character or her history. This is, again, an undermotivated plot development that signals an ideological need—in this case, to link Midwinter's potential for narrative agency (his growing skill and success as a writer) to a reduced vulnerability to Gwilt's powers as a plotter.

In reopening the diary, Gwilt claims to be turning to it purely to witness to her "woman's misery," which "*will* speak—here, rather than nowhere" (532). But eventually the diary itself begins to exert its narrative pull: "What am I to do with myself all the morning? . . . If I open the piano, I shall disturb the industrious journalist who is scribbling in the next room. . . . Shall I read? No; books don't interest me; I hate the whole tribe of authors. I think I shall look back through these pages, and live my life over again when I was plotting and planning, and finding a new excitement to occupy me in every new hour of the day" (534). Gwilt's resentment of her subordination to the "industrious journalist" who is her husband modulates into hatred of "the whole tribe of authors," and thence into a renewed hunger for her own plots, which are explicitly a substitute for the "excitement" of novelistic narrative. But the plotting exuberance and creativity on display in her letters is never recovered. The diary continues to convey a sense of fatalism about the progress of her plot, the conditions for which keep being fulfilled without any planning or effort on her part.

From here on, Gwilt's material plot also becomes increasingly dependent upon male accomplices who exercise some power over her, in contrast to her more equal relationship to Mother Oldershaw. Her first active step to forward the scheme—setting on her former husband Manuel to murder Armadale for his money—is one she is driven to by Manuel's threat to expose her to Midwinter. She later throws herself upon Dr. Downward for help, subordinating herself to his schemes for rescuing the situation, even though she is aware that he is putting her at risk to ensure the safety of his own reputation.

The end of the diary powerfully reinforces the sense that Gwilt is at the mercy of forces beyond her control: the diary is "broken off"—to use the terms of the chapter title— before any decisive conclusion to its plot has been reached:

> Are my energies wearing out, I wonder, just at the time when I most want them? Or is some foreshadowing of disaster creeping over me which I don't yet understand? I might be in a humour to sit here for some time longer, thinking thoughts like these, and letting them find their way into words at their own will and pleasure—if my Diary would only let me. But my idle pen has been busy enough to make its way to the end of the volume. I have reached the last morsel of space left on the last page; and whether I like it or not, I must close the book this time for good and all, when I close it tonight. (600)

There is a portentousness to her conclusion here that seems out of proportion to the trivial circumstance of running out of pages in the diary (why not keep writing on a separate sheet of paper, or buy a new diary?). Her readiness to submit herself to the material limitations of her diary is associated with the "foreshadowing of disaster" that saps her plotting energies. It is as if she has accepted on a more fundamental level that the ending will not be of her own inditing, "whether I like it or not."

And in fact Gwilt's desperate efforts to bring her plans to fruition are by this time driving her very much against her will: after coolly denying

Midwinter to his face (causing him to faint with shock), she gives way to "an agony of tenderness beyond all relief in tears . . . a passion of remorse beyond all expression in words" (614). Though she goes through with the plot to the bitter end, luring Allan to Downward's asylum and then piping poison fumes into the sealed room where she thinks he is sleeping, it is with almost a sense of relief that she discovers the plan has been foiled. Unknown to her, Midwinter has switched rooms with Allan at the last minute. While the fumes are at work, Gwilt discovers this, and overwhelmed by love and remorse, she drags the unconscious Midwinter from the room. In resolving to shut herself in the room to die instead, Gwilt recasts herself into Midwinter's providential plot of "atonement" and redemption: "The one atonement I can make for all the wrong I have done you is the atonement of my death. It is not hard for me to die, now I know that you will live" (653). In doing so, she recovers her femininity: "When she looked up again, the hard despair had melted from her face. There was something softly radiant in her eyes, which lit her whole countenance as with an inner light, and made her womanly and lovely once more" (652).

The first part of *Armadale* offers us an alignment of heredity, fatalistic plotting, and female writing. Although heredity seems here to be a matter of fathers and sons, it is associated with the figure of the mother through Lydia Gwilt: her part in the original crime was to forge a letter from Allan Armadale's mother—that is, she writes in the place of the mother.[36] Similarly, her plots in the present make her the (apparent) agent of Midwinter's hereditary fate to bring disaster to his friend: "the 'fatal' force of the father's prophecy and projected threat . . . turns out to be the power of manipulative female sexuality."[37]

But through the gradual empowerment of Midwinter and the corresponding incapacitation of Gwilt, this alignment modulates by the end of the novel into an alternative alignment of freedom, providential plotting, and *male* writing. As Midwinter says when he recovers from his faint, "She has denied her husband tonight . . . she shall know her master tomorrow" (616). Ultimately, Gwilt alone is mastered by fate, a process in which her womanliness—in the form of her love for Midwinter—becomes both agent and telos. Her entrapment frees Midwinter to face without fatalistic anxiety his own future as a successful writer (661). We are never told what Midwinter writes, but it is tempting to identify him with the omniscient narrator—a voice that has succeeded in claiming the narrative authority of providence through its transcendence of the struggling, contingent, embedded voice of a woman.

Six

THE DOCUMENTARY NOVEL

Struggles for Narrative Authority in
The Woman in White and *Dracula*

*Q*uestions of gender and narration come most clearly into focus in works that combine the narrative voices of both men and women and in which there is some competition between them to construct a master-narrative out of these narratives. Two closely connected late-Victorian novels, Wilkie Collins's *The Woman in White* and Bram Stoker's *Dracula*, are particularly interesting in this regard: both employ lurid plots and odd characters that are widely acknowledged to be profoundly influenced by gender anxieties, but their equally unusual narrative methods, in which the story is told by means of a varied assortment of documents collected by a key character, have not generally been considered in relation to these concerns. Both novels, I will argue, use their complex narrative structures to stage a gendered struggle for narrative mastery. The novels' thematization of the struggle to shape and deploy narrative reveals both the close association of narrative authority with other forms of social power and agency and, more particularly, an anxiety about the implications of women appropriating that power. At the same time, though, they suggest an anxious recognition of the potential fragility of the gender constructs on which their staged triumph of masculinity is founded.

In their narrative form, *The Woman in White* and *Dracula* have more in common with Richardson's epistolary novels than with the single-consciousness retrospective narration that predominates in the Victorian novel, or even more mixed narratives like those of *Bleak House* or *Armadale,* which still rely on a coordinating authorial voice located outside the fictional world. Like epistolary novels, these novels pose as collections of "real" documents: in *The Woman in White* these are a series of limited "narratives" written by participants in the story, plus selections from a diary; in *Dracula,* they are a broader-ranging collection of newspaper clippings, letters, diaries, professional journals, and so on. Since the letters or documents that

147

compose the novel are purportedly produced by its events—a production that must be motivated in plausible terms within the story—both types of novel necessarily foreground the process of writing, acquiring, reading, and interpreting the story's documents. Indeed, in these two novels, as in the best epistolary novels, this process is itself a key aspect of the plot.

The two genres, though, emphasize different aspects of this process. In Richardson's novels, what is at issue is precisely the consciousness of the narrating female voice; that is, what she actually thinks, feels, or knows, as against what she publicly says she thinks, feels, or knows. The "solution" of this mystery within the novel—that is, the recognition of Pamela's virtue by Mr. B., or of Clarissa's by her broader audience—is what makes possible a resolution of the novel's plot via Pamela's marriage to B., or via the vindication and beatification of the dead Clarissa. This solution is made possible through access to the heroine's private letters, which, at least in theory, give privileged access to her true feelings. Thus, while Richardson's novels necessarily foreground the *production* of the letters (which must take place in terms that guarantee their genuineness as a window on consciousness), as well as the circumstances of their acquisition by other characters (which must take place so as not to undermine belief in the former), the process by which the mass of letters is retrospectively recognized as a narrative is less important as an aspect of the plot. In the documentary novels, by contrast, the collection and collation of seemingly unrelated or irrelevant documents, and the identification of an explanatory narrative that links them together and hence solves the problem or mystery at the core of the novel, is itself a major element of the action the novel represents. In other words, while in the epistolary novel the collection of letters *witnesses* to a plot (which is sometimes carried on by the letters themselves), in the documentary novel the acquisition, collation, and interpretation of documents, to a large extent, *is* the plot.[1] This shift in emphasis necessarily gives a greater prominence to the role of the master-narrator, who becomes a key plotter both of and within the novel's story.

The shift is closely related to the different role of female consciousnesses within the novels. In these documentary novels, the struggle is largely between plotting men—over avowedly "innocent" women. The function of female-authored documents within the narrative, rather than being to certify the absence of female plotting to readers within and of the narrative, is to provide readers with access to the buried *male* plots of which the women have been witness and victim. Nonetheless, while in the latter novels the possibility of female plotting is a far less overt concern, it remains a source of covert anxiety: in both cases, stable gender roles come to be associated with men's and women's radically different relationships to plots and plotting. The quest for narrative mastery becomes linked to anxieties about the "proper" distribution of masculine and feminine qualities among characters.

In particular, in both novels the first movement of the plot generates an anxiously feminized male—Walter Hartright in *The Woman in White* and Jonathan Harker in *Dracula*—who is paired with a strong, admirable female who is granted explicitly and anomalously masculine intellectual qualities: Collins's Marian Halcombe is described as having, in grotesquely literal terms, a man's head on a woman's body, and possesses with it "the foresight and resolution of a man,"[2] while Stoker's Mina Harker has a "man's brain . . . and a woman's heart."[3] Although these M-women, as I shall call them,[4] are idealized by their (initially) feminized male counterparts in the novel, and although the "resolution" and intelligence they bring to the problem at hand in both cases proves a crucial supplement to the men's efforts, both novels eventually enact a refeminization of these women that complements the masculine reassertion of the men. By this process, gendered relationships to both narrative and material agency are first called into question and then reasserted. But rather than reasserting the absoluteness of gender categories by exiling, punishing, or discrediting the female figures who appear to challenge them—as occurs in *Armadale,* for example—these novels allow the constructedness of these categories to remain partially in view, while locating true masculinity in the power to reassert such constructions in the face of potential challenges. The assertion of gender roles becomes a source of pleasure akin to the assertion of narrative authority— indeed, they amount to the same thing, since the narratives are in part *about* the regendering of apparently ungendered or misgendered beings. By constructing narrative mastery *as* masculinity, Collins and Stoker safeguard manliness from the threat implied in the growing recognition that "reallife" gender experience does not readily fall into such absolute categories.

The male villains in both novels play an important role in this process. If the M-woman provides a counterpart to the male would-be hero by possessing the characteristics he needs to acquire (and simultaneously strip from her), the villain provides a model of mastery that is officially discredited and unofficially appropriated by the male heroes. The villains in both cases are amoral, foreign archplotters who possess a seemingly limitless power to feminize their opponents, due to both genuine intelligence and an almost impenetrable faith in their own greatness. Their power to reduce the M-woman to a purely feminized victim-tool magnifies their status as a threat to the virtuous heroes (whose own masculine power has had to be propped on that of the M-women) and, on a deeper level, does the dirty work for them in reasserting proper gender roles.[5] These novels thus recognize the violence required to enforce gender roles (in both cases the refeminization is carried out by means of a symbolic rape) while separating good and true men from such crude tactics.

"In Sorrow That She Cannot Compose": *The Woman in White*

The "Preamble" to Collins's 1860 novel *The Woman in White* offers a dual claim for the text it introduces. The opening sentence supplies the meaning or moral to be drawn from what follows: it is to be "the story of what a Woman's patience can endure, and what a Man's resolution can achieve"— with the capitalized nouns suggesting that this particular story will offer truths about Woman and Man in general (33). At the same time, though, the presentation is to be analogous to that in a courtroom, in which "the persons who have been most closely connected with [the events], at each successive stage, relate their own experience word for word," so that "no circumstance of importance . . . [is] related on hearsay evidence."

In fact, though, neither claim accurately represents the text that follows. If *The Woman in White* offers examples of "what a Woman's patience can endure and what a Man's resolution can achieve," it also offers equally significant examples of what a woman's resolution can achieve (Marian's rescue of Laura), what a man's patience can endure (Hartright's early sufferings), what a man's resolution *cannot* achieve (Sir Percival's and Count Fosco's nefarious plans), and so on through every conceivable combination of man and woman, resolution and endurance, success and failure. Nor does the narrative conform to the preamble's prescription on the presentation of evidence: Hartright speaks "for" several female witnesses, such as Laura and Mrs. Clements, whom he presumes unable to speak coherently for themselves. More notably, Hartright gives a "hearsay" account of Marian Halcombe's experiences between her illness and her meeting with himself, despite the fact that Marian has amply demonstrated her ability to commit her experiences to writing herself.

Rather than providing distinct and accurate preliminary descriptions of the text's content and presentation, the preamble's dual claims can best be read together as a means of marking the novel's concerns about gender and narrative. The opening sentence provides, not a description of what happens, but a desired result—namely, the reaffirmation of assumptions about differences between the sexes that the text itself—or at least the story it claims to reproduce—threatens to obscure. Specifically, the preamble's opening statement assumes that women are at the mercy of time: unable to "resolve," to plan actions for the future that will achieve certain results, they are thus also unable to act. Rather than exerting control over the future, women can only "endure" with "patience" the stream of events that washes over them. Men, on the other hand, stand to a certain extent outside the wash of time. Able to "resolve" and act according to their sense of how events will follow each other, they thus control the future through their ability to "achieve" a desired end. *Resolution* is thus closely linked to what I have elsewhere termed *plotting*.

Narration, too, of course, is concerned with one's relation to time—time past, rather than time future. The gender differences implied in the opening sentence can thus be readily aligned with the "masculine" and "feminine" forms of narration I have been discussing. If resolution involves the calculation of how one action will follow from another to reach a particular end, the narrative equivalent would be telling a story about one's experiences—the retroactive calculation of how events have followed each other to lead up to their "end" in the present. It would be equivalent, in other words, to the conventional mode of retrospective narration. Feminine narration, by contrast, would be simply the unprocessed, unshaped recounting of events as they succeeded one another in experience—as they were passively endured. And just as in life the woman's passive endurance implies dependence on a male protector who can resolve and act on her behalf, so a truly feminine narration would require the shaping and ordering efforts of a male master-narrator. Both male roles are assumed here by Hartright, who also declares himself the author of the preamble.

Hartright's own narrative provides several examples of such shaping and ordering of women's testimony. The limited sense he is able to make out of Laura's garbled memories of her journey is one, but his interview with Mrs. Clements provides the clearest evidence of the assumptions that underlie the process: "Knowing by experience that the plainest narrative attainable from persons who are not accustomed to arrange their ideas, is the narrative which goes far enough back at the beginning to avoid all impediments of retrospection in its course, I asked Mrs. Clements to tell me first what had happened after she had left Limmeridge, and so, by watchful questioning, carried her on from point to point, till we reached the period of Anne's disappearance" (479). To get Mrs. Clements's information into a usable form, Hartright finds it necessary to restrict her to the form of essentially feminine narration—the simple recounting of events in the order in which they happened. For someone, like Mrs. Clements, unable (or "not accustomed") to "arrange . . . ideas," the effort to establish relationships between events over time—the effect of "retrospection"—can only create "impediments" to Hartright's own, more logical, process of ordering the raw data of her experience. Hartright's "watchful questioning," by restricting the opportunities for anticipation or retrospection in her account, is intended to ensure that Mrs. Clements provides no more than such raw data, unconfused by her necessarily inadequate attempts at shaping and analysis. Hartright can then, using his own words, offer the reader "the substance of the information which I thus obtained" (479).

Mrs. Clements's presumed mental incapacity for narrative ordering is doubtless attributable at least in part to her lower social class, but, early in Hartright's first narrative, a similar incapacity is associated with women of any class—interestingly, by Marian Halcombe herself. Marian informs Hartright in their first conversation that "women can't draw—their minds are too flighty, and their eyes are too inattentive" (61). Though applied to the visual arts rather than narrative, Marian's comment points to similar cultural assumptions about women's inability to relate ideas to each other effectively by fixing their minds on a subject over time—and the link between visual and narrative ordering has already been implicitly made by master-narrator Hartright's profession as a "drawing-master."

Marian's own relationship to her numerous unflattering observations on her sex, though, is of course highly problematic. If the statements are true, they bespeak a capacity for observation, deduction, and generalization— for logical ordering—that their content would deny her. The logical conflict between Marian's presumed feminine disabilities and her "masculine" ability to analyze them (not to mention her decidedly masculine habit of misogynistic banter) is much like that experienced by Hartright when faced by the contradiction between her "feminine" figure and "masculine" face:

> Never was the old conventional maxim, that Nature cannot err, more flatly contradicted—never was the fair promise of a lovely figure more strangely and startlingly belied by the face and head that crowned it. The lady's complexion was almost swarthy, and the dark down on her upper lip was almost a moustache. She had a large, firm, masculine mouth and jaw; prominent, piercing, resolute brown eyes; and thick,

coal-black hair, growing unusually low down on her forehead. Her expression—bright, frank, intelligent—appeared, while she was silent, to be altogether wanting in those feminine attractions of gentleness and pliability, without which the beauty of the handsomest woman alive is beauty incomplete. To see such a face as this set on shoulders that a sculptor would have longed to model—to be charmed by the modest graces of action through which the symmetrical limbs betrayed their beauty when they moved, and then to be almost repelled by the masculine form and masculine look of the features in which the per- fectly shaped figure ended—was to feel a sensation oddly akin to the helpless discomfort familiar to us all in sleep, when we recognize yet cannot reconcile the anomalies and contradictions of a dream. (58–59)

There is more going on here than a purely visual contradiction between a delicate body and a coarse, swarthy face: Hartright's emphasis on the thick black hair "growing unusually low down on her forehead," which indirectly associates Marian with all the bestially hairy, low-browed villains of period fiction, and on the "repell[ent]" effect of her face overall, makes her out to be a curiously sinister figure. She reinforces these undertones herself, in a more lighthearted mode, when comparing herself to her half-sister: "In short, [Laura] is an angel; and I am—Try some of that marmalade, Mr. Hartright, and finish the sentence, in the name of female propriety, for yourself" (61). Since Marian is quickly established as both Laura's and Hartright's staunchest ally, the sinister threat seemingly posed by her masculine fea- tures never materializes on the level of narrative event, but it does institute, on a more covert level, a subtle alignment between Marian's "masculine" qualities and the other demons of the story that Hartright must battle.

The "contradictions" Marian poses are more suggestively developed in relation to the question of artistic control. In contrasting the "piercing, resolute" eyes with the "shoulders that a sculptor would have longed to model" Hartright is also contrasting two different relations to artistic shaping: while Marian's shoulders present an invitation to "model" them, her face crucially lacks such "pliability," threatening instead to impose its own "resolution" on the pierced object of her attention. For Hartright, such a blending of masculine and feminine characteristics seems inherently unstable, akin to "the anomalies and contradictions of a dream" that need to be "reconciled"— and we know that the best way to reconcile the anomalies and contradic- tions of a dream is to repress their more disturbing aspects.

Marian's appearance and conversation, then, both affirm and potentially challenge the assumptions about gender that underlie the novel. Her narrative, unsurprisingly, occupies a similarly ambiguous position in the novel. In one sense, Marian is Hartright's only real competition as a narrator. Whereas the other narratives are clearly fragmentary or limited in their perspective, and also clearly subordinate to the master-narrative by Hartright for which they have been solicited (the narrators themselves often make reference to this), Marian's diary provides a largely autonomous consciousness that gives us most of the story during the period of Laura's engagement and marriage (about one-fourth of the novel), and that includes some of the most suspenseful damsel-in-distress-type thrills and chills of the novel —its truly Gothic portion.

The diary form of Marian's narrative is, of course, a close literary approximation to what I have termed feminine narration, in that it recounts events as they occur and not with regard to some foreknown end that shapes the content and manner of the telling. Indeed, a good deal of the pleasure that Marian's narrative provides for a reader stems from her ignorance about the future. In the narratives by Hartright and Gilmore that precede the diary, the reader has been faced with a narrator who writes "with the shadows of after-events darkening the very paper" he writes on (50). Such foreknowledge is useful in building suspense and interest and in drawing the reader's attention to key facts, such as Laura Fairlie's resemblance to the madwoman Anne Catherick, or the disadvantageous financial settlement for Laura's marriage to Sir Percival Glyde, but it can become irritating and oppressive when we sense that we are being manipulated by heavy-handed foreshadowing and the deliberate withholding of information. In reading Marian's diary, by contrast, the reader is put in the position of knowing more, not less, than the narrator, in that the reader has at least the ominous hints of Hartright's and Gilmore's knowledge of "after-events" to go on. In this sense, Marian's diary provides an instance of the narrative "relief" I have suggested is one function of feminine narration.[6]

In a sense, then, the reader occupies in relation to Marian's diary the position of the male master-narrator, who has a framework of knowledge (which she lacks) by which to interpret her experience. This is particularly notable in the earlier portion of Marian's diary, before the marriage. Here Marian's ignorant efforts to conquer her forebodings about the marriage and bring herself to like Sir Percival are most clearly at odds with the hints of future trouble provided by Hartright and Gilmore. Indeed, the very variation of Marian's emotions becomes a reminder of her immersion in time and of the reader's transcendence of it. Her entry of December 19, for example, ends, "Really, I hardly know myself again in my new character of

Sir Percival's warmest friend" (213)—the culmination of a long process of forcing herself to think well of her sister's future husband. But in reading this, we can already see immediately following it the opening lines of the next day's entry: "I hate Sir Percival!" (213). Marian is hence perceived as at the mercy of shifts over which she has no control, while the reader occupies a distanced position as observer and interpreter of these shifts.[7]

But if the reader of the novel can obtain a certain degree of transcendence of time by reading over Marian's fluctuating account of her experiences, so can Marian, as reader of her own text. Indeed, the sustained effort to like Sir Percival (of which the above entry is the conclusion) is itself the result of a resolution Marian forms after reading over previous entries: "On looking back, I find myself always referring to Sir Percival in disparaging terms. In the turn affairs have now taken, I must and will root out my prejudice against him. . . . If it has got to be a habit with me always to write of him in the same unfavorable manner, I must and will break myself of this unworthy tendency" (208). Later, the fluctuations in tone that result from the breakdown of this effort become themselves the subject of a retrospective reinterpretation: "I have been writing, for the last few days, in a tone of levity which, Heaven knows, is far enough from my heart, and which it has rather shocked me to discover on looking back at the entries in my journal" (214).

Marian turns to earlier diary entries not only, as above, to generate resolutions for future behavior, but also to gain that sense of the relationship of her actions to future results that an immersion in time makes it difficult for her to see. When, for example, the disastrousness of Laura's marriage becomes obvious shortly after the couple's return, Marian again reads over her early diary "to see what my share in the fatal error of her marriage had really been, and what I might have once done to save her from it" (289).

It should be noted, though, that thus far both Marian's resolutions and her conclusions about her ability to affect the course of events are influenced primarily by a notion of feminine propriety that tends to reinforce a passive or simply reactive involvement with events. Marian judges her own and Laura's actions according to an abstract code of appropriate female behavior that is divorced from—even opposed to—any assessment of what that behavior has achieved. As for Clarissa and Helen Burns, the conclusion that one has behaved "properly" can even become a consolation for the failure of the results. It is only on these terms that Marian can conclude that her actions before the marriage were, as she says, "for the best" (289) despite their failure to prevent a marriage that is clearly for the worst. Small wonder that Marian finds herself on the eve of Laura's marriage "in sorrow that she cannot compose, in doubt that she cannot conquer" (216).

But as Laura's situation worsens, the need for planned opposition to the men of the house becomes critical. The women reach a point at which, as Marian says, "our endurance must end, and our resistance must begin" (321). In shifting her energies from feminine endurance to active resistance, Marian increasingly turns to her diary for data to aid in planning her actions most effectively. The diary now seems to be a way for Marian to split off her femininity into a separate text, a splitting that enables the "masculine" planner and achiever to go to work. The diary acts as a repository for the feminine narration of her experiences—as she records events and conversations in exhaustive detail regardless of how relevant they seem to her plans at the time—and can afterwards be used as raw material for a process of ordering carried out retroactively: it plays Mrs. Clements to her Hartright. For although Marian is often praised for her "faithful memory," its accuracy over time is a continual source of anxiety; she seems unwilling to rely on her memory for more than the few hours needed to get to her journal and write everything down: "It was almost as great a relief to my mind as to Laura's, to find that my memory had served me, on this occasion, as faithfully as usual. In the perilous uncertainty of our present situation, it is hard to say what future interests may not depend upon the regularity of the entries in my journal, and upon the reliability of my recollection at the time when I make them" (307). This is in contrast to Hartright, who comments frequently on the detailed vividness of his recollection even years after events (78), and who can rely on himself to recall later important details even of conversations that he says "wearied" him in their seeming irrelevance at the time (527). Marian even seems to need to resort to the same disciplining of her mind to avoid the confusing effects of "retrospection" that Hartright employs on Mrs. Clements: in one entry, she writes, "Let me get back first to the place at which I left off, or I shall lose myself in the confusion of my own thoughts" (290).

In keeping with the gendered split between herself and her diary, Marian becomes concerned about preserving the diary from the possibility of abduction and violation. At the same time that she recommends to Laura that she keep herself locked in her room for safety, it occurs to Marian to lock her own door—not to protect herself inside, but to protect her diary when she is out (325). While Marian thus presumes herself able to protect her own body, her diary is associated with the vulnerable—and ultrafeminine —Laura.

Marian's "resolution" reaches its peak with her decision to eavesdrop on the Count's conversation with Sir Percival, by sneaking out onto the roof over their room. This is also the peak of her defeminization: physically, as she strips off her "cumbersome" female clothing (342) to ensure that "no man could have passed through the narrowest spaces more easily than I," and psychologically, as she casts off any worries about the impropriety of her actions by reference to the "one motive" of protecting Laura's future interests (340). In other words, although previously, in reference to Laura's marriage, propriety of action had been the excuse for destructive results, now the need to achieve particular results provides the excuse for feminine impropriety. Significantly, as Marian gears herself up for this act, her ability to focus attention on completing "the day's record" in her diary leaves her: "In spite of my efforts to fix my thoughts on the matter in hand, they wandered away with the strangest persistency in the one direction of Sir Percival and the Count, and all the interest which I tried to concentrate on my journal centred instead in that private interview between them which had been put off all through the day, and which was now to take place in the silence and solitude of the night" (338–39).

At the point of her expedition over the roof, Marian is at her most masculine, determined to endure nothing patiently but to try what her "resolution can achieve." She is consequently at her most threatening, not only to the particular pair of male plotters she opposes, but also to the clear-cut gender boundaries that the master-narrator's preamble set out. Marian's failure, and subsequent silencing as a narrator, must be read in the context of this dual threat. The immediate consequence of Marian's expedition is her collapse into total physical vulnerability, through the illness caused by her soaking in the rain—a "refeminization" on the crudest level. Its secondary consequence is Fosco's reading of her diary, which D. A. Miller justly calls "by far the most shocking moment in the reader's drama."[8]

The very fact that Fosco has read the intimate and carefully guarded diary is sufficient to create some sense of "violation," but it is the nature of Fosco's reading that makes the occasion so effective as a marker for Marian's silencing and incapacitation. What makes Fosco's violation of the diary particularly chilling is his refusal to read it as a strategic tool in Marian's opposition to him: "I condole with her on the inevitable failure of every plan that she has formed for her sister's benefit. At the same time, I entreat her to believe that the information which I have derived from her Diary will in no respect help me to contribute to that failure" (359). Instead, Fosco insists on reading the diary in the light of his sexual desire for Marian: it provides him with an "unexpected intellectual pleasure" in affirming "how worthy Miss Halcombe would have been of ME" and in "awakening the finest sensibilities in my nature" (358–60). By denying the split between the feminized diary and Marian as masculine strategist—in other words, by reading both sides of the split together as grounds for aesthetic pleasure and sexual desire—Fosco eliminates the self-division that had enabled Marian's determined opposition, and ensures that violation of the diary will also be a psychic rape of Marian herself: in effect, he refeminizes Marian.

Fosco's approach to the diary is a confirmation of his own prescription for the maintenance of masculine domination over women. The secret of such domination, as he tells Sir Percival, is "never to accept a provocation at a woman's hands" (345)—that is, never to allow a woman to see her actions achieve a calculated effect. To "accept a provocation" from the diary would be to acknowledge Marian's potential to affect the outcome of events, and this would leave a far greater weapon in her hands than the text of the diary itself could ever be. His postscript takes the more effective course of subtly insisting on her status as the passive object of his desire.

What is remarkable, though, is the extent to which the novel as a whole adopts Fosco's strategy. One of the reasons that Fosco's postscript is so unnerving is that we tend to perceive the diary as utterly convincing on the subject of Sir Percival's and Count Fosco's guilt. If Fosco sees possession of the text of it (and for that matter, of his own, seemingly self-incriminating postscript) as nonthreatening, he must be terrifyingly confident of his power. But Hartright, too—or perhaps it would be more accurate to attribute this directly to Collins—considers the diary nonusable as a strategic document. When he is arranging materials to bring to Kyrle, Laura's family lawyer, Hartright includes only notes taken from Marian's reading of the diary aloud to him. In other words, it is treated as raw, informational data (and interestingly, as oral data), that turns out to be inadequate to establish the case (456). What that means is that the narrative force of the diary, its power in itself to carry conviction, its authority, has been closed out of the world of the novel.

This happens in other ways, too. For example, when she is recording in her diary the Count's words to Sir Percival about herself, Marian says, "I write the villain's words about myself because I mean to remember them—because I hope yet for the day when I may speak out once for all in his presence, and cast them back one by one in his teeth" (347). Generally speaking, the narrative function of a gesture like this—what might be called a *resolution*—is anticipatory: that is, given our experience of the way stories are structured, we naturally expect that Marian will indeed have the opportunity to "speak out once for all" in Fosco's presence. This expectation is actually reinforced a little later in Hartright's narrative, when Marian tells him that she is "worth trusting with my share in the risk and danger. . . . Remember that, if the time comes!,'" and after these words Hartright writes, "I did remember it when the time came" (454). The time does come, but if Hartright remembers this request then, he does so only to ignore it, because Marian is given no share whatsoever in the "risk and danger" Hartright comes into in his encounters with first Sir Percival and then Fosco. Indeed, when he resolves on his final confrontation with Fosco, in which he will be gambling his life to win a confession from the Count, Hartright actually tries to leave the house without telling Marian where he is going (603). The only thing he asks of her (once she has found him out) is "the courage to wait till I come back" (603). So, again, whatever "resolution" Marian has is closed out of any place in the trajectory of the narrative. This is in effect a continuation of Fosco's process of refeminizing her, but here the refeminization serves the purpose of empowering Hartright.

Hartright finally completes the refeminization of Marian by taking over her story. To explain why, I would like to take a look at his rather ambiguous relationship to his own "manhood." In the first part of the novel, when Marian confronts him with his impossible love for Laura, Hartright can be described only as *ir*resolute. It is Marian who provides the backbone Hartright needs to break away from Laura:

> Her large black eyes were rooted on me, watching the white change on my face, which I felt, and which she saw.
>
> "Crush it!" she said. "Here, where you first saw her, crush it! Don't shrink under it like a woman. Tear it out; trample it under foot like a man!"
>
> The suppressed vehemence with which she spoke, the strength which her will—concentrated in the look she fixed on me, and in the hold on my arm that she had not yet relinquished—communicated to mine, steadied me. We both waited for a minute in silence. At the end of that time I had justified her generous faith in my manhood—I had, outwardly at least, recovered my self-control. (96)

Manhood here is obviously a constructed category, something produced in response to the demand "be a man," and produced, not by eliminating, but by repressing "unmanly" irresolution, loss of control: "I had, *outwardly* [my emphasis] . . . recovered my self-control." Furthermore, the "will" to achieve manliness in this way is actually being poured into Hartright by Marian, in the form of "the strength which her will . . . communicated to mine." She, as it turns out, is the real man in this situation.

The Hartright who returns from various, dimly indicated perils abroad to resume his narration in the second part of the novel seems to be quite literally a "new man," one who has fully internalized the resolution and self-control Marian had earlier demanded that he at least try to fake: "In the stern school of extremity and danger my will had learnt to be strong, my heart to be resolute, my mind to rely on itself. I had gone out to fly from my own future. I came back to face it, as a man should" (427). Here again, "resolute" manliness implies an active, shaping relationship to the future. But when we look at the relationship of this form of mastery to narrative mastery, things get a little more complicated: "The history of the interval which I thus pass over must remain unrecorded. My heart turns faint, my mind sinks in darkness and confusion when I think of it. This must not be, if I who write am to guide, as I ought, you who read. This must not be, if the clue that leads through the windings of the story is to remain from end to end untangled in my hands" (433).

The first thing worth noting here is that we suddenly have a very different model of this narrator's job from that in the preamble. This is not the courtroom any more, or if it is, Hartright is not in the witness box—he is the lawyer orchestrating this parade of witnesses in the interests of a reading of the story that is to remain exclusively "in [his] hands." In other words, the master-narrator has stepped out of the closet.

But note, too, that becoming a narrator in this way is structurally akin to "being a man" in that earlier passage with Marian: it involves simply pushing away, repressing, a loss of control—if necessary, just dropping a week out of the narrative. In the light of this construction of the manly master-narrator, we should look at what happens to Marian's "story"—that is, the story of everything that happens between Marian's illness (the point where her diary ends) and the reunion of both women with Hartright over Laura's supposed grave. Hartright writes: "The story of Marian and the story of Laura must come next. I shall relate both narratives, not in the words (often interrupted, often inevitably confused) of the speakers themselves, but in the words of the brief, plain, studiously simple abstract which I committed to writing for my own guidance, and for the guidance of my legal adviser. So the tangled web will be most speedily and most intelligibly unrolled" (435).

I would argue that part of what is going on here, only a couple of pages after Hartright's earlier comment about "pass[ing] over" a confusing "inter-val" in his own story, is that the possibility of narrative confusion is being transferred to the women and made into a sex-specific "inevitability." Marian has proved again and again her clear-headedness and intelligence in writing and in action, not only in the diary, but in the very events Hartright now recounts on her behalf: she begins an investigation of the circumstances of Laura's (supposed) death, she discovers Laura in the asy-lum, and she plans and executes her rescue without a hitch. Yet her own narrative is presumed capable only of generating a "tangled web" that can only be "intelligibly unrolled" by Hartright, by replacing her "inevitably confused" account with his own "brief, plain, studiously simple abstract" (435). Marian has been reduced, like Mrs. Clements, Anne Catherick, and Laura, to feminine incoherence, in need of the resolute shaping hand of the masculine master-narrator.

Hartright's narrative concludes, "Marian was the good angel of our lives —let Marian end our Story." (646). In the terms of shared narration that the preamble set out, we might expect the expression "let Marian end our Story" to mean that Marian was to conclude the narrative herself. Of course, it means nothing of the sort; it means that Hartright's narrative, and with it the novel, is to end by placing the image of Marian before us. The process of resolving the "anomalies and contradictions" Marian repre-sented is now complete, with her reconstitution as purely the object of nar-rative—and consequently, I should add, as a "good angel."

"The Taste of the Original Apple": *Dracula*

The sensation novel and the Gothic novel are related forms: both gain much of their force by "daring to speak the socially unspeakable" and then offer-ing "modes of imaginary transcendence" to control its threat.[9] The sensa-tion novel differs from the Gothic partly in that it situates its action largely within the bourgeois family, within England, and within the bounds of natural possibility (if not of probability). The Gothic novel enacts broader displacements of social anxieties onto stranger forms, which are consequently harder to trace with any precision.[10] *Dracula* also differs from *The Woman in White* in that it has a less tightly controlled coalition of narrators. Whereas *The Woman in White* begins and ends with Hartright's retrospective narrative, so that potential challenges by other narrators are, as it were, framed by his narrative mastery, *Dracula* is composed entirely of documents produced while the events were taking place. No narrator within the novel writes from a position of authority equivalent to Hartright's. Since both men and women in the novel tell the story via letters and diaries, *Dracula* lacks the clear-cut distinction between masculine and feminine modes of narration that are identifiable in *The Woman in White*. But I will argue that the novel does carry out a similar process of refeminizing an androgynous female figure, in part by restricting her right, or power, to order the unfolding narrative.

Critics have generally accepted that anxieties about gender and sexuality are central to *Dracula;* indeed, as Kathleen Spencer points out in a recent article, "interpreting *Dracula*'s sexual substrata has become something of a cottage industry lately."[11] If a focus on Dracula and his victim-cohorts suggests that issues of sexuality are central to the novel, a focus on his opponents and their methods suggests an equal emphasis on questions of knowledge. Dracula as a figure threatens not only the stability of contemporary sexual roles but also the sense-making capacity of science and rationalism.[12] The story of his defeat at the hands of Mina and her "little band of men" is in large measure one about collecting, collating, and interpreting information. By such means, his opponents can determine the Count's whereabouts, his limitations, his mental character, and his future plans, reducing him from an otherworldly embodiment of all that threatens rationality and social order to a predictable, and hence defeatable, "criminal type" (361).

In *Dracula,* knowledge is power, and not only power over Dracula himself. The opening note, with its tantalizing promise that "[h]ow these papers have been placed in sequence will be made manifest in the reading of them" (xxi), asks that we read with a consciousness not only of the emerging story but of the process by which it has been recognized and organized as such. This process turns out to be crucial to the plot: for characters within the novel, the ability to identify and organize an explanatory narrative—to *plot* it—carries with it the ability to plot more effectively against the sinister figure at its center, as well as to shape the moral or ideological significance of the story as a whole. The figure who organizes these documents is hence a key plotter in both senses of the term. To place a woman in this position —as *Dracula* at least temporarily does—potentially poses as great a threat to traditional gender roles as all the ambiguities of "vampire sexuality."

Dracula has often been read as a largely reactionary response to the threat of autonomous female sexuality posed by the phenomenon of the New Woman, with its anxieties about female sexuality being most clearly visible in Lucy Westenra's story. Particularly once she has been "vamped," Lucy's sexual assertiveness seems to link her with the New Woman. But

Lucy's actions as a vampire, like those of the "awful women" (42) Jonathan encounters at Dracula's castle, perhaps owe less to the specific threat posed by the New Woman's insistence on sexual autonomy than to the ambivalences built into the model of Victorian womanhood from the start. Since ideal womanhood (and the ground of male desire) was characterized by a combination of total sexual purity and at least the potential for passionate devotion to a man, this model risked undermining the supposed grounds of male love at the moment of its consummation. The only genuine Angel in the House is a wife who has literally joined the angels. Van Helsing's description of the rationale for remurdering Lucy in her coffin could equally well describe a more general preference for an idealized dead fiancée over a sexually initiated wife: "Instead of working wickedness by night and growing more debased in the assimilating of it by day, she shall take her place with the other Angels" (226). In driving the stake through Lucy's heart—a right granted to her betrothed because his is "the hand that of all she would herself have chosen" (227)—Arthur, improving on the experience of the average bridegroom, gets to deflower his bride and simultaneously restore her forever to "unequalled sweetness and purity" (228). From here on, Lucy's ennobling influence emanates from a securely "separate sphere." If Lucy does represent the sexual aspect of the New Woman, that representation explicitly resists late Victorian feminist efforts to reconceive the mutually exclusive terms in which womanhood was judged. Either way, as inspiring angel or as "voluptuous" vampire-whore, Lucy remains squarely within High Victorian gender categories.

Jonathan and Mina

While Lucy is ambiguously linked to the New Woman through her sexual assertiveness, Mina shares many of the figure's other qualities: she begins the story as a self-supporting professional (a schoolmistress) with no family ties, and she is in the process of learning typewriting and shorthand, professional skills often associated with the New Woman. She also proves to have intellectual and organizational abilities at least equal to those the men bring to their joint task. As Senf points out, she is "the kind of woman who could not have existed much before the period in which Stoker wrote."[13] At the same time, as we have seen, Mina herself is outspokenly critical of the New Woman's assertiveness in sexual matters, and she abandons her career in favor of the more traditional role of wife and mother. Even her typing and shorthand have been taken up to be "useful to Jonathan" (65) in his career.

Her marriage to Jonathan Harker, too, significantly departs from the High Victorian model, while retaining much of its emotional dynamic. Jonathan and Mina share talents and interests that prove interchangeable and mutually reinforcing. Both are orphans who have risen by their own talents and innate authority—Jonathan from "clerk to master" and Mina to schoolmistress. After their marriage, Mina intends to bring her professional skills to the assistance of Jonathan's business. Such details reveal both their equivalent professional competence and their relative freedom from the social and dynastic interests that would circumscribe a more traditional courtship and marriage. In one sense, Stoker seems to be affirming this professional and personal symbiosis, which dissolves the "separate spheres" in which the High Victorian husband and wife ideally operated. All the novel's good characters—and particularly the authoritative Van Helsing—admire the couple, and it is the Harkers who ultimately provide the traditional novelistic closure of domestic marital happiness. In this light, Mina herself can be read, as Senf does, as a merging of what Stoker saw as "the best of the traditional and the new,"[14] combining the intelligence and resourcefulness of the New Woman with a traditional feminine commitment to providing emotional support and nurturance to men and their children.[15] But the dynamic of both Mina's and Jonathan's shifting status and activities as characters and narrators indicates that this merging and crossing of gender categories is more unstable than the final endorsement of the couple suggests. Although the Harkers' marriage is the only model of gender relations still standing at the end of the novel, it has been reaffirmed by a rather strange route, which restates traditional gender positions in the most lurid terms. Along the way, Mina's "New-Womanly" qualities are not so much affirmed as dissolved and then reshaped, suggesting that the New Woman's intellectual agency raises almost as great an anxiety about masculinity (if a less obvious one) as does her sexual self-assertion.

The symbiotic quality of the Harkers' marriage is evident in the remarks each makes about the function of their own writings. Jonathan's first journal entry (which opens the novel) indicates that he views his journal less as place for private reflection or a professional record than as a sourcebook to be used when he "talk[s] over [his] travels with Mina" on his return (8). Accordingly he takes extensive notes on local culture and history, resolving to fill in gaps in his understanding by questioning the Count (8), and even writing "memos," or reminders, to pick up recipes "for Mina" for interesting local dishes (7). His efforts to record, organize, and interpret information on his journey are thus explicitly motivated by Mina's role as potential audience and interlocutor. Mina, too, in the letter that immediately follows the journal, sees her husband as the potential audience of her own planned journal "if there is anything in it worth sharing" (65). She reveals another motive for both in explaining that they have decided to write both letters and journals in shorthand, by way of practice in the newly acquired skill. Their (planned) correspondence and journals, then, show the couple embarking on a joint, interdependent process of intellectual and professional self-improvement.

There are, of course, significant gender differences in the potential use of such skills. For Mina, stenography is primarily a way of being "useful to Jonathan": "if I can stenograph well enough I can take down what he wants to say in this way and write it out for him on the typewriter, at which also I am practising very hard" (65). Stenography, combined with typewriting, provides a way of recording oral information and then rendering it comprehensible in a written document, but only in the most unmediated way —one that, at least in theory, provides no interference with or reinterpretation of what the speaker "wants to say." Jonathan is less explicit about what he plans to do with shorthand professionally, but in the course of his journal the system takes on significance less as a secretarial convenience than as a secret code.[16] Like the shorthand Lovelace employs in his letters to Belford, Jonathan's shorthand closes down the circuit of information that, in the documentary as in the epistolary novel, is also the circuit of power.[17] Imprisoned and prevented from communicating with outsiders, Jonathan's only real advantage over the Count is that he knows more about his own dire situation than the Count believes he does. Keeping the journal—which proves essential to retaining his own sanity and self-control—in shorthand ensures that his own efforts to organize his thoughts effectively can give no further advantage to the Count.

But Mina, too, hints at more ambitious uses for her recording skills. Though she hopes her journal may prove "of interest" to Jonathan, she intends it primarily as "an exercise book" for herself: "I shall try to do what I see lady journalists do: interviewing and writing descriptions and trying to remember conversations. I am told that, with a little practise, one can remember all that goes on or that one hears said during a day" (65). Mina's goal in seeking to record "all that goes on or that one hears said" seems an extension of, rather than a departure from, her stenographic ambitions, but the shift from the role of secretary to that of "lady journalist" suggests a significant shift also in the relation between recorder and source. The "lady journalist" actively seeks information (by "interviewing"), and, because of her memory skills, is able to obscure her own recording of it from the subject's knowledge. Left unstated in the comment is the implication that the journalist gathers data toward her own construction of a story, rather than in the service of whatever it is the speaker "wants to say."

"I Felt Impotent": The Feminization of Jonathan's Voice

Thus far I have provided parallel accounts of Jonathan's journal opening and Mina's first letter, as if they appeared at the same point—and indeed they are roughly contemporaneous within the chronology of the novel, being dated "3 May" and "9 May," respectively. Discussing the documents together illuminates what might be termed the opening status of the relationship. But within the narrative, Mina's letter appears only after the entire text of Jonathan's journal, which covers a period of nearly two months and comprises the first four chapters of the novel. To understand the shifting gender dynamics of narrative authority in the novel, we must see how Jonathan's position as a narrator alters over the course of the diary, since it is his shift in position that frames the introduction of Mina's narrative voice.

What begins as an intellectual exercise for Jonathan quickly evolves into a journal of captivity, bearing generic—and gendered—affinities with both Marian Halcombe's diary at Blackwater Park and Pamela's journal in Lincolnshire. Indeed, Jonathan's position at Dracula's castle closely parallels Pamela's at Mr. B.'s: initially drawn in by deference to his wealthy, upper-class employer, Jonathan soon finds himself imprisoned and subjected to quasi-sexual threats at the hands of Dracula and his monstrous female cohorts. Vampirism even reproduces the moral logic of female sexual violation in Richardson, not only in its explicit erotic associations—Jonathan, entranced and prone, waits in "languorous ecstasy" for the vampire-woman's teeth to penetrate his throat (48)—but also in that even an unwilled physical violation has moral consequences, turning an innocent victim into a future fellow fiend. Jonathan's "soul" is under the same kind of threat as Pamela's "virtue."[18]

The diary kept by a captive diarist comes to be in itself a key focus of the captive's resistance, and it is for this reason that the diaries become to some degree equated with the bodily self of the writer. Jonathan, like Pamela and Marian, worries about the potential violation of his diary. Awakening after his encounter with the vampire women, he is relieved to find his journal as much intact as his neck. But the nature of the resistance implied—and hence the stake involved in secrecy—varies significantly in the three cases mentioned, each of which involve different relationships between gendered narration and the sex of the narrator.

Pamela's "journal" remains an extension of her earlier correspondence with her parents. Even in the absence of any possibility of reply—or even of an opportunity to dispatch what she's written—Pamela continues to write with her parents as her primary audience. Thus, while her journal challenges Mr. B.'s construction of her story, it does not substantially challenge the principle of subjecting her experience to the judgment of a "higher" moral authority; when Mr. B. is content to occupy *that* position, he can fully appropriate her story. Pamela's journal, in other words, poses no real challenge to male narrative mastery. Marian's diary does pose such a threat, but one that can be defused by a renewed emphasis on her sexual identity. The diary, as we have seen, enables a strategic splitting of "masculine" strategist and "feminine" recorder of experience. Its potential as a source of resistance is determined by its place within her practice of material plotting. This is why Marian's resistance is effectively disabled when Fosco reads her diary —as B. read Pamela's—as no more than a witness to her admirable character, and thus a justification of his own sexual attraction to her as a woman.

Jonathan's anxiety about losing his journal is unrelated to its contents— again, its shorthand form ensures secrecy on that front. Nor does the diary prove of any practical value to him in planning an escape from the Count. Rather, it becomes a way of asserting some kind of psychological control over his own unnerving experiences. Thus, for Jonathan, the journal becomes a site for efforts to regain the sense of mastery that his feminized plight has stripped from him. Confronted with the first glimmerings of such experiences, Jonathan sees the journal as a way of controlling his anxieties about the very reality of what he observes, as he resolves to "begin with facts . . . verified by books and figures, and of which there can be no doubt," and to avoid "confus[ing] them with experiences which will have to rest on my own observation, or my memory of them" (39). By treating the "facts" about the Count's business plans and inquiries as something that "may somehow or sometime be useful to me" (39), Jonathan reasserts his power to make a strategically useful order out of his experiences in the face of his growing fears about his own possible unreliability as an observer. After the more overtly supernatural (and terrifying) scene with the vampire women, the journal becomes Jonathan's only link to sanity: "Up to now I never quite knew what Shakespeare meant when he made Hamlet say:— 'My tablets! quick, my tablets! / 'Tis meet that I put it down,' etc., for now, feeling as though my own brain were unhinged or as if the shock had come which must end in its undoing, I turn to my diary for repose. The habit of entering accurately must soothe me" (46).

Nonetheless, as a captive with little to do but scribble secretive complaints about his treatment and fears about the titillating "fate worse than death" that awaits him, Jonathan clearly has more in common with literary damsels in distress than with their rescuing heroes. The parallel is apparently not lost on Jonathan himself: the turning point in his fortunes at the castle is marked by a moment of rejected identification with a helpless woman. The scene comes after a series of particularly Pamela-esque disappointments: the Count's foiling of Jonathan's attempt to smuggle out a letter to Mina via the gypsies (52), and his subsequent theft of Jonathan's writing materials, traveling clothes, and papers (53); a failed appeal to the Slovak drivers, who prove indifferent to Jonathan's "piteous cry and anguished entreaty" (54); and finally, another brush with his would-be rapists, the vampire-women (55)—all events with direct parallels in *Pamela*. Finding himself "locked in my prison" and able to "do nothing," Jonathan writes, "I sat down and simply cried." He is immediately startled from his tears, though, by hearing "the agonised cry of a woman" outside (55). This is the woman who comes to demand her child from the Count, and whom Dracula quickly has torn to pieces by wolves. Jonathan's final commentary on the scene is, oddly, that he "could not pity her" (56).

This scene has been commented on as evidence of Jonathan's (and Stoker's) equation of women with their maternal function[19]—"I knew now what had become of her child, and she was better dead"—but it seems more significant as the moment of Jonathan's re-gendering of himself. He is initially identified with the woman through their joint "cry." Hence his refusal to "pity" her becomes a refusal to dwell upon what is pitiable in his own condition. Already his closing questions, "What shall I do? What can I do?" have become less a cry of despair than questions open to productive answers. Beginning with the next day's entry, Jonathan's energies begin to focus on "Action!" rather than reflection (57), and he makes his first foray onto the outer walls of the castle, the method he will eventually use for his escape. The journal ends with his resolution to stop writing in favor of action that will at least allow him to die "as a man" (64).

Jonathan's escape effectively puts an end to Dracula's material threat to his identity "as a man." But the lack of a coherent frame within which his experiences can be made sensible continues to debilitate him afterward. Mina, nursing him in his convalescence, writes that "[a]ll the resolution has gone out of his dear eyes" (119). Even upon his recovery and return to

England, she notes, he remains crucially unmanned by "the grave shock that he experienced." It is a wound precisely to his sense of mastery: his "sweet, simple, noble, strong nature . . . which enabled him . . . to rise from clerk to master in a few years . . . [is] so injured that the very essence of its strength is gone" (177). What is missing, apparently, is the force that transformed him from the "clerk," who merely records what others intend, to the "master," who directs and interprets their work. As Jonathan succinctly puts it later: "I felt impotent" (210). But this is an impotence of intellect, a fear that his constructions of reality have no natural authority. Jonathan's real fear is that his diary, rather than being a reliable account of what he has done and experienced, is a witness against his sanity. "Manly" and "resolute" as his final actions in the castle may seem within that account, they can be seen that way only within a framework of knowledge that acknowledges his judgment of his situation as accurate.

Giving the diary to Mina, then, is a loaded gesture. In one sense, it signals Jonathan's abdication of the effort to make sense of the past, an effort that makes his "head spin round." His real desire is simply to cut off the past altogether, to start the story over, to "take up my life here, with our marriage" (120). Thus, although handing over the diary is a gesture of trust, it is not overtly a transfer of responsibility for interpreting the past: Mina can "read it if [she] will," but only if she does not allow the reading of it to have any impact on their relationship: "never let me know" (120).

Mina's sealing of the diary with her wedding ring appears to indicate her acceptance of this trust on Jonathan's own terms, converting the diary from a disturbing mystery requiring interpretation to "an outward and visible sign for us all our lives that we trusted each other" (121). Nonetheless, the abdication of narrative authority signaled by Jonathan's rejection of the diary and the memories it contains provides the context for Mina's growing importance as a compiler and interpreter of her own and others' stories. When Jonathan responds to her gesture by telling her "that he would go through all the past again to win [her hand], if need be," Mina glosses his words to Lucy: "The poor dear meant to have said a part of the past, but he cannot think of time yet, and I shall not wonder if at first he mixes up not only the month, but the year" (121). Like her first letter, this one slides from dutiful subordination toward a more subtle impulse to take charge: Mina, not Jonathan, is now the authority on what he "meant to say," as well as the only one capable of putting in proper order the months, and even the years, of the past.

Upon Jonathan's "relapse" after seeing the Count in London, Mina decides that it is time to gain a better command of her husband's story by reading the sealed diary. This will enable her, "if it be wanted," to "speak for him, and never let him be troubled or worried with it at all." Jonathan, like Laura after her asylum experience, has become the helpless, disordered center around which interpretive efforts must be mobilized by others. If he is to be disturbed at all by recollections of his ordeal, it is so that Mina, equipped now with a fuller grasp of background details than Jonathan can bring to consciousness, can "ask him questions and find out things" that he may not understand himself (201).

At this point, Mina's position is comparable to that of Marian in the first half of *The Woman in White,* stepping in to provide the "resolution"—both judgment and willpower—that a weakened male counterpart lacks. Although the unmanning of Jonathan seems to be quickly reversed—Van Helsing's confirmation of the truth of his diary, like Hartright's adventure abroad, makes "a new man" of him (210)—the refeminizing of Mina that will ultimately confirm it is a longer and more complex process.

"I Want You to Believe": Science and Narrative Authority

By the time Mina meets with Van Helsing, another struggle of interpretation has already taken place around Lucy's mysterious illness and death. Centering as it does on the efforts of the two doctors, Seward and Van Helsing, this section first brings into focus the novel's concern with science as both an intellectual activity and a practical tool, and establishes the relationship between scientific and narrative authority. Science, particularly that of practicing physicians also engaged in experimental research, involves an interaction akin to that between narrative and material plotting, between the organization of experience or data into a meaningful form (scientific knowledge, or narrative plotting), and the effective application of that knowledge for material (i.e., therapeutic) ends. Unsurprisingly, then, scientific skill is closely associated with other "manly" qualities, and particularly the old standby, *resolution.* Lucy, on first meeting Seward, describes him as "one of the most resolute men I ever saw" (66), and Seward himself, in praising the scientific genius of his mentor Van Helsing, attributes to him, along with his intellectual qualities, "an iron nerve, a temper of the ice-brook, an indomitable resolution, [and] self-command" (128).

Seward, whose journal provides most of the narrative in this section, is initially largely closed out of the construction and deployment of scientific authority. In the two cases that dominate his journal entries—Lucy's illness and Renfield's madness—Dracula's influence renders his scientific efforts ineffectual. The vampire, as a causal factor that his science cannot recognize or allow for, renders the observable data incoherent, and hypotheses incomplete.[20]

Interestingly, though, Seward is also hampered by an absent "cause" of another sort. Reflecting on Renfield's case, he feels frustrated by the "humanitarian" considerations that prevent him from gathering more data by allowing Renfield to follow his grotesque impulses to their logical conclusion: "Men sneered at vivisection, and yet look at its results today! Why not advance science in its most difficult and vital aspect—the knowledge of the brain? Had I even the secret of one such mind . . . I might advance my own branch of science to a pitch compared with which Burdon-Sanderson's physiology or Ferrier's brain-knowledge would be as nothing. If only there were a sufficient cause!" (83).

Cause hence takes on the same kind of double meaning as *plot*. It is both the origin that can organize an explanatory narrative (or theory) and the telos that can organize and justify material efforts. Dracula as an enemy will eventually be able to fill both roles, in that, as both an alien physical force and the incarnation of evil, he provides a means of unifying scientific and moral authority.

Seward's scientific confusion provides the necessary framework for the introduction of Van Helsing, the novel's embodiment of scientific mastery and the counterfigure to Dracula. Like Dracula, Van Helsing initially appears only through the eyes of others: an inaccessible figure whose plots can only be dimly perceived through the narration of those ignorant of them. Seward is as confused by Van Helsing's remedies as he is by Lucy's ailment. Van Helsing is the only figure who possesses the same clue as to what ails Lucy as the reader does, but it remains unclear just how much he knows—or can do.

Aside from its obvious narrative function in prolonging suspense, Van Helsing's initial secretiveness also foregrounds the novel's thematization of sharing and withholding information, an issue that becomes central with Mina later on. Van Helsing seems to feel that knowledge is always more valuable when it is not shared. He explains his refusal to share his early thoughts even with Seward by comparing them to grain that has not yet begun to form—suggesting that the time will come when Seward will need to be told—but his rationale for keeping their proceedings secret from everybody else is more absolute: "All men are mad in some way or the other; and inasmuch as you deal discreetly with your madmen, so deal with God's madmen, too—the rest of the world. You tell not your madmen what you do nor why you do it; you tell them not what you think. So you shall keep knowledge in its place, where it may rest—where it may gather its kind around it and breed" (135).

By this logic, the less "knowledge" is shared, the greater it becomes: Van Helsing tends to respond to requests for information by demanding trust instead. The principle is reinforced by Seward's initial description of Van Helsing. He is a "seemingly arbitrary man," he writes, but only because his frame of reference always exceeds that of his hearers: "he knows what he is talking about better than anyone else." In other words, Van Helsing's refusal to explain himself fully reinforces the sense of his mastery even when it makes him incomprehensible, or "seemingly arbitrary." Thus he gains the reputation of being "one of the most advanced scientists of his day" (128). The mechanisms that establish Van Helsing's scientific authority thus parallel those of masculine narrative authority as exercised by Walter Hartright in *The Woman in White:* the benevolently manipulative withholding of information and the self-conscious staging of its revelation at the moment when it will carry greatest force.

The "So Clever Woman": Mina and Van Helsing

While Van Helsing seems to stand for the principle of knowledge, or theorizing, withheld, Mina, as we have seen, has been aligned with the gathering of information. The instant alliance and mutual admiration between them, then, would seem to invite a situation in which Mina could dutifully provide informational raw material that Van Helsing would then "process" and put to work in ways she might not intend or understand: this, of course, would reproduce precisely the relationship between masculine and feminine narration established in *The Woman in White.* But Mina complicates the model on their first meeting. Van Helsing has come to her looking for data relevant to Lucy's death—letters from Lucy to Mina, Mina's recollections of her visit with her, and so forth—and she seems happy to oblige, offering him her own diary for the period of the visit. But initially Mina— inspired, she says, by "some of the taste of the original apple that remains still in our mouths" (204)—hands him the original diary, written in shorthand. "For an instant his face fell," she writes, but he quickly recovers, praising her as a "so clever woman" and requesting translation (205). Mina, now "almost ashamed" of her "little joke," hands over the typed copy she has already prepared, and all is well. The incident seems minor, but it is significant. With this gesture, Mina inserts herself, as an active, thinking force, between Van Helsing and the passive data provided by her diary, making clear to him that her mediation is required before her documents can be put to intellectual use. She thus casts her assistance as a pooling of intellectual resources rather than merely as a contribution of data. Like the eater of the "original apple," she claims a higher level of understanding than has been officially permitted to her.

Though he is effusive throughout the novel in his praise for Mina's "cleverness," Van Helsing never seems quite comfortable with this aspect of her character. After reading her diary, for example, he tells her that he is "dazzle, with so much light," but adds "that you do not, cannot, comprehend" (205). From here on, Mina's efforts to pool information compete with Van Helsing's—and the other men's—attempts to shield her from a comprehension perceived as threatening to her.

Mina proves able—and eager—to comprehend more than he thinks, becoming the active force behind the accumulation and organization of documents in the case. In this sense, she takes upon herself the role of master-narrator that Van Helsing, concerned as he has been with the withholding of knowledge, has declined. Her acquisition of Seward's diary is characteristic. In trying to evade her request to hear the portion of it relating to Lucy's death, Seward has already stumbled upon a key flaw in his phonographic recording method: the impossibility of finding "any particular part of it in case I [want] to look it up" (246–47). Thus, though ostensibly a scientist's casebook, the diary as it stands lacks the potential for retroactive self-reflection and reinterpretation that could lift it above a mere passive recording of experience. Mina offers to correct the defect by transcribing it, but her offer is motivated largely by her desire to integrate the diary with her own knowledge: "my mind was made up that [it] might have something to add to the sum of our knowledge" (247). In overcoming Seward's resistance to opening his diary to other readers, Mina stresses the subordination of his personal story—a story that he claims "[n]o one need ever know"—to the larger plot "of poor Lucy's death and all that led to it." More importantly, she stresses the story's place in the developing plot "to rid the earth of this terrible monster." In making these arguments, Mina also makes clear that she has already begun the process of reinterpreting the data that Seward unknowingly transcribed: "the cylinders you gave me contained more than you intended me to know; but I can see that there are in your record many lights to this dark mystery" (248). Her final appeal is for the kind of open sharing of knowledge and thoughts that the men of the novel have often resisted: "We need have no secrets amongst us; working together and with absolute trust, we can surely be stronger than if some of us were in the dark." Interestingly, though, Seward casts his acquiescence less as a matter of agreeing with her argument than as one of "giving in" to the "courage and resolution [manifested] in her bearing" (249).

Again, Mina's activity here hovers ambiguously between an effort to appropriate and take charge of the materials on her own terms—to "master" them—and the mere provision of a kind of subordinate assistance. This ambiguity in itself is significant, but I want to point out the way the text seems to stress the former beneath the guise of the latter. Even in offering to transcribe Seward's diary—a task that seems purely secretarial—Mina stresses the difference produced by her mediation between the voice on the cylinders and the typed transcription. The spoken diary, she says, "told me, in its very tones, the anguish of your heart . . . like a soul crying out to Almighty God." Her transcription mutes the anguish, so that "none other need now hear your heart beat, as I did" (248). Without changing the words, Mina has altered the meaning of the diary. By casting this alteration as a protection of Seward's privacy, Mina makes this transcription another effort to speak "for" a weakened male.

From here on, Mina takes charge of the effort to gather and collate all the documents bearing on the case. She even thinks to check the newspapers for relevant news items, remembering how much her "cuttings" at Whitby had "helped us to understand the terrible events . . . when Count Dracula landed" (250). Though the project of weaving the gathered documents into a "whole connected narrative" (251) is referred to at the time as a joint effort of the Harker couple, it is undertaken on her initiative, and retrospectively viewed, even by Jonathan, as her achievement: "it is due to her energy and brains and foresight that the whole story is put together in such a way that every point tells" (276). Similarly, although Mina seems to subordinate the project to Van Helsing's own plans, telling Seward that preparing the documents is a way of getting "ready for Dr. Van Helsing when he comes" (250), it is clear later that she could have carried it out only in his absence and without his knowledge: his first act upon his return is to forbid her further involvement in the case.

Indeed, Van Helsing seems more disturbed than pleased by her initiative. He interrupts Seward's enthusiastic account of it with an outburst that, while ostensibly in praise of her, ultimately suggests that there is something anomalous or perverse about her abilities and involvement:

> Ah, that wonderful Madam Mina! She has man's brain—a brain that
> a man should have were he much gifted—and a woman's heart. The

good God fashioned her for a purpose, believe me, when He made that so good combination. Friend John, up to now fortune has made that woman of help to us; after to-night she must not have to do with this so terrible affair. It is not good that she run a risk so great. We men are determined—nay, are we not pledged?—to destroy this monster; but it is no part for a woman. Even if she be not harmed, her heart may fail her in so much and so many horrors; and hereafter she may suffer—both in waking, from her nerves, and in sleep, from her dreams (262).

Though initially claiming that her androgynous qualities must serve some divine purpose, Van Helsing seems determined to grant her none in the current enterprise. The "man's brain," he feels, is overruled by the woman's body, which makes her too vulnerable to nervous ailments to sustain any stress of conflict with Dracula. By casting even Mina's current contribution as a matter of "fortune" making her "of help to us," he both excludes her from the central "us" and suggests that her fortuitous involvement thus far, though useful, may have been ill-advised, or even improper. Seward later reinforces the association with sexual impropriety and its potential to "taint" a woman morally, suggesting that only "men of the world" can be safely involved in the case, and that if Mina "had remained in touch with the affair, it would in time infallibly have wrecked her" (285).

The decision to exclude Mina from further plotting is cast explicitly as a reassertion of conventional gender roles and a reappropriation of narrative authority. Indeed, it would be difficult to justify it on any other terms. Though feminine weakness, whether physical or mental, might conceivably provide a rationale for leaving Mina out of the actual pursuit of the Count, it is hard to see, given how much she already knows, how keeping her wholly in the dark subsequently could measurably increase either her safety or her peace of mind; in fact, it notably fails to do either. The decision seems intended, rather, to increase the men's confidence in the power of their own masculinity, and to force Mina into the role of silent inspiration. "We are men and are able to bear," Van Helsing assures her, "but you must be our star and our hope" (270). To fill this passive role, Mina must be excluded from the kind of active research and theorizing she has hitherto excelled in ("you no more must question," he tells her) and limit herself to providing an audience for a retroactive account of the completed story: "we shall tell you all in good time" (270). Though the decision is initially Van Helsing's, the other men embrace it eagerly, with Seward even expressing concern lest his mentor "weaken" in his resolve (285). It is as if Van

Helsing's invocation of "we men" as a category suddenly reminds them all of how much Mina has already encroached on the territory of manliness.

The value of his decision in propping up masculinity can be most clearly seen in the shift it produces in Jonathan's relationship to Mina. Although previously he had turned his own diary over to her rather than deal with its contents himself, he now claims to be "glad" that "henceforth our work is to be a sealed book to her, till at least such time as we can tell her that all is finished" (283). And though he anticipates difficulty in abandoning the intellectual communion he had previously relied on, the challenge makes him determined to "be resolute" (283).

Mina's exclusion also produces a significant change in the tone and function of her own journal. Instead of using it as an "exercise book" for the development of her own intellectual skills, which may or may not be shared with Jonathan, she now conceives of it solely as a source of testimony to Jonathan of her own state of mind at any given moment: "lest it should ever be that he should think for a moment that I kept anything from him, I still keep my journal as usual. Then if he has feared of my trust I shall show it to him, with every thought of my heart put down for his dear eyes to read" (286). A similar change appears in the content of the diary, in which Mina begins to focus on thoughts and feelings that she can neither understand nor control. Mina's failure to grasp the sinister significance of her own experience, which is immediately apparent to a reader, is particularly interesting in that by this time both possess identical background information —indeed, Mina has by now been assigned the full credit for its organization and presentation. Her diary, in other words, has become a more thoroughly feminized narrative in response to the men's pronouncements.

I have dwelt in such detail on the admittedly short-lived state of affairs produced by Mina's exclusion from the men's plans because it represents a central moment in the novel's complex treatment of gender and plotting. Though it takes place amid the overt praise and encouragement of her male allies, rather than alone in a hostile, threatening situation, Mina's accomplishment in organizing the narrative thus far—bringing it into being *as* narrative—closely parallels Marian's challenge to male plotters in her rooftop expedition. Both represent the greatest assertion of the M-women's "masculine" qualities, and with it, a certain defeminization—most obvious in Marian's stripping off of female clothing, but also suggested in Mina's involvement of herself in concerns that are "no part for a woman." In both cases, the women's masculine intelligence and "resolution" have been called into play due to the absence or incapacity of male allies, in this case due to

Harker's nervous illness and Seward's confusion. More significantly, both evoke a similar response, in the violence and silencing to which Mina, like Marian, is subsequently subjected. The sequencing of events and the distribution of agency among heroes and villains differ somewhat, but I would argue that the underlying symbolic functions are similar in their operation: in both cases the assertion of plotting abilities coded as "masculine" leads immediately to a reassertion of "feminine" vulnerability to the plots of others. In *The Woman in White* this vulnerability is achieved initially through a plot device: the heavy rain that causes Marian's fever, disordering her thoughts, disabling her from writing, and rendering her physically defenseless. In *Dracula* the doctors achieve the same effect by merely invoking such frailty: even Jonathan, who has hitherto relied on Mina's strength, becomes convinced that to keep her even minimally informed would be to risk having "her nerve broken" (291). And just as Marian's physical frailty enables Fosco's reading of her diary, the purposeful isolation of Mina enables Dracula's attack, a scene that, with its emphasis on violent compulsion, its overtones of "enforced fellatio,"[21] and the subsequent feelings of humiliation and guilt experienced by its victim, more clearly evokes rape than any other episode of vampirism in the novel.[22]

These pseudo rapes—in both novels arguably the single most horrifying moment—catalyze a refiguration of the women's relationship to plotting whose logic is surprisingly similar. In both cases the attack is explicitly a response to the threat the M-women pose as counterplotters. Fosco vehemently warns Percival of the danger Marian poses to their plans (346); Dracula accuses Mina of trying to "play your brains against mine . . . [and] help these men to frustrate me in my design!" (319). At the same time, both counts proclaim or instate a special bond with the women based precisely upon these abilities. Fosco drinks toasts to Marian even while plotting against her, and fantasizes about what he could do "with that woman for my friend" (346). Dracula, rather than merely "vamping" Mina, exchanges blood with her to get access to her thoughts, and looks forward to the day when she will become "my companion and my helper." While the counts view the ultrafeminine women of both novels primarily as a kind of raw material—Laura represents a potential source of money and a body to be disposed of, and Lucy is largely a food source—the M-women prove attractive for the power of their minds. Because they recognize this, the counts cast themselves, oddly, as the champions of the very women they victimize: Fosco sings Marian's praises; Dracula promises Mina, "You shall be avenged in turn; for not one of them but shall minister to your needs" (319).

In one sense, then, the villains seem to recognize the M-women as equals, Fosco noting "how worthy I should have been of Miss Halcombe— how worthy Miss Halcombe would have been of ME" (359), and Dracula calling Mina "flesh of my flesh; blood of my blood; kin of my kin" (319). But in another sense the whole function of their contact with them is to institute the kind of clearly gendered dominant/subordinate relationship the women have hitherto inverted in their relationships with the heroes. Marian's fear of Fosco is a recognition of precisely this ability: "If he had married a tigress, instead of a woman, he would have tamed the tigress. If he had married *me,* I should have made his cigarettes, as his wife does" (239). Similarly, Dracula glories in the power he now has to command absolute obedience from Mina: "When my brain says 'Come!' to you, you shall cross land or sea to do my bidding" (319).

This complex relationship serves three related purposes. First, the counts' recognition of the M-women's potential as allies indirectly associates the women's strengths with the evil forces the villains represent.[23] At the same time, the villain's power effortlessly to subdue—and potentially even recruit —the very women on whose masculine "resolution" the weakened male heroes have relied emphasizes the extent of their mastery, their power to subordinate others to their own plots. If they can so easily refeminize such resolute women, they can potentially feminize men as well.[24] Finally, the "good" men can only neutralize this threat by, as it were, acquiescing in the refeminization of the women, recasting what had been a threat to the joint interests of a male/female team as an attack on a woman that demands an exclusively masculine—and explicitly "manly"—response.[25]

The discovery of the Count's attack initially invalidates the men's decision to exclude Mina, a decision that has in fact put her at risk. Yet its ultimate effect is to produce a replay of the same decision on stronger grounds and with Mina's full concurrence. While initially Mina had been frustrated by her exclusion, calling it "a bitter pill for me to swallow" and noting that the arrangement "did not seem to me good" (256), she now makes Jonathan promise "not [to] tell [her] anything of the plans formed for the campaign against the Count" (344), since the Count now has access to her thoughts. Similarly, while previously she felt silenced by the archaic gender roles the men enforce—"I could say nothing, save to accept their chivalrous care of me" (256)—now that she has been literally silenced by the Count she calls the men together for a chivalric-style group vow to protect her soul (350).

The effect of this replay-with-a-difference is both to place the enforcement of gender roles on a firmer footing and to hide their explicit association with gender.[26] Mina's vampire "taint" becomes both the marker and the mask of an essentialized femininity.[27] Because of it, her role in the narrative becomes split into what might be termed the good and the bad (or artless and artful) feminine narrator. Under hypnosis, she represents the epitome of feminine narration, a purified version of what Hartright obtains from Mrs. Clements in *The Woman in White,* as she spills forth unedited sensory experiences whose significance must be interpreted by the men. Rather than organizing and interpreting others' data, her chief contribution now is to tell "that which even I myself do not know" (362). And rather than providing the "resolution" herself to prop up weakened males, Mina can now help only by subjecting herself wholly to Van Helsing's powerful "will"; as Jonathan observes, "He seems to have power at these particular moments to simply will, and her thoughts obey him" (368).[28] Appropriately, then, Mina's reliability in this state becomes threatened as soon as she begins to think about what she says: Seward grows suspicious of her testimony when he notices "that her imagination is beginning to work": "Whilst she has been in the trance hitherto she has confined herself to the simplest of facts. If this goes on it may ultimately mislead us" (382).

At the same time, Mina's reliability outside hypnosis is also affected by the Count's presumed influence. When Van Helsing voices to Seward his suspicions about the Count's possible access to Mina's consciousness, he also notes that she herself is "changing": "I can see the characteristics of the vampire coming into her face. . . . Her teeth are sharper, and at times her eyes are more hard" (357). As the detail of the hardened eyes suggests, Van Helsing's observations indicate that Mina is undergoing a moral as well as a physical transformation. She potentially poses a threat not only as a passive microphone for the Count, but in her own words and actions.

Amid this uncertainty, Mina's intervals of freedom from the Count's influence—at sunset and sunrise—create a brief space in which the "original," reliable Mina can potentially make herself heard. This device makes it possible for Mina herself to endorse—and even insist upon—the alterations in her status and role in relation to the men that the attack has produced. She uses the first of these intervals to suggest the experiment in hypnosis that first reveals her mental link to the Count, and later to insist on her exclusion from the men's plans. The next are devoted to warnings about her own untrustworthiness in her "changed" state. In insisting that she be brought along on the pursuit of the Count instead of being left at home with Jonathan, she confirms the same possibility Van Helsing had already suspected: "I can tell you now, whilst the sun is coming up; I may not be able again. I know that when the Count wills me I must go. I know that if he tells me to come in secret, I must by wile; by any device to hoodwink— even Jonathan. . . . You men are brave and strong. You are strong in your numbers, for you can defy that which would break down the human endurance of one who had to guard alone" (362).

Mina is essentially warning the men to distrust anything she says or does. Her allegiance is now crucially uncertain, and what seems an effort to help may be only a "device to hoodwink." The men's joint efforts are required to protect her, and themselves, from the sinister, plotting self she feels taking over her personality. She even makes the men promise to kill her when her transformation has clearly gone too far, and reminds them that here, too, her own judgment or will is not to be relied upon: "At such a time I myself might be—nay! if the time ever come, *shall be*—leagued with your enemy against you" (367).

Thus, again, Mina's vampire taint operates to reproduce, in disguise, a more traditional model of femininity than she initially appeared to represent. Any form of agency, any effort to "plot," is rendered suspect, while reliability is associated with passive acquiescence to the "will" of a male guardian in her periods of hypnosis.[29] Mina not only grants the men the responsibility for assessing her adherence to this model, she explicitly endorses the violence required to enforce it, even representing it as an act of kindness. She compares the situation to that of men who "have killed their wives and their womankind, to keep them from falling into the hands of the enemy" (366), thus relating it directly to the question of men's right to enforce their prerogatives over "their" women.

This process of refeminization is complicated, however, by the fact that the "original" Mina does make a further appearance in the novel: first when she offers, with Van Helsing's coaching, an analysis of the Count's "child-brain," and immediately afterward, when, on her own initiative, she succeeds in deducing the Count's probable route back to his castle. Thus Mina's "great brain which is trained like man's brain" (376) asserts its value even at the very last stage of plotting against the Count. This episode consequently resists any effort to read Mina's intellectual agency simply as destroyed or negated in the course of the novel. Throughout the novel, Mina's intelligence forms part—if a highly ambivalent part—of her idealization.[30] In this sense, Senf is right in seeing the characterization of Mina as an effort to incorporate, rather than merely reject or punish, the intellectual qualities of the New Woman. While the effects of her "vamping" have thus far worked to dissolve the challenge to male authority seemingly posed by those qualities, this episode seems a brief effort to recuperate what is lost when gender roles are so violently reasserted. It thus represents a buried acknowledgement that something *is* lost.

Nonetheless, the episode is framed in terms that stress the need for masculine judgment and authority as a context for Mina's efforts. It occurs just after the most definite evidence yet that Mina poses a threat to the plan against the Count: the trance she enters, in which he is able to use her knowledge to escape the trap laid for him at Varna. The reason given for the men's renewed trust in her, and her renewed activity, is the hypothesis that the Count has distanced himself from Mina in his efforts to escape quickly. This move represents yet another recapitulation of her initial exclusion from the men's councils. Just as that earlier decision had been justified by invoking traditional gender categories regardless of their applicability to the case at hand, the Count's move now represents an unreflecting return to ingrained habit. In both cases, the exclusion of Mina on one side makes possible the appropriation of her mind by the other: if the men's first major mistake is believing that they can protect Mina by excluding her, the Count's is that he can protect himself by doing the same thing. Rejecting Mina comes to be seen as the Count's fatal error, the point at which his reversion to criminal habit (abandoning his forces when threatened) reveals his imperfectly developed mind, and hence his vulnerability. Van Helsing and company, by contrast, are able to assess the situation attentively enough to change their policy toward Mina when it may prove useful to do so. In fact, the very ground of their ability to make such assessments is faith in what might be termed Mina's transparency as a character: the belief that they can tell the difference (even if she cannot) between sincere helpfulness and a clever "device to hoodwink."

Rather than simply reaffirming Mina's reliability or power, then, this episode seems in part to exemplify the men's superior ability to take advantage of all the shifting resources at their disposal. Van Helsing and Seward remain suspiciously watchful of her, and as we shall see, such watchfulness remains necessary in reading her narrative.

"Let Us Go to Meet My Husband": Mina as Ambivalent Narrator

Once she has been cast as a figure of uncertain allegiance, the status of Mina's narrative voice necessarily also changes. Like the men of the novel, the reader becomes attuned to signs of a possible "change." Throughout the novel, because of the absence of a clear master-narrator, the narrative mode has invited a form of suspicious reading: we are constantly being presented with narrators who do not understand the full significance of their own experience. A great deal of the pleasure—and terror—of *Dracula* is generated by this technique. But with Mina, for the first time, the reader must begin to wonder whose side the narrator is really on, or if she understands the implications of her own thoughts. When, for example, she repeatedly asks "if it were really necessary that they should pursue the Count" once he has left England (353)—ostensibly because she dreads being left behind without Jonathan—she clearly does not consciously intend to act as an advocate for the Count's safe escape, but we are invited to suspect that this is her unconscious motive. This effect is more obvious later, when her text confesses to her hesitation in writing the word *Vampire,* preceding it with a kind of written stutter: "the . . . the . . . the . . . " (391).[31] It becomes most disturbingly pronounced near the end of her diary when, complaining about the suspicious countrywoman who loads her food with garlic, she remarks without further comment that she "can't abide garlic" (398).

It is not that we need ever actually suspect Mina of evil or deceitful motives. In fact, her frequent outbursts in her diary of gratitude to the "brave men" for their devotion to her cause, submission to God's will, and shame and revulsion at her own tainted state, emphasize the extent to which her conscious will remains devoted to the cause of opposing Dracula's influence. What these suspicious moments do is to indicate how insidious the threat to her is without undermining the image of a fundamentally virtuous woman that validates the men's heroic efforts to save her. Only by seeing her as out of control of, and relatively unselfconscious about, her own feelings or motives at these moments—reading them as the expression of the will of an alien male, impinging on her own—can she be retained as an admirable or sympathetic figure. It is partly for this reason that Mina's diary halts at the point on her journey with Van Helsing where she begins incorporating vampire characteristics more fully into her personality.

The halt in Mina's journal is the culmination of a process of converting her from an interpreter to an object of interpretation. It is hence appropriate that her interrupted narration should be taken over by Van Helsing himself. His "Memorandum" displays an even greater ambiguity about Mina's status than her narrative, as the physical and behavioral evidence of incipient vampirism becomes more pronounced. But rather than indicating a failure to recognize these sinister signs—her loss of appetite, heavy daytime sleep, and nighttime vivacity are all pointedly noted—Van Helsing's account displays a conscious refusal to pursue in writing the implications of what he perceives. After a night in which it is dimly suggested that Mina may even be "vamping" him already—he wakes a few times to find her watching him with "so bright eyes," and in her daytime sleep afterwards she looks "more healthy and more redder than before"—he voices no overt suspicions, but writes, "I like it not. And I am afraid, afraid, afraid! . . . even to think." But Van Helsing's reticence in this case is validated by the power he still has to *act:* "The stake we play for is life and death, or more than these, and we must not flinch" (402). He avoids pursuing the implications of Mina's changing behavior because he still believes he will be able to alter the conclusion.

Unlike Marian Halcombe's, Mina's narrative voice does reappear to "end our story": her last journal entry narrates the dramatic climax of the hunt for Dracula, and except for a brief postscript by Jonathan, ends the narrative. I would argue, though, that part of the function of this entry is to extend the implications of her new relationship to the narrative beyond the unnatural conditions that initially produced it. Since it is written retrospectively, after Dracula's death has erased her vampire taint, the entry ought to display none of the suspicious qualities previously detectable in her journal. But in fact her account of the chase and battle is curiously ambiguous. Until the moment in her narrative when the Count's body crumbles into dust, dissolving his influence over her, Mina's words are potentially subject to a double reading.

Her final entry is immediately preceded by Van Helsing's account of their exchange just before going to meet Dracula and his pursuers, an account that introduces further doubts about her loyalties. Van Helsing has just finished his "butcher work" on the vampire women in the castle. Seeing him afterwards, he writes, Mina "cried out in pain that I had endured too much," but her words as quoted leave unclear whether the pain is for him or the butchered "sisters." She then urges him to go with her "to meet my husband who is, I know, coming towards us" (409). Mina's unexplained "I know" here recalls the previous scene described by Van Helsing in which she instinctively "knows" the correct route to Dracula's castle. Challenged on this, she replies, "Of course I know it," then pauses to think before adding, implausibly, that she got the information from Jonathan's journal (400)—which, of course, Van Helsing has read as well. He finds the episode "somewhat strange." In both cases Mina seems to be under some special influence: at the pass she is "all on fire with zeal," and in the later scene "her eyes . . . glowed with fervour" (409), but zeal or fervour for what is unclear. Since the implication in the first scene is obviously that Mina's bond with the Count is what guides her toward his home, this later instance suggests that she may be rushing to meet the wrong "husband"—the Count, after all, is now "flesh of [her] flesh . . . kin of [her] kin." Van Helsing's concluding sentence, with its floating "whom," leaves the ambiguity of her statement intact while underlining the oddness of her knowledge: "And so . . . we go eastward to meet our friends—and *him*—whom Madame Mina tell me that she *know* are coming to meet us" (409).

Mina's journal entry, which follows this, is produced *after* the Count's influence has been removed, but it is framed here simply as a continuation of Van Helsing's narrative, with no overt reference to this fact. Within the entry, the "husband" of whose approach she had such mysterious knowledge is now directly identified with Jonathan (412), but other aspects of her narrative remain subtly ambivalent. At the first glimpse of the cart bearing Dracula's coffin, she writes, "My heart leaped . . . for I felt that the end was coming. The evening was now drawing close, and well I knew that at sunset the Thing, which was till then imprisoned there, would take new freedom and could in any of many forms elude pursuit" (411). The surge of joy suggested by "my heart leaped" initially seems associated with Dracula's approaching "end," and revulsion is further suggested by the reference to him as a "Thing," rather than "he." But the remainder of the passage, without any rhetorical indication of a shift in emphasis, focuses on the Count's potential escape, with terms like "imprisoned" and "new freedom" suggesting sympathy and hope for him. Later she expresses puzzlement that she "felt no fear" at "seeing Jonathan in such danger," though she retroactively attributes this to "the ardour of battle," which "must have been upon me" (413).[32] Finally, there is her anguished "shriek" as Jonathan's knife shears through Dracula's throat (415).

In these ambivalent moments, the psychological vantage point of the narration is made more contemporaneous with the events narrated than with the time of narration, despite the (presumably) drastic change in perspective that takes place between the two. This technique certainly heightens the narrative effect of the description: any perceived ambivalence in Mina's account only emphasizes further how much hangs on this final confrontation. Until the very moment in the narrative when the Count's body crumbles to dust, Mina's words, like her loyalty, could go either way. They literally take their final meaning from the telos provided by the men's efforts. But such moments also emphasize how Mina's narrative role has changed. If the earlier episode in which she deduced the Count's route home represented a holdover from her original self into her "vampirized" state, this passage shows a similar leakage of the latter state into her final self. The ordeal of partial vampirization thus transforms the terms under which Mina can recover her "old" self. In particular, this final entry shows how fully Mina has become the object of interpretation rather than a reliable interpreter herself, even after the conditions that rendered her suspect have been eliminated. For these ambivalent moments to make sense, we must assume that Mina herself is not fully aware of the significance of the feelings she remembers having at the time. Rather than being the interpreter of others' unconsciously meaningful words, she now produces such a text herself. In his postscript, Jonathan completes the exchange of roles by speaking "for" Mina, and by quoting Van Helsing's summary of her value as lying in what she inspired in men: "Already [her son] knows her sweetness and loving care; later on he will understand how some men so loved her, that they did dare much for her sake" (416).

The threat of vampirism, then, serves to displace Mina from her position of narrative mastery, converting her into (alternately) someone who can provide only the raw material of a plot, or someone whose potential plots are inherently dangerous. Mina, like Marian before her, is transformed by the novel's end from a potential devil to a good angel, a transformation made possible by the refeminization of her narrative voice, and the renewed "resolution" of the men enabled by it. While Mina's more "masculine" efforts are not quite as thoroughly negated as Marian's are—being appropriated by and subordinated to male efforts instead—the violence unleashed by the prospect of genuine female agency, narrative or material, is also much greater in this novel.

The transgression of conventional gender roles, whether sexual or intellectual, is clearly central to *Dracula*'s power and appeal as a narrative, as it was to a lesser degree in *The Woman in White,* and it may seem like an open question whether the play in gender roles it allows ultimately undermines the security of such roles more than the novel's eventual reassertion of them reinforces them. Stoker, even more than Collins, keeps us cognizant to the end of the *constructedness* of his narrative: though the novel's documentary format bespeaks a concern with creating an effect of authenticity, the thematization of copying, transcribing, and translating stresses the artificiality of that effect. As Jonathan remarks in his final "Note," "in all the mass of material of which the record is composed, there is hardly one authentic document" (400). The same might be said of gender roles in the novel. If Van Helsing seems to stabilize gender attributes by labeling Mina's intellect "male," Mina herself traces the genealogy of her intellectual curiosity in the female line—to the "lady journalists" who are her contemporaries, and to Eve, taster of the "original apple." But a covert recognition of the constructedness and potential instability of gender roles need not constitute a critique of their enforcement.[33] In both these novels, the gender dynamics of narration in fact play a crucial role in such enforcement. In refeminizing an androgynous female figure partly by means of restricting her right or power to order the unfolding narrative, both Collins and Stoker make the assertion of gender roles a source of pleasure linked to the assertion of narrative authority. The interplay of narrative voices ultimately enlists the reader's own sense-making efforts in the task of subordinating, or reading against, the female voice, and reinforcing masculine efforts at narrative "mastery." By constructing narrative mastery *as* masculinity, Collins and Stoker safeguard manliness from the threat implied in the growing recognition—made explicit in the phenomenon of the New Woman—that real-life experience does not naturally fall into such absolute gender categories. Men and women, like narrative, and *through* narrative, can be constructed from the most unlikely materials.

Seven

INNOCENT OF LANGUAGE
The Feminine Narrator as Fantasy Ideal

For me,
'Tis otherwise: let men take, sift my thoughts
—Thoughts I throw like the flax for sun to bleach!

—Pompilia, from Robert Browning, *The Ring and the Book*

*W*hen Clarissa—and perhaps her author—is feeling most hemmed in by the rhetorical contradictions of her state, whereby it seems impossible for her to convince anyone of anything without being immediately discredited by virtue of her artful capacity to convince, she engages in a brief fantasy of complete, unmediated self-exposure: "I should be glad that all the world knew my heart. Let my enemies sit in judgement upon my actions: fairly scanned, I fear not the result. Let them even ask me my most secret thoughts, and, whether they make for me or against me, I will reveal them" (822). However the epistolary structure of the novel may seek to approximate such a state, it necessarily remains an approximation. Self-exposure unmediated by the veil of language is never really available—who could check the accuracy of a claim to have revealed one's "most secret thoughts," anyway? But the fantasy of a kind of pure representation remains a powerful one, for author as well as character. If the mobilization of feminine narration often seems disciplinary in its force, a matter of reasserting what women ought not to or cannot do—plot or preach—I would like to suggest that feminine narration also speaks to a fantasy of linguistic transparency, an imagined escape from the difficulties involved in the project of constructing powerful fictions in order to tell "the truth."

The most powerful evocation of this fantasy in the Victorian period occurs not in the novel but in narrative poetry, in Pompilia of Robert Browning's *The Ring and the Book*. If, as I have argued, the self-consciousness of Clarissa's willed self-exclusion from narrative and material agency makes her a limit-case for feminine narration in one direction, the illiterate, dying

Pompilia might stand as the opposite extreme, the feminine narrator imagined as pure, unselfconscious witness.

Pompilia is a witness in the most literal terms. Her narrative is the written document of oral testimony in the murder case against her husband Guido Franceschini, which forms part of the documentary evidence in the case presented to the pope for judgment. It is spoken as she lies dying of the twenty-two stab wounds delivered by her husband's hired assassins, who killed her parents at the same time. Pompilia's narrative is only one (though the only exclusively female one) among the wide variety of conflicting perspectives the twelve books of *The Ring and the Book* offers, but it stands out from them in the complete absence of the kind of problems in the relationship of language to truth that seem to have inspired *The Ring and the Book* to begin with.

The poet himself,[1] in the opening and closing books of the poem in which he addresses the audience directly, puts the issue of language's power to distort the truth at the center of the poem. The poem's "one lesson," he writes, is

> that our human speech is naught
> Our human testimony false, our fame
> And human estimation words and wind.
>
> (12. 832–36)

The problem is not that truth is nonexistent, unknowable, or even merely inexpressible (the poet, after all, claims to have both the "truth" and a way to "speak" it). Rather, the poet is concerned with a seemingly irresistible human temptation to use language to distort the truth: to deceive others or to deceive oneself. "Speech," which here encompasses writing as well, becomes not just a tool of man's sinfulness but the very symbol of original sin. The poet calls it "the primal curse / Which bids man love as well as make a lie" (1. 637–38); the pope, his most authoritative speaker, reflects that "barren words . . . / More than any deed, characterize / Man as made subject to a curse" (10.348–50), and believes that at the "judgement-bar" of God language will be dispensed with altogether: there will be "nor question nor reply" (10.346–47). In keeping with the association of language with original sin, speakers seem both culpable for their sinful misuse of speech and unable to escape its distorting power: the poet does not hide his dislike or disapproval of the lawyers, the defendant, and the gossips of Rome, but his sweeping condemnation at the poem's end encompasses *all* "human speech." The pope gains his authority only by recognizing and repenting in advance the possible limitations of his judgments of others' speech and of his own speech-act, the sentence on Guido and his accomplices.

But Pompilia emerges as a special case. "Perfect in whiteness," as the pope calls her (10.1001), she is considered exempt from the sinful stain of language, and her speech is allowed to be perfectly transparent, effortlessly sincere. For the pope, saddened by encountering all around him "these filthy rags of speech" (10.372), there emerges from Pompilia's testimony an uplifting possibility of purity: she is "one blossom . . . / Born 'mid the briars of my enclosure" (10.1029–30); "the one prize vouchsafed unworthy me" (10.1025).

In one sense, the transparency of Pompilia's speech is derived simply from her moral (i.e., sexual) purity. Having nothing to hide—no sin to be ashamed of and no self-interest to further—she has no motive to fall into the distortions of speech the other speakers engage in. Her sinlessness in the flesh guarantees her sinless (sincere) speech. But in another sense, it is precisely the apparent artlessness of her speech that guarantees her purity, which external evidence is not sufficient to establish. The perceived absence in her testimony of internal signs of evasion or distortion—the telltale marks of speech's "filthy rags"—is what inspires the pope's (and the poet's) conviction of her innocence.[2]

From this perspective, it could be argued that the sincerity of Pompilia's speech is guaranteed not so much by her "goodness" as by her lack of access to language as a tool to shape or misshape the expression of experience. The sinful use of speech that the poet concerns himself with in *The Ring and the Book* is not outright lying—the basic facts of the case being readily available and incontrovertible—but the subtle distortions that take place through a process of revision. The most explicit examples of this are the lawyers' written arguments. In introducing them, the poet stresses, with heavy irony, the way the written arguments make possible the careful construction of an artificial mask, a "simulated tongue" (1.1111) that, representing a "sound / Which never was," (1.1112–13) hides the absence of the human speaker behind it, and most particularly of his thoughts, presumed to be "too immense [at] odds" (1.1114) with the product to appear. The poet's description of the lawyers' sections emphasizes the process of shaping and revision: "How he turns, twists, and tries the oily thing" (1.1152); and the calculated artistry of the finished product, the "masterpiece" incubated in "law's bosom" (1.1119). Of all the lawyer's artful gifts—the "ready smile and facile tear, / Improvised hope, despairs at nod and beck"—it is "language . . . the gift of eloquence" that serves him best: "Language that goes, goes, easy as a glove, / O'er good and evil, smoothens both to one" (1.1169–73).

This is a kind of language to which Pompilia has no access. As the pope says of her, "It was not given Pompilia to know much, / Speak much, to write a book, to move mankind" (10.1015–16). While the pope speaks of her purity as a kind of compensation for her ignorance, it would seem just as accurate to call the latter the condition of the former. Unable even to write, let alone to shape, polish, and adorn her writing as the learned lawyers do, Pompilia is immune to the temptations such powers would offer. She herself says she is "glad" to be unable to write when she sees the results of "vile pens / Scribbling a charge against" her rescuer, Caponsacchi (7.1473–74).

Writing, though, is not the only means by which truth is corrupted in *The Ring and the Book*. The poet describes the gossips of Rome as carrying out a similarly distortive process of revision, although less self-consciously, in talking over and passing on the events of the story. Here the revision takes place through the subtle "swerve" brought about by the speaker's predispositions, "The instinctive theorizing whence a fact / Looks to the eye as the eye likes the look" (1.855–56). It is made possible by the circumstances of sharing information through gossip: the sense of authority provided by being the one "in the know," the feeling of confirmation at being agreed with by one's listener, and the increasing distance from the bare facts of the event itself provided by the passage of time.

This is, again, a process unavailable to Pompilia, in this case not so much through her ignorance as through her position with regard to the other characters. From the start, she is isolated from the possibility of a sympathetic listener: the first result of her marriage is that she is forbidden to confide in her friends or her father. Once she is settled in Arezzo with her husband, her isolation is complete. She is surrounded by people who either reject her confidence (the archbishop) or invite it with too-apparently destructive intent (her maid Margherita). Guido himself distorts her every word and action into a proof of sexual guilt. "Used to such misconception day by day" (7.1025), Pompilia abandons the attempt to communicate with her persecutors, and consoles herself by repeating—uselessly, as she knows—"the mere truth" (7.1028). At the time of her testimony, Pompilia's speech is conditioned throughout by her knowledge of her approaching death, which denies her the opportunity of gaining the kind of distance from the events she describes that the gossips have. She lacks the time to seek explanations, to reconsider, to decide to say "more" or "less"—in short, to shape her experience in telling it: "Think it out, you who have the time! for me,— / I cannot say less; more I will not say" (7.703–4).

The effect of her isolation and approaching death points to the link between the perceived transparency of Pompilia's speech and her status as victim. Indeed, her entire story emphasizes her passivity in relation to the multiple plots others mount around and against her.[3] As a "victim stripped and prostrate" for an "obscene" rite (1.575–76), she is stripped also of the "filthy rags" of distorting speech. The poet himself equates her physical exposure on her deathbed—the result of Guido's violence against her—with her linguistic transparency as two forms of nakedness: Pompilia has "scarce more privacy at the last / For mind than body" (1.1093–94).

For the other reliable speakers of this poem—the poet/master-narrator and the pope—language is a corrupt medium that cannot be escaped on earth any more than one can escape humanity's fallen state. But both struggle with it, struggle to find the truth within the distorted speech of others, or to find the form that can communicate that truth without further distortion to others. They seek to transcend the corruption of language by actively and self-consciously engaging with the problems of communication and sincerity, and their learning and the wisdom of past experience stand them in good stead in the effort. But Pompilia, far from "transcending" language, seems almost to have never entered the arena of human speech. As ignorant, passive victim, or as struggling mother acting under the "prompting" of the instinctual forces she shares with "brute and bird . . . reptile and the fly / Ay and . . . even tree, shrub, plant / And flower o' the field" (10.1068–74), Pompilia never seems to achieve the self-consciousness and linguistic skill that would entangle her in the complexities of human speech. She is innocent of language in every sense of the term.

As a pure witness, Pompilia acts as a safe grounding for the poet's exploration of the seemingly ungrounded permutations of language-as-power. Pompilia thus points up what the strange narrative dynamic of Collins's and Stoker's novels also suggests—that the "masculine" narrative confidence, competence, and control to which feminine narration is opposed is itself an increasingly precarious construct. In *The Ring and the Book,* feminine narration not only acts to counterpoint and reinforce masculine narrative mastery, it *mobilizes* it. Just as, within the narrative, Pompilia's transparent purity in person inspires Caponsacchi's courageous rescue, so the faith in her purity as a witness makes possible both the pope's courageous interpretation of the textual evidence in his verdict and, arguably, the writing of the poem itself. Similarly, the feminine narration of Pamela and Clarissa helps to mobilize the "reform" of Mr. B. and Belford and their subsequent authorization as master-narrators, while the refeminization of Marian, Lydia, and Mina enables and even inspires the renewed material and narrative "resolution" of Hartright, Midwinter, and Harker. By contrast, Jane Eyre's and Aurora Leigh's achievements of narrative mastery are accompanied by the textual and material incapacitation of the male lovers who had earlier tried to define the trajectory of their lives: in both cases, blinding produces a literal erasure of the masculine "point of view" and constitutes the women as the master-narrators of their own and their husbands' worlds.

But if this suggests the positive power of feminine narration (though not of feminine narrators) within these texts, we should keep in mind the close association of that power with these same figures' positioning as the object of physical violence as well as of narrative interpretation. For the artless feminine narrator, the two are usually bifurcated between male villains and heroes, but for the artful woman they readily merge, as in Dickens's (and by implication the reader's) "dissection" of Miss Wade.

The persistent parallels between material and narrative agency in all of these texts are not coincidental. The need to transform the data of experience into coherent, meaningful narratives took on greater urgency in this period—when received narratives like those of the Bible were being persistently called into question but the very possibility of producing adequate explanatory narratives was not—than at any time before or since: Ruskin's morally charged histories of artistic development and decline, Darwin's (proclaimed) transformation of a welter of biological data into a profoundly meaningful narrative of development, Macauley's progressive history of Britain, and numerous other works of the period all testify to the power of a shapely and coherent narrative to convey not only pleasure but cultural convictions with substantial instrumental power—as indeed does the rise and social influence of the novel as a literary form. For the Victorians, narrative agency, to a large extent, *is* material agency, and the power to plot confers the authority to preach.

Feminine narration as a convention both reflects and helps to define the "proper" relationship of women to this process, and in general works to reinforce the perception of masculine narrative power, not only over women, but over experience itself. Because this convention is encoded in the formal structures of novels, and in the dynamic of reading those structures produce, it is less readily apparent, and arguably more powerful, than the gender thematics of mimetic representation. My examination of female narrators in these texts suggests that a woman's power to define the shape and meaning of her story—or further, her power to define herself as having that power—was considerably more elusive in the eighteenth and nineteenth centuries than the proliferation of women's voices in the novels of the period would suggest—even in texts that seem to escape or actively resist the stereotype of the helpless, incoherent woman.

At the same time, as we have seen, novels with female narrators in this period often engage more fully and dynamically with the problems and possibilities of narrative mastery—by men *or* women—than their single-voiced, authoritative counterparts. Attention to the gender dynamics of narration illuminates how much is at stake in the struggle to shape and deploy narrative: there is considerably more involved in telling our stories than being able to write *I*.

Notes

Introduction

1. Blackmore, *Lorna Doone*, 21. (Subsequently referenced parenthetically in the text.)

2. In shortening characters' names, I have tried to adopt the form that will be most easily recognizable to a reader of the novel in question—for the most part, this means adopting the form of the name commonly used in the novel itself. In practice, the result is that men are generally referred to by their last names, and young women, at least, by their first names, though there are exceptions, such as Darsie and Alan in *Redgauntlet,* and Gwilt in *Armadale.*

3. This is what Rabinowitz terms "authorial reading" (*Before Reading,* 21).

4. See Rabinowitz, *Before Reading.*

5. In conformity with the practice, now common, of using "feminine" to refer to cultural norms of womanhood and "female" to refer to women per se (i.e., to the female sex), I will use the term *female narrator* to refer to any female figure who narrates, and "feminine narrator" to refer to one, whether male or female, who conforms to the conventions of feminine narration.

6. Warhol, "The Look, the Body," 21.

7. Phelan, *Reading People.*

8. Rabinowitz, *Before Reading.*

9. Richter, *Narrative/Theory,* 94.

10. Lanser, *Narrative Act,* 47.

11. Ibid., 86. Lanser divides her consideration of "point of view" into three aspects: "*status,* the relationship between narrator and speech act; *contact,* the relationship between narrator and audience; and *stance,* the narrator's relation to the discourse content or 'message' or narrated world" (18).

12. Lanser, *Fictions of Authority,* 3.

13. Warhol, *Gendered Interventions,* 6.

14. Ibid., 1.

15. Mezei, "Contextualizing Feminist Narratology."

16. Lanser, *Fictions of Authority,* 5.

17. Warhol, *Gendered Interventions,* 15.

18. Two recent critical books that do not directly associate themselves with feminist narratology do address the use of female narrators in texts by men. Madeleine Kahn's *Narrative Transvestism* uses psychoanalytic accounts of transvestism as a model for exploring the psychological functions fulfilled by the adoption

of female voices for Defoe and Richardson; the book is not concerned with gendered narration as a broader literary convention, or with these texts' influence by or on a literary tradition. Linda Kaufman's *Discourses of Desire* identifies a genre, the "amorous epistle," composed of fictional or actual letters from an abandoned woman to her lover. The genre spans many centuries and includes texts written by both men and women (and some for which authorship is uncertain). I discuss Kaufman's work in the last section of this introduction.

19. Nor should this tendency on the part of feminist narratologists be overstated. Feminist narratological critics have been attentive to and insightful about the ways women's writing influences and is influenced by men's. Lanser, for example, notes that women's deployment of autodiegetic narrators—what she terms "personal voice"—has been complicated by the fact that male authors have also used female narrators, who might be said to compete with female authors' versions (*Fictions of Authority,* 19). Warhol's book discusses the interplay of engaging and distancing direct address in both male and female authors.

20. Lanser, *Fictions of Authority,* 19.

21. The alternative would be an instance like *The Sound and the Fury,* where the narratives appear to be windows into the consciousness of the characters, and no occasion of autodiegetic narration is given—or in Benjy's case, is even possible.

22. As the opening passages from *Lorna Doone* suggest, narrative authority is inflected by class as well as gender. But these inflections are much harder to generalize about usefully, since the category itself is so unstable. Definitions of classes, the location of boundaries between them, and the values attached to membership in particular classes or to mobility between them vary enormously over this period, and from writer to writer at any one time. In the works I discuss, while lower-class status usually exacerbates the narrative disabilities of female narrators, its impact on male narrators is much more unpredictable. I address issues of social class more particularly as they come up in readings of individual novels.

23. Nancy K. Miller, "Emphasis Added."

24. Brooks, *Reading for the Plot,* xiii.

25. Winnett, "Coming Unstrung."

26. Phelan, *Reading People,* 107–16.

27. Brooks, *Reading for the Plot,* 12.

28. Barthes, *S/Z,* 17–18. The proairetic code, which concerns the mapping of events over time into a pattern of cause and effect, can be readily equated with plotting. My linking of the hermeneutic code, associated with the development of *enigma* and the disclosure of meaning, with what I have termed *preaching* is obviously looser.

29. Warhol, *Gendered Interventions,* 18.

30. *Letters,* 8: 15n, quoted in Krueger, *Reader's Repentance,* 58. This advice predates the ban on women preachers, which covered even such unpreaching as this.

31. Richardson, *Pamela,* 173–75. (Subsequently referenced parenthetically in the text.) Significantly, though, the most important audience for this sermon turns out to be the one Pamela does not know she has—Mr. B., who is hiding in the room in disguise.

32. Doody, in *A Natural Passion,* contrasts this view with that of Allestree's

Gentleman's Calling (1660), in which "masculine virtue is shown as active, powerful in the world," (16). Davidoff and Hall quote Rev. T. Binney's *Mothers and Maidens* (1850) as an example of the view that women should "inspire and animate, sooth and resuscitate their men, so that 'the mighty engine of masculine life may be aided in its action and its results,'" (118). Ruskin's "Of Queens' Gardens" also exemplifies the commonplace Victorian view that man is "eminently the doer, the creator, the discoverer, the defender," whereas the woman must be "wise . . . for self-renuncia- tion" (140–42).

33. Brooks, *Reading for the Plot*, 12.

34. Lanser, *Fictions of Authority*, 357: "I would be eager for narratology to talk about such a crossing of the plot of narration with the story plot."

35. See McKeon, *Origins of the English Novel.*

36. Brooks, *Reading for the Plot*, 154.

37. Ibid., 155.

38. Sue, *Mysteries of Paris*, 14.

39. Brooks, *Reading for the Plot*, 19.

40. See my discussion of Clarissa's "mad papers" in chapter 1.

41. Defoe, *Moll Flanders* 1: vii. (Subsequently referenced parenthetically in the text.)

42. Watt, *Rise of the Novel*, 113–14.

43. Van Ghent, *English Novel*, 57.

44. Defoe's *Roxana* lacks such distancing gestures in its preface. *Roxana,* though, clearly still adheres to the opposition between narration and feminine *virtue.*

45. As Rader points out, in the development of the novel Defoe has "ancestors but no posterity" ("Defoe, Richardson, Joyce," 7).

46. Altman suggests that, since it is not told from the ending but rather pur- ports to follow events as they are experienced daily, the epistolary novel may be to some degree inherently antiteleological, at least to the extent that it reaches for verisimilitude (*Epistolarity*, 161). But in fact it could be equally well argued—à la Frank Kermode—that any novel is antiteleological to the extent that it reaches for verisimilitude, just as it is teleological to the extent that it aims to be a novel. Indeed, without the reassuring presence of a narrating consciousness, the epistolary novel- ist must work harder to reassure the reader that a story is indeed progressing. A novel like *Tristram Shandy* can be more easily and successfully antiteleological than *Pamela* or even *Humphrey Clinker.*

47. Richardson, *Pamela* 2: 130.

48. Rader elucidates in some detail the way the novel's form necessarily gener- ates "the ambiguity of Pamela's status as heroine-hypocrite" ("Defoe, Richardson, Joyce," 35), though he does not identify the gender issues that influence the choice of this form in the first place. Eagleton makes a similar point in terms of class ide- ology: "Pamela is both realist character and bearer of Richardson's ideological project of integration with the gentry; so it is not her fault, so to speak, if she is sometimes forced by those textual exigencies to act suspiciously. . . . If the reader is to be in full possession of the work's motives, it is vital that Pamela should not be in full possession of her own" (*Rape of Clarissa,* 35).

49. Rader, "Defoe, Richardson, Joyce," 35–38.

50. Warner does this in some detail in anatomizing Clarissa's account of her brother James (*Reading Clarissa*, 11–12). The widespread critical suspicion of Esther Summerson of *Bleak House* is another example of this pattern, though as we shall see it is something of a special case.

51. Phelan, *Narrative as Rhetoric*, 81.

52. Lanser, *Fictions of Authority*, 14.

53. Ibid., 33.

54. Booth, "Narrative Choices."

55. As Rabinowitz observes, even the most clear-cut narratives can usefully be seen as "unassembled" (*Before Reading*, 38). A "kit" differs from an "unassembled" item in the assumption that the process of assembly is a pleasurable end in itself.

56. *Bentley's Monthly Review*, in Dyson, *"Bleak House" Casebook*, 67.

57. Lanser argues that male mastery of "the female 'I'" in the eighteenth century rendered women novelists "superfluous" (*Fictions of Authority*, 38).

58. Collins, *Armadale*, 41.

1. The Triumph of the Antiplotter

1. Castle, *Clarissa's Ciphers*, 22.

2. Warner, *Reading Clarissa*. Interestingly, Warner's 1979 analysis of the novel, and particularly his animus toward Clarissa herself, reproduces precisely the cultural anxiety about female narrative authority that I am arguing shaped Richardson's (and others') representations of female narrators. The very terminology Warner uses in describing the battle of meanings between Clarissa and Lovelace casts the linguistic skills Warner attributes to her as illegitimate (and sneaky) usurpations, while Lovelace's are merely the playful exercise of his rightful powers. Hence, while Clarissa is described as "appropriat[ing] immense authority to herself," Lovelace merely "asserts his own very considerable powers of authorship" (28–30).

3. Castle, *Clarissa's Ciphers*, 22.

4. Eagleton, *Rape of Clarissa*, 52–53.

5. In saying that she excludes herself, I do not mean to suggest that Clarissa has such powers readily available to her all the time. But her grandfather's estate does represent the availability of such power, and Clarissa not only resigns it voluntarily, but frequently reaffirms the correctness of her decision to do so even in the face of its painful consequences.

6. Eagleton, *Rape of Clarissa*, 52–53.

7. Warner, "Reading Rape," 17.

8. Richardson, *Clarissa*, 441. (Subsequently referenced parenthetically in the text.)

9. Eagleton, *Rape of Clarissa*, 54.

10. Ibid., 66.

11. Ibid., 79.

12. Eagleton does recognize that there is an intimate connection between Lovelace's "political violence" and his approach to language: "Linguistic lawlessness is the other face of his sexual libertinism: a writing which brooks no closure is a desire which knows no mercy" (*Rape of Clarissa*, 83), but his emphasis on Lovelacean *jou-*

issance tends to obscure the element of calculation and control involved in this connection.

13. By contrast, Clarissa, like Pamela, really does try to "retire . . . to put down every sentence as spoken," and candidly acknowledges any gaps or breaks in her narration. Thus, while both Lovelace and Clarissa achieve the same "lively present-tense" *effect* in their letters, for Lovelace (as for Richardson) it is precisely a literary effect to be self-consciously achieved, while for Clarissa it is only, as it were, a *side-effect* of her diligence and honesty in recording her experiences and thoughts.

14. Todd, *Women's Friendship,* 49.

15. Another would be Warner's plea for recognition of "the chancy moments in the genuine proposal scenes where the story of Clarissa and Lovelace suddenly opens out to comedy and love," moments that "resist the impositions of Clarissa's (and Richardson's) tragic design" (*Reading Clarissa,* x). Since Warner aligns Lovelace with comedy, this "chanciness" is represented as being somehow to Lovelace's credit, the sunny side of his fluidity. But in fact it is Lovelace himself who subsequently displays the most anxiety in the face of these openings, and who works hardest to close them down. If he is on the side of comedy, he wants nobody's comic plot but his own.

16. Eagleton, *Rape of Clarissa,* 62.

17. Ibid., 63. See also Castle, *Clarissa's Ciphers,* 99.

18. See Doody, *Natural Passion,* 69.

19. Eagleton, *Rape of Clarissa,* 63.

20. Gwilliam, *Fictions of Gender,* 58.

21. Ibid., 62.

22. Ibid., 61.

23. Wilt, "He Could Go No Farther."

24. Todd also reads Lovelace's attribution of all evil to the women of the house as a form of patriarchal self-defense; she notes that even in the midst of railing against them, Lovelace reiterates his own intention of putting Clarissa to the final test: "before the rape [Lovelace] speaks of his own divided psyche in terms of a fight between himself and the women, forgetful that he has made them whores and that he alone brought Clarissa to the house . . . the infernal women allow Lovelace the exquisite pleasure of brutality with high motives and they allow him also the comfort that, because society refuses their remorse, the women must exceed himself in dreadfulness. Sinclair the silent can become his scapegoat as well as society's" (*Women's Friendships,* 39).

25. Another way of putting this is that Lovelace casts women as habitually desiring what he believes he has—linguistic and sexual mastery—as a way of reassuring himself that he does indeed have it. This formulation casts the phallic psychology of Lovelace's compulsive libertinism in a slightly different light than Eagleton's account of it. What Lovelace seeks to unveil in woman after woman is not her lack of a phallus but her denied desire for it in *him.* As Lovelace says himself, it is not the sexual act itself, with its purely genital revelations, that delights him, so much as it is the psychological triumph of "seduction," the revelation of the woman's desire for him. If "the whole sex love plotting," such triumphs reassure him, they "love plot-*ters*" more (792). Clarissa's triumph, then, is not that she either *has* the phallus

or *is* the phallus, but that she can live without whatever *he* has. So doing, she ultimately unveils Lovelace to himself as a posturing, castrated stand-in for the Real Thing.

26. As Todd notes about Clarissa's comment on her sister, "Arabella is condemned not only for being cruel, but also for trespassing on male ground" (*Women's Friendships*, 32–33).

27. Eagleton, *Rape of Clarissa*, 59.

28. Warner, *Reading Clarissa*, 49.

29. Eagleton similarly characterizes Anna as a "symptomatic" reader of her friend's texts, though he sees this as something done against Clarissa's will (*Rape of Clarissa*, 41).

30. Castle, *Clarissa's Ciphers*, 77.

31. Todd sees this quality as the source of the friendship's threat to patriarchy: "Anna insists that the friendship is unique—fervent, erotic, generous, judicious, and critical. Within the patriarchal scheme there cannot be its equal and there are few people daring enough to reject this scheme to enter into a relationship so potentially subversive, questioning as it does the values, polarities, and inclusiveness of patriarchy" (*Women's Friendships*, 49).

32. Castle, *Clarissa's Ciphers*, 78.

33. This is another version of what Kinkead-Weekes terms her "safety-valve" function (*Samuel Richardson, Dramatic Novelist*, 158). Nonetheless, in representing Anna as a "human norm" whose "more likeable" qualities implicitly cast doubt on the value of Clarissa's "absolutisms" (163), Kinkead-Weekes ignores the extent to which Richardson undermines the legitimacy of Anna's viewpoint—perhaps because he is unwilling to recognize how profoundly gendered Richardson's constructions of "human norms" are.

34. It is worth noting the difference between this and the male ethic of responsible stewardship later promulgated in *Sir Charles Grandison*, an ethic that presupposes certain kinds of social power that it would be irresponsible to abdicate or ignore.

35. As Van Ghent points out, "it is not the daughter's rebellion that is thematically paramount, but the daughter's obedience; for her father's curse is far more effective emotionally upon her than the attraction of the lover, or than her desire to escape [marriage with Solmes]" (*English Novel*, 79).

36. Castle, *Clarissa's Ciphers*, 119. For Castle, the rape marks a radical break in Clarissa's "relation to 'Nature,' to signs, to the 'discourse of the heart,'" impelling her away from the "struggles of interpretation" and hence toward death (*Clarissa's Ciphers*, 118). Because I see Clarissa's relationship to her narrative as more ambivalent from the start, and her final abdication of control over the presentation of her story as an act more of hermeneutic faith than of despair, the rape seems to me only to highlight and exacerbate the contradictions of narrative authority that have been inherent in Clarissa's position from the beginning.

37. Warner sees the post-rape scenes between Clarissa and Lovelace as self-consciously staged "melodrama," in which Clarissa acts such a "nice part" that she outdoes Lovelace in strategic staginess. That Richardson draws heavily on melodra-

matic effects in these scenes is clear enough, but Warner's discussion of them seems to me to assume what it claims to prove—that these scenes are self-consciously plotted or staged by Clarissa in the same way that Lovelace admits he frequently stages his interactions with her (*Reading Clarissa*, ch. 3). In a later reference to the "penknife scene," for example, Clarissa suggests that the suicidal resolution she "staged" in that scene was heartfelt enough: "More than once, indeed, was I urged by thoughts so sinful [i.e. to hasten her own death]: but then it was in the height of my distress" (1117).

38. Of course, a thoroughly suspicious reader could always conclude that Clarissa knows exactly what effect these written hysterics will produce, and is confident that the maid will retrieve them, but I know of no one who has actually argued this.

39. The first question is not entirely rhetorical: Belford later declines to help Lovelace with his plans on the grounds that his professed good intentions toward Clarissa are not trustworthy: "thou writest that in thy *present* mood thou thinkest of marrying; and yet canst so *easily* change thy *mood*" (958). Lovelace's reply again reveals the self-serving calculation behind his professedly "protean" qualities: "*hadst* thou undertaken the task, and I had afterwards though fit to change my mind, I should have contented myself to tell thee that that *was* my mind when thou engagedst for me" (958).

40. Eagleton, *Rape of Clarissa*, 75; Castle, *Clarissa's Ciphers*, 26.

41. Warner, *Reading Clarissa*, 93–94.

42. Eagleton, *Rape of Clarissa*, 85.

43. Ibid., 78–79.

44. Belford is conspicuously absent from Eagleton's discussion, perhaps because Eagleton has unconsciously cast himself in this role. Warner suggests this identification in "Reading Rape," in counter to Eagleton's charge of a Lovelacean bias on his part. One might also say that Showalter's criticism of *Rape of Clarissa*, in "Critical Cross-Dressing," stems from Eagleton's failure to examine critically the potential slippage from a genuine "male feminism" to the more ambivalent role of a Belfordian defender of "the Sex."

45. Aikins, in a review of *Clarissa's Ciphers*, takes issue with Castle's portrayal of Clarissa as a "helpless fool," arguing that, far from "losing her voice," Clarissa "creates for herself a voice that is heard within her novel even beyond her death—in her posthumous letters that so powerfully affect their readers" ("The Power of Clarissa," 116).

2. Comic Femininity

1. Altman, *Epistolarity*, 86. Jack notes that for Smollett "there are as many Baths as people to view them," but also observes qualities in the narration that point to "incontrovertible truths," ("Appearance and Reality," 223–24).

2. Zomchick notes that Melford and Bramble both "speak a language of tradition and continuity" that is "punctuated and counterpointed" by that of the women ("Social Class," 176). Spector also notes that Smollett "uses his fictional women

primarily as adjuncts to the interests of his heroes" (*Smollett's Women*, 8), though he is concerned primarily with the characterization of women across a range of novels rather than with their status as narrators.

3. Smollett, *Humphrey Clinker*, 154. (Subsequently referenced parenthetically in the text.)

4. See my discussion of Marian Halcombe's diary in *Woman in White*, in chapter 6.

5. Scott, *Redgauntlet*, 367. (Subsequently referenced parenthetically in the text.) Sutherland, introduction, xii.

6. Ibid.

7. See Sutherland on "the dominance of interpretation over event" in the novel (introduction, xv), and Kerr on the novel's shift "away from the depiction of actual events" and toward an emphasis on "strategies of emplotment" as his "central subject" ("Fiction against History," 238).

8. Politi notes that Darsie, like Pamela, becomes "the object of another's quest" ("Ideological," 350).

9. Wilt, *Secret Leaves*, 148.

10. See Politi on Redgauntlet as "imprisoned within the grammar of his narrative," "Ideological," 354.

11. Sutherland, introduction, xvi.

12. Kerr, "Fiction against History," 253.

13. See Daiches, on the novel's exposure of "the gap between sentimental Jacobitism and actual rebellion," ("Scott's *Redgauntlet*," 52). See also Wilt, *Secret Leaves*, 128.

14. Wilt discusses this exchange, though her conclusions about the role of women and femininity in the novel are different from mine (*Secret Leaves*, 127–28).

15. This relative lack of anxiety, which contrasts strongly with so many Victorian authors, may be the root of an 1898 reviewer's sense that "there is less of the accepted cant about women in [Scott's] novels than in the works of some who are supposed to know better," quoted in Merryn Williams, *Women in the English Novel*, 56.

16. I am indebted to Harry Shaw for my understanding of the terms of Scott's historical vision in *Redgauntlet*.

3. Redeeming the Plotting Woman

1. Moglen suggests a deeper motivation: that "she is still bound to the ambivalent attitudes of adolescence and accepts automatically the male point of view as the 'official' perspective" (*Self Conceived*, 88).

2. Moglen, for example, writes of it that "what is most interesting . . . are its flaws: the subterranean eruption of materials which will become the foci of Brontë's later work" (*Self Conceived*, 85).

3. Brontë, *The Professor*, 5–6. (Subsequently referenced parenthetically in the text.)

4. There are, of course, circumstances in which a retrospective narrator needs to cite his own letters—as for example when a writer of memoirs seeks to verify his account of his feelings at a particular point in his life by reference to letters he

wrote at the time. This, though, is really a special case of the rationale for interpolated letters I have already given: in effect, the memoirist confesses that, given the
vicissitudes of memory, he cannot be sure, without outside evidence, of genuine
access to the consciousness of a previous self. This does not seem to be the case
with Crimsworth, for there is no perceivable qualitative distinction between the
consciousness presented in the letter and the one that takes over the narrative afterwards. Indeed, if the letter serves any characterological purpose at all, it is to show
us Crimsworth's sameness over time, the product of his grim determination to
allow nothing to affect him deeply.

5. Rodolff sees this recognition emerging in the final chapters of *The Professor,*
when interest shifts to the development of Frances Henri's consciousness, though
the shift is rendered awkward by being presented still through Crimsworth's narration ("From the Ending," 85).

6. Lanser, *Fictions of Authority,* 177.

7. Brontë, *Jane Eyre,* 9. (Subsequently referenced parenthetically in the text.)

8. For clarity, I will throughout refer to Jane Eyre's narrating self as "the narrator" and the narrated self as "Jane."

9. The ambiguous social status implied by Bessie's practice here is counteracted
years later with her surprise visit to Jane at Lowood, at which point she acknowledges Jane's superiority to her cousins in all ladylike accomplishments and pro-
nounces her "quite a lady" (93). Bessie also tells her she has given the name Jane to
her own daughter (91), thus confirming the maternal qualities of her feelings for
Jane at the same time that she reestablishes the social distance between them.

10. Spens details the many correlations of plot in her 1929 article "Charlotte
Brontë," in Garrod, *Essays and Studies,* 54–70.

11. See Freeman, "Speech and Silence."

12. That Bertha is a kind of alter ego for Jane, representing or acting out the
qualities she fears or wishes to repress or deny in herself, has been accepted ever
since Gilbert and Gubar's influential reading of the novel, though what exactly
those qualities are remains a subject of critical discussion. See Gilbert and Gubar,
Madwoman, 336–71.

13. Lanser, *Fictions of Authority,* 182.

14. See Spens, "Charlotte Brontë."

15. Kaufman, *Discourses of Desire,* 180.

16. Lanser, *Fictions of Authority,* 186.

17. Peterson provides a detailed account of the multiple narratives Rochester
employs to redefine Jane to himself and to her (*Determined Reader,* 100–103).

18. See Peterson, *Determined Reader,* 105–6.

19. The equation of artistic and narrative skill has been made earlier, not only
in Jane's comment that Mrs. Fairfax has "no notion of sketching a character" (106),
but in Rochester's recognition of Jane's imaginative and skillfully executed draw-
ings as prefiguring her power to reshape his life.

20. This shifting of agency is actually shadowed earlier during Jane's thought
processes in leaving Lowood: the willed brainwork proves fruitless until, in a brief
pause to look out the window, "a kind fairy . . . dropped the required suggestion on
my pillow" (87). The reference to a "kind fairy" is clearly not meant to be taken

literally—it is a metaphor for a common mental phenomenon—but the effect is still to suggest that Jane is moved forward passively by an external force.

21. The reference, of course, is to Scheherezade, but in this case it is the male audience in need of "security."

4. "My Broken Tale"

1. Mermin, *Origins of a New Poetry,* ch. 7; Friedman, "Gender and Genre Anxiety"; Stone, "Genre Subversion and Gender Inversion." See also Cooper, *Woman and Artist,* ch. 6.

2. Radley, *Elizabeth Barrett Browning,* 125.

3. Castan, "Structural Problems," 77. Castan's argument transfers to the female author the presumed incapacity for narrative ordering conventionally attributed to feminine narrators.

4. This is particularly true, of course, of a poet's *Künstlerroman* written in verse. According to Mermin, "the poetry . . . proves . . . by its energy, zest, and exuberance, the heroine's vocation" (*Origins of a New Poetry,* 215).

5. See Barthes, *S/Z,* 17–18.

6. See especially Cooper, *Woman and Artist,* and Zonana, "The Embodied Muse."

7. Barrett Browning, *Aurora Leigh,* 1: 2–8. (Subsequently referenced parenthetically in the text.)

8. Dickens, *David Copperfield,* 1.

9. This is particularly the case in the last two books. As Castan establishes, although books 8 and 9 seem to provide an unbroken retrospective record of a single conversation between Aurora and Romney, Aurora makes various present-tense statements early in her narration of it that suggest she does yet not know what will emerge from the conversation later ("Structural Problems," 76–77).

10. Review of *Aurora Leigh, North American Review* 85 (1857): 415–41.

11. There is also a veiled suggestion of sexual impropriety: the unsuspecting male reader is led astray and then "trifled with" by a woman whose ends are obscure.

12. Here, as in so many ways, Victorian life was more flexible than its art. Both Barrett Browning and George Eliot, at least, seem to have been able to maintain relationships with men who were substantial figures in their own right without either sacrificing their own commitment to their art or impugning their companions' masculinity.

13. David, "Woman's Art as Servant of Patriarchy," 143–58.

14. Leighton sees this passage as reflecting Aurora's obsession with her absent father, but notes that the invocation "ring[s] false" (*Elizabeth Barrett Browning,* 130–31).

15. Cooper argues that the passage demonstrates to Aurora "her inability to give and take as the male poets . . . can from their mistresses or wives," and hence "the fact that love is essential for art" (*Woman and Artist,* 169–70). But again, these do not seem like relationships of "give and take" so much as examples of women's selfless adoration.

16. Cooper, acknowledging the discomfort critics such as Kaplan, Gilbert and Gubar, and Showalter have felt with this apparent capitulation, argues that it rep-

resents "a logical stage in her maturation," which Aurora eventually "reject[s]" as a "delusion" (*Woman and Artist*, 183–84). But this rejection is never indicated in the poem.

17. Nancy K. Miller, "Emphasis Added," 41–42.

5. Femininity and Omniscience

1. Lanser usefully suggests *authorial* as a more accurate term than *omniscient* for a narrator who is "heterodiegetic, public, and potentially self-referential" (*Fictions of Authority*, 15). I use *omniscient* in this chapter, despite its limitations, because *authorial* might confusingly suggest that the two voices are not the product of the same author, and because these narrators' superhuman access to knowledge (i.e., of the thoughts and private actions of a wide range of characters) is a particularly significant feature of their contrast with the novels' female narrators.

2. *Armadale* has a number of interpolated letters and personal narratives other than those of Lydia Gwilt, but the diary is distinctive both in its length and in its freedom from the explicit framing of the omniscient voice.

3. F. R. and Q. D. Leavis discuss the debt in terms of plot and characterization, in *Dickens the Novelist*, 108–10, and L. R. Leavis explores the issue in more detail in "David Copperfield and Jane Eyre."

4. Moers suggests that *Bleak House* was written "in a spirit of rivalry with Charlotte Brontë," noting that Esther "stands opposed to that abrasive and egotistical orphan girl, Jane Eyre" ("The Agitating Woman," 22).

5. I focus for now on the surface image of Esther as narrator—the image produced by taking her various narrative pronouncements at face value. The question of whether, or how far, Esther should be seen as self-consciously producing this image is addressed later.

6. Unframed in the sense that there is no explicit introduction—or even reference—to Esther's narrative by the omniscient voice that opens the novel. But as Moseley has convincingly argued, Esther's narrative is marked as "subordinate" to that of the omniscient narrator ("Ontology").

7. Dickens, *Bleak House*, 15. (Subsequently referenced parenthetically in the text.)

8. See Moseley, "Ontology," for a detailed discussion of Esther's narrative "subordination." See Kearns, "'But I Cried Very Much,'" on the "involuntary" quality of her narration.

9. *Bentley's* 67 (October 1853), reprinted in Dyson, *"Bleak House" Casebook.* Is *Bentley's* protesting too much? The faults this reviewer insists even a "dull-witted" reader could never see in Esther had of course already been attributed to her by earlier reviews (e.g., the *Athenaeum* on September 17, 1853, and the *Spectator* on September 24, 1853).

10. *Westminster Review,* October 1853, reprinted in Dyson, *"Bleak House" Casebook,* 71.

11. *Blackwood's Edinburgh Magazine* 77 (April 1855), reprinted in Dyson, *"Bleak House" Casebook,* 87.

12. *Spectator,* September 24, 1853, reprinted in Dyson, *"Bleak House" Casebook,* 57.

13. Forster, *Life of Charles Dickens,* 610.

14. Anticipatory comments like "It touched me then to reflect, and it touches me now, more nearly, to remember (having what I have to tell)" (182) make explicit her consciousness of a future withheld from her reader. And Esther at least once overtly defers sharing data from the narrative present, signaling her recognition of a need to shape her telling by actively manipulating the order in which information is revealed: "What more the letter told me, needs not be repeated here. It has its own times and places in my story" (513).

15. Harvey, *Character and the Novel* (1965), reprinted in Dyson, *"Bleak House" Casebook,* 227–28.

16. *Blackwoods,* in Dyson, *"Bleak House" Casebook,* 87, and the *Athenaeum,* in Dyson, *"Bleak House" Casebook,* 54.

17. Kearns, "'But I Cried Very Much,'" 121.

18. See Zwerdling, "Esther Summerson Rehabilitated"; Wilt, "Confusion and Consciousness"; and McCusker, "The Games Esther Plays," among others.

19. Graver, "Double Vision of *Bleak House,*" 4. Sadrin makes a similar argument in "Charlotte Dickens."

20. It is striking that *Jane Eyre* itself beautifully exemplifies that slide from a "safe" version of feminine moral influence to a form of female judgment potentially threatening to male authority that Graver suggests Dickens was anxiously managing in his portrayal of Esther.

21. see Dyson, *"Bleak House" Casebook,* 225–27.

22. J. Hillis Miller, *Charles Dickens: The World of His Novels,* reprinted in Dyson, *"Bleak House" Casebook,* 189.

23. Frazee, "Character of Esther," 233.

24. Dickens, *Little Dorrit,* 663. (Subsequently referenced parenthetically in the text.)

25. Harry Stone, *Working Notes,* 301.

26. Bock situates Miss Wade more broadly within "the novel's thematic interest in psychic self-imprisonment." Her narrative then becomes a "fable" that "makes a cautionary statement by depicting [her] as a victim of her own unlicensed, and therefore, perverted, self will" ("Miss Wade and George Silverman," 114).

27. Hughes, *Maniac in the Cellar,* 155, quoted in Peters, introduction to *Armadale,* xi.

28. See for example the *Spectator,* June 9, 1866, and the *Athenaeum,* June 2, 1866, both reprinted in Page, ed., *Collins: The Critical Heritage,* 146–50.

29. T. S. Eliot, *Selected Essays,* 468, quoted in Peters, introduction, xi.

30. See chapter 6.

31. See Sutherland, introduction to *Redgauntlet,* xii.

32. Collins, *Armadale,* 41. (Subsequently referenced parenthetically in the text.)

33. Kent argues that Collins does not align himself with the fatalism of many of his characters and first-person narrators; he is instead interested in "the representation of probability," particularly as it is subjectively experienced. But Kent's argument, which relies in part on "the absense of the authorial presence as narrator" ("Probability, Reality, and Sensation,") in many of the novels, seems problematic

as applied to *Armadale,* where an authorial presence as narrator predominates, and often explicitly reinforces the characters' fatalism.

34. O'Neill argues rather oddly that the consonance between the dream's predictions and Gwilt's and Oldershaw's plots undercuts Midwinter's fatalistic interpretation of the dream by revealing that events he sees as "supernatural intervention" are the product of the women's perfectly rational plots (*Women, Property, and Propriety,* 24). How this would constitute a "rational" explanation for the predictive accuracy of Allan's dream itself is unclear, though, since Allan knows even less than Midwinter of what Gwilt and Oldershaw are up to. In general, O'Neill's focus on individual characters' highly unstable and necessarily partial interpretations obscures the high level of consistency among the novel's predictive structures, a consistency that the omniscient narrator frequently underlines.

35. See Taylor, who notes that Gwilt "becomes in both senses the author of the plot" (*Secret Theatre of Home,* 163).

36. Gwilt's association with motherhood carries through to the ending, with its bizarre parody of childbirth—the mother dying to deliver the beloved and unconscious child from a deadly, enclosed space.

37. Taylor, *Secret Theatre of Home,* 154.

6. The Documentary Novel

1. It might be argued that, in *Pamela,* the acquisition and interpretation of Pamela's letters is also a key element of the plot. But the relevance of her papers to B's concerns is obvious throughout, so that the key question concerns whether the circumstances of her production of them and his acquisition of them can certify their genuineness as proof of her virtuous intentions.

2. Collins, *Woman in White,* 346. (Subsequently referenced parenthetically in the text.)

3. Stoker, *Dracula,* 262. (Subsequently referenced parenthetically in the text.)

4. The *M* refers both to their shared first initial and to their "masculine" traits. I use the term to refer to the qualities the two figures share. In general, the pairing of names and roles in the two novels—Marian/Mina, Hartright/Harker, Laura/Lucy, the two foreign counts, and the two foreign professors who provide the keys to the counts' undoing—seems too consistent to be coincidental.

5. While the heroes in these novels are initially feminized in ways that suggest weakness, the villains are also slightly—in Fosco's case, decidedly—"fey." But as with Lovelace's claim to have "a good deal of the soul of a woman," their effeminate qualities suggest a strategic *mastery* of gender codes, since they enhance their self-conscious ability to fascinate and unnerve both men and women.

6. See my discussion of *Humphrey Clinker* in chapter 2.

7. If Marian's changes of tone are uncontrollable, they are not wholly incomprehensible. Her instinctive distrust of Sir Percival invokes the category of "feminine intuition": like Laura's dog, Marian just somehow *knows* that there is something wrong with this man. On this level, given the confirmation provided by Hartright's foreshadowing, Marian's instincts have a certain reliability or authority. What is significant, though, is that such instincts remain at odds with her own

more self-conscious efforts to make sense of what she is observing, or to plan any active intervention in events.

8. D. A. Miller, "Sensation and Gender," 117.

9. Punter, *Literature of Terror,* 73. Quoted in Cranny-Francis, "Sexual Politics," 64.

10. A good example would be the question of what "socially unspeakable" concerns vampirism—and Dracula in particular—represents, since it can be read compellingly in relation to oedipal anxieties, as in Richardson, "Psychoanalysis of Ghost Stories"; fears about "reverse colonization," as in Arata, "Occidental Tourist"; male homoerotic desire, as in Craft, "'Kiss Me'"; female sexuality in general, as in Roth, "Suddenly Sexual Women"; or the New Woman in particular, as in Senf, "Stoker's Response to the New Woman," and Cranny-Francis, "Sexual Politics." Stevenson suggests, in "Vampire in the Mirror," that it is the very amorphousness of "vampire sexuality" that is threatening.

11. Spencer, "Purity and Danger," 197.

12. Jann gives a good account of the novel's promotion of science and rationalism in "Saved by Science?" Greenway also provides useful background on the novel's engagement with contemporary scientific and pseudoscientific debates in "Seward's Folly."

13. Senf, "Stoker's Response to the New Woman," 45.

14. Ibid., 49.

15. Men and children are equated in the scene in which Mina comforts Arthur, and in the end, when Mina's and Jonathan's child is named after all the men. See Senf, "Stoker's Response to the New Woman," 46. Cranny-Francis argues that the novel uniformly negates any "New-Womanly" qualities in Mina, but she tends to dismiss the novel's promotion of Mina's professional and intellectual qualities too readily ("Sexual Politics").

16. Wicke sees the use of shorthand as a reference to "the standardization of mass business writing" and all it implies ("Vampiric Typewriting," 471). My point is that shorthand, like the other variations on writing in the novel, can take on widely different functions in different contexts, and that the manipulation of these contexts is a key site of contestation in the novel. Here, I would argue, shorthand refers as much back to Richardson and the epistolary novel as forward to modern business practices.

17. Mina briefly exploits the same potential of shorthand as a secret code when she plays a "little joke" on Van Helsing by handing him her shorthand diary to read; see below.

18. This analogy is carried further with the "law" that a vampire can enter a house only after he has once been invited by an inhabitant (267), just as Jonathan must "enter freely" into Dracula's own house to be fair game (23). Whatever wiles or violence the vampire eventually resorts to, his victim has always somehow "asked for it" first.

19. Cranny-Francis, "Sexual Politics," 66.

20. Greenway suggests that Stoker's portrayal of Seward as a scientist is ironic, intended as a critique of rigid adherence to the current scientific "paradigm." Though he makes a good case for seeing the boundaries between science and what is now perceived as pseudoscience as more fluid in Stoker's period, Seward's reluc-

tant path to conviction seems necessary to mediate between Van Helsing's early hypothesis of a paranormal "cause" and a more naturalistic response. Nor does resistance to paradigm challenges necessarily make a scientist bad, provided he is prepared to succumb when the weight of evidence becomes overwhelming—as Seward does ("Seward's Folly").

21. Bentley, "Monster in the Bedroom," 30.

22. The other obvious "rape scene" is of course one not of vampirism but of its cure: the gang staking of Lucy.

23. This is foreshadowed in *Woman in White* by Hartright's description of Marian's sinister face. Its implications for Mina will become clearer later on.

24. As indeed they do. Fosco tells Sir Percival that "quiet resolution is the one quality the animals, the children, and the women all fail in" (345). Sir Percival fails in it, too, and thus Fosco manages him as readily as he does his wife. Dracula, as we have seen, is highly successful in reducing Harker (at least temporarily) to the status of a hysterical woman.

25. Craft suggests that the male "Crew of Light," as the men are called in the novel, appropriate vampirism, rather than defeat it: "We may say that Van Helsing and his tradition have polished teeth into hypodermic needles, a cultural refinement that masks violation as healing" ("'Kiss Me,'" 126). This reading parallels, at the level of sexual symbolism, the claims I wish to make about the operations of plotting in the novel. In general, the ways in which the novel stages a violent and punitive reassertion of male sexual agency has been amply documented by Craft, Cranny-Francis, and others.

26. The first exclusion of Mina could usefully be seen as in itself a replay-with-a difference of Van Helsing's earlier secretiveness, which excluded *everyone,* ostensibly for their own good, but also to consolidate his own authority. Mina's efforts at unifying and sharing documents thus serve the purpose of defusing potential competitive tensions between the men, enabling them to work together. This applies not only to Van Helsing's stranglehold on interpretation, but also to the male competition for Lucy's affection, which Mina simultaneously makes public and subordinates to the common goal. That done, though, continued male cooperation is ensured by transferring the struggle for mastery *among* the sex to one *between* the sexes, buried behind the concern of "we men" for the welfare of "a woman."

27. Feminist critics who focus largely on issues of sexuality in the novel tend to read incipient female vampirism as a threat to male prerogatives. Mina's *intellectual* assertiveness, though, unlike Lucy's sexual assertiveness, pre-dates her "vamping" by Dracula. His attack constitutes a solution to, rather than a source of, her threat to the men's authority over the narrative.

28. Greenway points out that hypnosis was believed to be the exercise of the power of a stronger mind over a weaker one. His first attempt to hypnotize Mina leaves Van Helsing with "great beads of perspiration" on his forehead (345), and as she becomes harder to hypnotize, he must "throw his whole soul into the effort" (381). Hypnotizing Mina becomes, quite literally, a battle of wills between Van Helsing and the Count ("Seward's Folly," 222–24).

29. After Mina has delivered her warnings, all subsequent periods of freedom are used solely for hypnosis.

30. Cranny-Francis argues that Mina's intelligence is negated by being "nominated male," cast as "a masculine attribute to which she has somehow gained access" ("Sexual Politics," 72–73). This is certainly true, but it is also worth noting that, in both instances where Van Helsing refers to her intelligence as masculine, the fact that it is also "of sweet woman" (376), or combined with "a woman's heart" (262) actually adds to its intellectual value.

31. How does one stutter in writing, anyway? A truly visceral, bodily resistance to articulating a particular word, a pause before writing, would be virtually unrepresentable in writing. Mina's written stutter, like Esther's written flutterings over Woodcourt, associates her written narrative with oral testimony.

32. Interestingly, if we read this passage "straight," it becomes an instance of resistance to the role of passive observer to which Mina has been relegated.

33. Particularly in a fin-de-siècle setting in which traditional gender roles have already been greatly destabilized by the cultural figures of the New Woman, the aesthete, and so on. In that context, the novel's ultimate reassertion of active, resolute manliness and passive femininity stands out more than its previous exploration of potential gender reversals.

7. Innocent of Language

1. I refer to the narrator-figure of these books as "the poet," rather than "Browning," because the structure of The Ring and the Book—not to mention Browning's lifelong insistence that his poetic speakers were dramatic masks— invites us to assume that this speaker, too, is a dramatized voice. Nonetheless, I see nothing explicit within these books to suggest that this speaker is ironically distanced from Browning as poet, and a great deal that would associate him, poetically and philosophically, directly with him.

2. Pompilia, of course, has her skeptical readers, both within the poem (most of the people of Rome, whether they side with her or Guido, assume that she had an affair with Caponsachi) and among critics. Walker, in an article that displays in classic form the possibility of reading any seemingly artless narrator as artful, argues, despite the poet-narrator's explicit claims to the contrary, that Pompilia is in fact "a subtle rhetorician who on occasion is cynical and ironic, and who deliberately employs various strategies to achieve her ends," and lumps her with Guido and the lawyers for her rhetorical sophistication and consequent unreliability ("Pompilia and Pompilia"). One is tempted to add that Pompilia cannot be as ignorant as she claims, since she manifestly speaks in very competent blank verse.

3. Pompilia mounts an active resistance at only two points: like Clarissa, when her sexual purity is threatened (by Guido's insistence that she consummate their marriage despite the lack of any emotional or spiritual union between them), and later to save her unborn child.

BIBLIOGRAPHY

Aikins, Janet. "The Power of Clarissa." *University of Toronto Quarterly* 54 (1984): 106–19.

Altman, Janet. *Epistolarity: Approaches to a Form.* Columbus: Ohio State Univ. Press, 1982.

Arata, Stephen D. "The Occidental Tourist: *Dracula* and the Anxiety of Reverse Colonization." *Victorian Studies* 33 (1990): 621–45.

Barthes, Roland. *S/Z.* Trans. Richard Miller. New York: Hill & Wang, 1974.

Baugman, Cynthia. "Epistolary Epistemology." Unpublished paper delivered at Cornell University, 1985.

Bentley, C. F. "The Monster in the Bedroom: Sexual Symbolism in Bram Stoker's *Dracula.*" *Literature and Psychology* 22 (1972): 27–34.

Bock, Carol. "Miss Wade and George Silverman: The Forms of Fictional Monologue." *Dickens Studies Annual* 16 (1987): 113–26.

Blackmore, R. D. *Lorna Doone.* London: Pan Books, 1967.

Bloom, Clive, et al., eds. *Nineteenth Century Suspense.* New York: St. Martin's, 1988.

Bold, Alan, ed. *Smollett: Author of the First Distinction.* New York: Barnes & Noble, 1982.

Booth, Wayne. "Are Narrative Choices Subject to Ethical Criticism?" In Phelan, ed., *Reading Narrative,* 57–78.

Brontë, Charlotte. *The Professor.* Oxford: Clarendon, 1987.

———. *Jane Eyre.* Oxford: Oxford Univ. Press, 1975.

Brooks, Peter. *Reading for the Plot: Design and Intention in Narrative.* New York: Random House, 1984.

Browning, Elizabeth Barrett. *Aurora Leigh and Other Poems.* Ed. Cora Kaplan. London: Women's Press, 1978.

Browning, Robert. *The Ring and the Book.* In *The Collected Works of Robert Browning,* ed. Jack W. Herring, vols. 7–9. Athens: Ohio Univ. Press, 1988.

Castan, C. "Structural Problems and the Poetry of *Aurora Leigh.*" *Browning Society Notes* 7 (1977): 73–81.

Castle, Terry. *Clarissa's Ciphers: Meaning and Disruption in Richardson's Clarissa.* Ithaca: Cornell Univ. Press, 1982.

Collins, Wilkie. *The Woman in White.* New York: Penguin, 1985.

———. *Armadale.* Oxford: Oxford Univ. Press, 1991.

Cooper, Helen. *Elizabeth Barrett Browning, Woman and Artist.* Chapel Hill: Univ. of North Carolina Press, 1988.

Craft, Christopher. "'Kiss Me with Those Red Lips': Gender and Inversion in Bram Stoker's *Dracula*." *Representations* 8 (1984): 107–33.

Cranny-Francis, Anne. "Sexual Politics and Political Repression in Bram Stoker's *Dracula*." In *Nineteenth Century Suspense,* ed. Clive Bloom et al., 64–79.

Daiches, David. "Scott's *Redgauntlet*." In *From Jane Austen to Joseph Conrad,* ed. Robert C. Rathburn and Martin Steinmann Jr. Minneapolis: Univ. of Minnesota Press, 1958.

Davidoff, Leonore, and Catherine Hall. *Family Fortunes: Men and Women of the English Middle Class, 1780–1850.* Chicago: Univ. of Chicago Press, 1987.

Defoe, Daniel. *Moll Flanders.* 2 vols. Oxford: Blackwell, 1927.

Dickens, Charles. *Bleak House.* Oxford: Oxford Univ. Press, 1987.

———. *David Copperfield.* Oxford: Oxford Univ. Press, 1989.

———. *Little Dorrit.* Oxford: Oxford Univ. Press, 1953.

Doody, Margaret Anne. *A Natural Passion: A Study of the Novels of Samuel Richardson.* Oxford: Oxford Univ. Press, 1974.

———. "The Man-made World of Clarissa Harlowe and Robert Lovelace." In *Samuel Richardson: Passion and Prudence,* ed. Valerie Grosvenor Myer. New York: Barnes & Noble, 1986.

Dyson, A. E., ed. *Dickens "Bleak House": A Casebook.* London: Macmillan, 1969.

Eagleton, Terry. *The Rape of Clarissa: Writing, Sexuality and Class Struggle in Samuel Richardson.* Oxford: Blackwell, 1982.

Forster, John. *Life of Charles Dickens.* London: Chapman & Hall, 1907.

Frazee, John P. "The Character of Esther and the Narrative Structure of *Bleak House*." *Studies in the Novel* 17 (1985): 227–40.

Freeman, Janet H. "Speech and Silence in *Jane Eyre*." *Studies in English Literature* 24 (1984): 683–700.

Friedman, Susan. "Gender and Genre Anxiety: Elizabeth Barrett Browning and H.D. as Epic Poets." *Tulsa Studies in Women's Literature* 5 (1986): 203–28.

Garrod, H. W. *Essays and Studies.* London: Clarendon: 1929.

Genette, Gérard. *Narrative Discourse: An Essay in Method.* Trans. Jane E. Lewin. Ithaca: Cornell Univ. Press, 1980.

Gilbert, Sandra, and Susan Gubar. *The Madwoman in the Attic.* New Haven: Yale Univ. Press, 1979.

Graver, Suzanne. "Writing in a 'Womanly' Way and the Double Vision of *Bleak House*." *Dickens Quarterly* 4 (1987): 3–15.

Greenway, John L. "Seward's Folly: *Dracula* as a Critique of 'Normal Science.'" *Stanford Literature Review* 3 (1986): 213–30.

Gwilliam, Tassie. *Samuel Richardson's Fictions of Gender.* Stanford: Stanford Univ. Press, 1993.

Harvey, W. J. *Character and the Novel* (1965). Reprinted in A. E. Dyson, ed., *Dickens "Bleak House": A Casebook,* 227–28.

Jack, R. D. S. "Appearance and Reality in *Humphrey Clinker*." In *Smollett: Author of the First Distinction,* ed. Alan Bold, 209–27.

Jann, Rosemary. "Saved by Science? The Mixed Messages of Stoker's *Dracula*." *Texas Studies in Language and Literature* 31 (1989): 273–87.

Kaufman, Linda S. *Discourses of Desire: Gender, Genre and Epistolary Fictions.* Ithaca: Cornell Univ. Press, 1986.

Kearns, Michael S. "'But I Cried Very Much': Esther Summerson as Narrator." *Dickens Quarterly* 1 (1984): 121–29.

Kent, Christopher. "Probability, Reality, and Sensation in the Novels of Wilkie Collins." *Dickens Studies Annual* 20 (1991): 259–80.

Kerr, James. "Fiction against History: Scott's *Redgauntlet* and the Power of Romance." *Texas Studies in Literature and Language* 29 (1987): 237–60.

Kinkead-Weekes, Mark. *Samuel Richardson: Dramatic Novelist.* Ithaca: Cornell Univ. Press, 1973.

Krueger, Christine L. *The Reader's Repentance: Women Preachers, Women Writers, and Nineteenth-Century Social Discourse.* Chicago: Univ. of Chicago Press, 1992.

Lanser, Susan S. *Fictions of Authority.* Ithaca: Cornell Univ. Press, 1992.

———. *The Narrative Act: Point of View in Prose Fiction.* Princeton: Princeton Univ. Press, 1981.

———. "Toward a Feminist Narratology." *Style* 20 (1986): 341–63.

Leavis, F. R., and Q. D. Leavis. *Dickens the Novelist.* London: Chatto & Windus, 1970.

Leavis, L. R. "David Copperfield and Jane Eyre." *English Studies* (1986): 167–73.

Leighton, Angela. *Elizabeth Barrett Browning.* Bloomington: Univ. of Indiana Press, 1986.

Mermin, Dorothy. *Elizabeth Barrett Browning: The Origins of a New Poetry.* Chicago: Univ. of Chicago Press, 1989.

Mezei, Kathy, ed. *Ambiguous Discourse: Feminist Narratology and British Women Writers.* Chapel Hill: Univ. of North Carolina Press, 1996.

———. "Contextualizing Feminist Narratology." In *Ambiguous Discourse,* ed. Kathy Mezei, 1–20.

McCusker, Jane. "The Games Esther Plays—Chapter Three of *Bleak House.*" *Dickensian* 81 (1985): 163–74.

McKeon, Michael. *The Origins of the English Novel (1600–1740).* Baltimore: Johns Hopkins Univ. Press, 1987.

Miller, D. A. "*Cage aux folles:* Sensation and Gender in Wilkie Collins's *The Woman in White.*" *Representations* 14 (1986): 107–36.

Miller, J. Hillis. *Charles Dickens: The World of His Novels* (1959). Reprinted in *Dickens "Bleak House": A Casebook,* ed. A. E. Dyson.

Miller, Nancy K. "Emphasis Added: Plots and Plausibilities in Women's Fiction." *PMLA* 96 (1981): 36–48.

Moers, Ellen. "*Bleak House:* The Agitating Woman," *Dickensian* 69 (1973): 13–24.

Moglen, Helene. *Charlotte Brontë: The Self Conceived.* New York: Norton, 1976.

Moseley, Merrit. "The Ontology of Esther's Narrative in *Bleak House.*" *South Atlantic Review* 50 (1985): 35–46.

Myer, Valerie Grosvenor, ed. *Samuel Richardson: Passion and Prudence.* Barnes & Noble, 1986.

O'Neill, Philip. *Wilkie Collins: Women, Property, and Propriety.* London: Macmillan, 1988.

Page, Norman, ed. *Wilkie Collins: The Critical Heritage.* Boston: Routledge, 1974.

Peters, Catherine. Introduction to *Armadale,* by Wilkie Collins.

Peterson, Carla. *The Determined Reader: Gender and Culture in the Novel from Napoleon to Victoria.* New Brunswick, N.J.: Rutgers Univ. Press, 1986.

Phelan, James. *Narrative as Rhetoric: Technique, Audiences, Ethics, Ideology.* Columbus: Ohio State Univ. Press, 1996.

————. *Reading People, Reading Plots: Character, Progression, and the Interpretation of Narrative.* Chicago: Univ. of Chicago Press, 1989.

————, ed. *Reading Narrative: Form, Ethics, Ideology.* Columbus: Ohio State Univ. Press, 1989.

Politi, Jina. "The Ideological Uses of Intertextuality: *Redgauntlet.*" In *Scott in Carnival: Selected Papers from the Fourth International Scott Conference, Edinburgh, 1991,* 345–57. Edinburgh: Association for Scottish Literary Studies, 1993.

Rabinowitz, Peter J. *Before Reading: Narrative Conventions and the Politics of Interpretation.* Ithaca, Cornell Univ. Press, 1987.

Rader, Ralph. "Defoe, Richardson, Joyce, and the Concept of Form in the Novel," in *Autobiography, Biography, and the Novel,* ed. William Matthew and Ralph Rader, 31–72. Los Angeles: Clark Memorial Library, 1973.

Radley, Virginia. *Elizabeth Barrett Browning.* New York: Twayne, 1972, 125.

Rathburn, Robert C., and Martin Steinmann Jr., eds. *From Jane Austen to Joseph Conrad.* Minneapolis: Univ. of Minnesota Press, 1958.

Richardson, Maurice. "The Psychoanalysis of Ghost Stories." *The Twentieth Century* 166 (1959): 427–28.

Richardson, Samuel. "Advice to Unmarried Ladies." *Rambler* 97 (19 February 1751).

————. *Clarissa, or, the History of a Young Lady.* New York: Penguin, 1985.

————. *Pamela, or, Virtue Rewarded.* New York: Houghton Mifflin, 1971.

————. *Pamela in Two Volumes* [Richardson's continuation, sometimes known as *Pamela in her Exalted Condition*], vol. 2. London: Dent, Everyman, 1984.

Richter, David. *Narrative/Theory.* White Plains, N.Y.: Longman, 1996.

Rodolff, Rebecca. "From the Ending of *The Professor* to the Conception of *Jane Eyre.*" *Philological Quarterly* 61 (1982): 71–89.

Roth, Phyllis. "Suddenly Sexual Women in Bram Stoker's *Dracula.*" *Literature and Psychology* 27 (1977): 113–21.

Ruskin, John. *Sesame and Lilies: Three Lectures.* Charles E. Brown, [1865].

Sadrin, Anny. "Charlotte Dickens: the Female Narrator of *Bleak House.*" *Dickens Quarterly* 9 (1992): 47–57.

Scott, Walter. *Redgauntlet.* Oxford: Oxford Univ. Press, 1985.

Seed, David. "The Narrative Method of *Dracula.*" *Nineteenth-Century Fiction* 40 (1985): 61–75.

Senf, Carol. "*Dracula:* Stoker's Response to the New Woman." *Victorian Studies* 26 (1982): 33–49.

Showalter, Elaine. "Critical Cross-Dressing: Male Feminists and the Woman of the Year." *Raritan* 3 (1983): 130–49.

Smollett, Tobias. *Humphrey Clinker.* Oxford: Oxford Univ. Press, 1984.

Spector, Robert D. *Smollett's Women: A Study in an Eighteenth-Century Masculine Sensibility.* Westport, Conn.: Greenwood Press, 1994.

Spencer, Kathleen L. "Purity and Danger: *Dracula,* the Urban Gothic, and the Late Victorian Degeneracy Crisis." *ELH* 59 (1992): 197–225.

Spens, Janet. "Charlotte Brontë." In *Essays and Studies,* ed. H. W. Garrod, 54–70.

Stevenson, John Allen. "A Vampire in the Mirror: The Sexuality of *Dracula.*" *PMLA* 103 (1988): 139–49.

Stoker, Bram. *Dracula.* New York: Bantam, 1981.

Stone, Harry, ed. *Dickens's Working Notes for His Novels.* Chicago: Univ. of Chicago Press, 1987.

Stone, Marjorie. "Genre Subversion and Gender Inversion: *The Princess* and *Aurora Leigh.*" *Victorian Poetry* 25 (1987): 101–27.

Sue, Eugene. *The Mysteries of Paris.* Routledge, 1897.

Sutherland, Kathryn. Introduction to *Redgauntlet,* by Walter Scott.

Taylor, Jenny Bourne. *In the Secret Theatre of Home: Wilkie Collins, Sensation Narrative, and Nineteenth-Century Psychology.* Boston: Routledge, 1988.

Todd, Janet. *Women's Friendship in Literature.* New York: Columbia Univ. Press, 1980.

Van Ghent, Dorothy. *The English Novel: Form and Function.* New York: Harper & Row, 1967.

Walker, William. "*Pompilia* and Pompilia." *Victorian Poetry* 22 (1984): 47–63.

Wall, Geoffrey. "'Different from Writing': *Dracula* in 1897." *Literature and History* 10 (1984): 15–23.

Warhol, Robyn R. *Gendered Interventions: Narrative Discourse in the Victorian Novel.* New Brunswick, N.J.: Rutgers Univ. Press, 1989.

———. "The Look, the Body, and the Heroine of *Persuasion.*" In *Ambiguous Discourse,* ed. Kathy Mezei, 21–39.

Warner, William Beatty. *Reading Clarissa: The Struggles of Interpretation.* New Haven, Conn.: Yale Univ. Press, 1979.

———. "Reading Rape: Marxist-Feminist Figurations of the Literal." *Diacritics* 13 (1983): 12–32.

Watt, Ian. *The Rise of the Novel: Studies in Defoe, Richardson, and Fielding.* Berkeley: Univ. of California Press, 1957.

Wicke, Jennifer. "Vampiric Typewriting: *Dracula* and its Media." *ELH* 59 (1992): 467–93.

Williams, Merryn. *Women in the English Novel 1800–1900.* New York: St. Martin's, 1984.

Wilt, Judith. "Confusion and Consciousness in Dickens's Esther." *English Language Notes* 16 (1978): 285–309.

———. "He Could Go No Farther: A Modest Proposal About Lovelace and Clarissa." *PMLA* 92 (1977): 19–32.

———. *Secret Leaves: The Novels of Walter Scott.* Chicago: Univ. of Chicago Press, 1981.

Winnett, Susan. "Coming Unstrung: Women, Men, Narrative, and Principles of Pleasure." *PMLA* 105 (1990): 505–18.

Zomchick, John P. "Social Class, Character, and Narrative Strategy in *Humphrey Clinker.*" *Eighteenth-Century Life* 10 (1986): 172–85.

Zwerdling, Alex. "Esther Summerson Rehabilitated." *PMLA* 88 (1973): 429–39.

Index

agency, 125–26, 149; denial of, in feminine narrators, 47, 49, 56, 69, 104–5, 106, 122, 128, 151, 180, 187, 203n. 20; and female villainy, 15, 140; and feminine propriety, 155–56, 198n. 5, 210n. 3; and history, 77, 138; intellectual, in female characters, 164, 172–74, 209n. 27; narrative and material, association between, 10, 192 (*see also* plotting; power, relation of narrative and interpersonal); reclaiming of, by men, 33, 168, 209n. 25; —, by women, 91, 96, 99–101, 157, 180–81
Aikins, Janet, 201n. 45
Allestree, Richard, 15
Altman, Janet, 197n. 46, 201n. 1
androgyny: in *Clarissa*, 38, 42–45; in *Dracula*, 162, 175, 207n. 5, 210n. 30; in "M-women," 149–50, 186; in *Redgauntlet*, 83; in *Woman in White*, 152–53, 207n. 5
Arata, Stephen D., 208n. 10
Armadale. *See under* Collins, Wilkie
artfulness and artlessness, 10, 28–30, 192, 210n. 2; in *Aurora Leigh*, 120; in *Bleak House*, 125, 127, 129–30, 131–32; in *Dracula*, 179; in *Jane Eyre*, 92–93, 94, 97, 99. *See also* plotting
Atkinson's Casket, 29
Aurora Leigh. *See under* Browning, Elizabeth Barrett
authority
    moral, 22; in *Clarissa*, 35, 39, 50, 69; in *Jane Eyre*, 93–94; in *Lorna Doone*, 5; in *Moll Flanders*, 19–20; of novels, 16. *See also* preaching
    narrative, 13, 105; and class, 91, 135–37, 152, 196n. 22; denial of, to feminine

narrators, 30, 92, 190; disruptions of, 88–89, 111, 204n. 9; gender and, 29, 32, 72, 138, 166 (*see also* competition, for narrative control; gender, dynamics); of historian in *Redgauntlet*, 84; for Lovelace, 40–41; of "mad papers" in *Clarissa*, 59–63; in *Pamela*, 26; as pleasure, 149; recovery of, by male narrators, 138, 146, 175–78, 209n. 27; refusal of, by feminine narrators, 2–3, 25, 69, 128, 136; of women, 10–12, 32–33. *See also* narration, epistolary, as display of authority; *and under individual titles*
    scientific: in relation to narrative, 170–72, 208nn. 12, 20, 209n. 28
    social: in relation to narrative, 8, 12–14, 144, 192

Barth, Roland, 13, 196n. 28
Baughman, Cynthia, 24–25
Bentley, C. F., 177
Bentley's. *See* Dickens, Charles, *Bleak House*, reviews of
Blackmore, R. D.: *Lorna Doone*, 1–6, 13, 15, 196n. 22; Lorna as feminine narrator, 2–6; Ridd's authority, 2
Bleak House. *See under* Dickens, Charles
Bock, Carol, 206n. 26
Booth, Wayne, 7, 30–31
Brontë, Charlotte, 85; *Jane Eyre*, 33, 89–90; —, Bertha as plotter, 101–2; —, and *Bleak House*, 10, 33, 125–26, 132, 134; —, and *Clarissa*, 95–96, 101; —, construction of narrative authority, 96–97, 106; —, Helen as Clarissa-figure, 95–96; —, influence on *David*